Welfare and Religion in 21st Century Europe

Volume 1

Configuring the Connectic

Edited by

ANDERS BÄCKSTRÖM
Uppsala University, Sweden

GRACE DAVIE
University of Exeter, UK

With

NINNA EDGARDH
PER PETTERSSON

ASHGATE

Published by
Ashgate Publishing Limited
Wey Court East
Union Road
Farnham
Surrey, GU9 7PT
England

Ashgate Publishing Company
Suite 420
101 Cherry Street
Burlington
VT 05401-4405
USA

www.ashgate.com

British Library Cataloguing in Publication Data
Welfare and religion in 21st century Europe.
    Volume 1, Configuring the connections.
    1. Public welfare – Europe – Cross-cultural studies. 2. Public welfare – Religious aspects. 3. Church and social problems – Europe – Cross-cultural studies.
    I. Bäckström, Anders, 1944– II. Davie, Grace, 1946– III. Edgardh, Ninna, 1955–
    IV. Pettersson, Per, 1952–
    261.8'32'094–dc22

Library of Congress Cataloging-in-Publication Data
Welfare and religion in 21st century Europe / [edited by] Anders Bäckström and Grace Davie ; with Ninna Edgardh and Per Pettersson.
        p. cm.
    Includes bibliographical references and index.
        ISBN 978-0-7546-6020-0 (v. 1 : hardcover : alk. paper) – ISBN 978-0-7546-6030-9 (v. 1 : pbk. : alk. paper)
        1. Public welfare—Europe—Religious aspects. 2. Welfare state—Europe.
    I. Bäckström, Anders, 1944– II. Davie, Grace, 1946– III. Edgardh, Ninna, 1955–
    IV. Pettersson, Per, 1952–

    HV238.W426 2009
    361.7'5094—dc22

                                                                2009020283

ISBN 9780754660200 (hbk)
ISBN 9780754660309 (pbk)
ISBN 9780754692560 (ebk)

Mixed Sources
Product group from well-managed
forests and other controlled sources
www.fsc.org Cert no. SA-COC-1565
© 1996 Forest Stewardship Council

Printed and bound in Great Britain by
MPG Books Group, UK

WE
21ST CENTURY EUROPE

The editors would like to thank the Bank of Sweden Tercentenary Foundation and the Foundation Samariterhemmet, without whose generosity this book would not have been possible.

Contents

List of Figures and Tables

Figures

Tables

Preface

This book is the first of two volumes, both of which can be read in three ways. At their simplest, they constitute an account of a comparative study on welfare and religion across eight western European nations. This study – Welfare and Religion in a European Perspective: A Comparative Study of the Role of Churches as Agents of Welfare within the Social Economy (WREP) – is itself the second of three related projects, all of which have emerged from the Centre for the Study of Religion and Society at Uppsala University in Sweden.[1] The genesis of each of these projects is set out in the following chapter, as are the details of WREP itself.

These books quite deliberately bring together very different fields of social-scientific enquiry – welfare, religion, gender and the social economy – which have, all too often, been kept apart. The reasons for these enforced separations are not hard to find. In terms of the first two (welfare and religion), they lie in an understanding of the modernization process in which one of these replaces the other as the dominant player in the field. This is especially true in those parts of Europe where the welfare state has substantially taken the place of the church as the effective means of care for European people – a process unlikely to be reversed in the foreseeable future. Why, then, should there be a study which focuses specifically on the interconnections between welfare and religion in the early years of the twenty-first century? Has something significant happened to demand this? And if so, how can this shift be explained? These are the questions addressed in the following chapters.

The question of gender adds a further dimension. Even a cursory glance at the institutions of welfare and religion in Europe reveals a strikingly similar pattern: in both systems, women are disproportionately present at the point of delivery, but under-represented in management. Once again, it is important to ask why this is the case and how it is best understood. Is this a persistent pattern, or is it likely to change; and, if so, when? How, moreover, is this pervasive imbalance legitimized? Is the legitimization process the same in each area of enquiry, or is something rather different at stake? Such questions will resonate repeatedly.

All of these interests come together in a specific 'field' – the sector that is variously termed civil society, the third or voluntary sector, or the social economy. Welfare is 'relocating', but in different ways in different places (see Chapter 2 for a detailed discussion of these shifts); the churches have increasingly ceased to be a 'sacred canopy' for the whole of society, but remain both active and effective at

---

[1]   In 2010, the Centre for the Study of Religion and Society will become the Uppsala Religion and Society Research Centre. It will be housed in the Faculty of Theology at the University of Uppsala. See http://www.impactofreligion.uu.se/ for more details.

local level; and women – both paid and unpaid – are more likely than men to be engaged at the level of delivery which is necessarily local. It is this that accounts for the stress in our writing on both the individuals and organizations that make up the social economy and the variety of forms that this takes in different parts of Europe.

There is, however, a further dimension to our work: that is, its *theoretical* significance. The logic of WREP demands that we address not only the changing nature of the institutions in question, but also the conceptual frameworks that must be brought into play if we are to understand fully what is happening in late modern European societies. It is clear that conventional theorizing about the welfare state has come under strain in recent decades. Pressures from within the system (notably the marked changes in European demography) and outside it (a shifting global economy) require that we rethink the assumptions on which the welfare state is built – a fact that becomes ever more urgent, almost by the day. Coincidentally, or perhaps not, standard theorizing about religion has been subject to similar pressures. No longer is it possible to talk simply in terms of secularization. The patterns of religion across Europe are changing rapidly as the religious factor once more asserts itself in public as well as private life – the outcomes of this situation are increasingly uncertain.

Hence one of the central questions of the WREP enquiry: what is the place of religion in Europe at the start of the third millennium, and what role does it play in the wider society? In engaging these issues, the final chapter of this volume not only analyses the data emerging from the case studies within WREP, but begins to place these findings in a theoretical perspective. In so doing, it draws on a range of theoretical ideas, some of them innovative, and becomes in itself a creative exercise. At the same time, it reveals the incompleteness of the work and the need for further developments in the field. The first stage in these developments can be found in the material contained in the companion volume to this one; a second lies in a further study from the Uppsala stable – Welfare and Values in Europe (WaVE) – which is introduced in Chapter 1; a third lies in the work currently being initiated in the newly established Centre of Excellence at the University of Uppsala.

It is important to grasp that the two volumes emerging from the WREP project embody different approaches. Volume 1 sets out the parameters of the project. The introductory chapters describe the background to the study, including its genesis, structure and scope. They also explain the details of the methodology – not least the advantages and disadvantages of the comparative method. The core of the book resides, however, in the eight case studies, each of which describes the connections between welfare, religion and gender in a 'representative' town in eight European societies. The final chapter – as has already been indicated – reflects on these data from a theoretical perspective. Volume 2 tackles the same material from a thematic point of view. Three approaches are taken in turn to identify and to explain the various strands within the data. A sociological analysis comes first, followed by an approach which concentrates on gender. The third way of working is somewhat different: it looks at the material from a theological perspective, asking in particular what motivates and sustains the actions of the churches in the field of welfare, and how the formal or 'official' statements of the churches are worked out in practice.

The last point requires a little expansion. The theological dimension is not an optional extra tagged on as an afterthought; it has been integral to the study right from the start, and will be carefully referenced in almost all of the case studies. As the churches engage in welfare, for example, theological ideas are present in the motivations of both individuals and organizations – though not always in similar or predictable ways. Quite apart from this, it is clear that different theologies account for both commonality and difference across Europe. Greeks and Finns, for instance, quote similar verses from the Bible in seeking justification for their work, or more precisely their care for those in need; conversely, Luther's doctrine of the 'two kingdoms' leads to a considerably more amicable division of labour between church and state in the Nordic countries than that found in, say, France.

None of these activities would have been possible without a number of key people – most of all the international and interdisciplinary team brought together in Uppsala in order to carry out the project. The details of the team and their respective responsibilities can be found in Appendix 1. Here, however, it is important to acknowledge the core group – those who conceived of the idea in the first place, set about finding the necessary resources and dealt with both the intellectual organization and the day-to-day management of the project. They are Anders Bäckström, Grace Davie, Ninna Edgardh, Per Pettersson and Thomas Ekstrand. Between us we represent a range of different disciplines and have – consequently – made different contributions to the project, which has been housed in the Centre for the Study of Religion and Society. The support staff of the Centre, notably Barbro Borg and Maria Essunger, deserve our warmest thanks; in sustaining the ongoing administration of the Centre, not to mention the numerous research meetings held there, they have played a vital role in the success of the whole undertaking. It is important, thirdly, to acknowledge the financial support given to the project from the Bank of Sweden Tercentenary Foundation and the Foundation Samariterhemmet – without whose exceptionally generous assistance very little of the work would have been possible. Additional grants came from the Academy of Finland (for the Finnish research) and the Diakonische Werk Württemberg (for the German case study). When it came, at last, to publication, Sarah Lloyd at Ashgate has proved an imaginative and very helpful editor. Rebecca Catto and Susannah Cornwall have put in long hours perfecting our English.

This preface must include a final point, which reflects our way of working: that is, the training element built into the WREP project and its successor, WaVE. Each national team has a senior and junior member: the senior member is an established scholar in the field (trained for the most part in sociology or theology); the junior researchers are doctoral or post-doctoral students. One of the most pleasing aspects of the whole venture has been the emergence of a new generation of scholars, as, one by one, these 'junior' researchers acquire their doctorates and launch their careers. Their enthusiasm, and a growing rapport between them, has been a crucial factor in sustaining not only themselves, but their senior partners – indeed, in permitting the project as a whole to come to a successful conclusion. In total, 24 researchers from Sweden, Norway, Finland, England, France, Italy and Greece have been involved – a team with growing competence in the field. Their names, the institutions in which they are based, and their disciplinary backgrounds are listed in Appendix 1.

As the Director and Assistant Director, we would like to thank all those who have contributed to WREP in whatever way and have helped us to bring the project to a successful conclusion.

Anders Bäckström
Grace Davie
2010

Chapter 1
The WREP Project:
Genesis, Structure and Scope

Anders Bäckström and Grace Davie

This book, together with its partner volume (Bäckström et al. 2010), is concerned with the project known as Welfare and Religion in a European Perspective – or WREP for short. The goal of the project is easily summarized: it is to discover exactly what happens on an everyday basis in the fields of welfare and religion in Europe in the first decade of the twenty-first century, and to ask what this can tell us about the changing nature of European societies.

This chapter outlines what WREP stands for and how the project came about. The first section reflects on the background to the study: what were the changes taking place both in Europe and beyond which prompted an enquiry of this nature? The second section is more concrete in that it presents the building blocks of the project – that is, the concepts and ideas that have underpinned our thinking. The third begins from a different starting point, in the sense that it explains the organizational environment from which WREP emerged; how, more precisely, the project found its inspiration in the ongoing work of the Centre for the Study of Religion and Society in Uppsala. The final section sets out the research methods employed in the study: how were the various elements in the project operationalized, and how were they examined empirically?

Introducing WREP

Welfare and Religion in a European Perspective deals with three closely interrelated questions: the current 'challenges' to the welfare state in Europe; the place of religion in modern European societies; and the role of voluntary organizations within the social economy. Each of these questions has already been the focus of extensive enquiry, and each of them has generated a considerable research literature – but almost always as *separate* fields. WREP is unique in the sense that all three aspects are brought together in order to analyse 'the function of majority churches as providers of social welfare in a comparative European perspective' (Bäckström 2003b: 52).

The background to this work lies, essentially, in the new flows of technology, capital, people and ideas that are transforming the economic, political and religious landscape of Europe in ways that were unthinkable until relatively recently.

Such flows have had multiple and far-reaching effects on the economies and societies of Western Europe. New divisions of labour, and therefore of inclusion and exclusion, have emerged as these influences make themselves felt. Quite clearly, many have benefitted: economic élites have grown (in size and wealth) alongside an expanding middle class – and both have gained from innovative economies and new forms of employment. Others, however, are not so lucky, in the sense that they have become increasingly dependent on various kinds of support (Hoogvelt 2001). Among the latter, new forms of poverty can be identified which have little to do with old class distinctions, exacerbated by the fact that, as the global market exposes European companies to new forms of competition, costs of production become paramount. As a result, those who cannot contribute are increasingly excluded. Castells (1998; 2000) has called this sector of society a 'fourth world', recognizing that the 'excluded' are not only present in the developing world, but exist in almost all European countries.

Such pressures both derive from and are specific to the late modern economy. That said, however, the transformations taking place at the start of the new millennium can be seen in some senses to mirror those that occurred some hundred years or so ago – above all in the movement of people. As industrial societies gathered pace, large sections of the European population moved rapidly from the countryside to the cities. Given the extent of these dislocations, it was hardly surprising that traditional forms of social care – those that depended on the household and the churches – no longer functioned effectively. Here, in fact, was the stimulus for new forms of social support. As the old order disintegrated, new institutions emerged – in, for instance, the systems of social security which began in Germany in the 1880s and which developed variously in different parts of Europe in the following decades (Esping-Andersen 2002; van Kersbergen and Manow 2009). These are institutions that find their roots in an emerging industrial society. Hence an inevitable question: can a similar process be seen in the early decades of the twenty-first century, but this time on a larger scale – a development that urges us to find solutions which not only are national but transnational? This idea is by no means a new one; it has already generated considerable discussion in the social sciences (for an overview, see Bäckström et al. 2004).

What *is* new in WREP is the inclusion of religion as a central factor in these debates, recognizing that religion is part and parcel of the transformations taking place. Clearly, the migration of different groups of people into Europe – though economically motivated – has important implications for religion, expressed most obviously in a growing religious pluralism in almost every European society. That, in turn, has made religion more visible – disturbingly so for many people. Even a cursory glance at the literature reveals a renewed, and not always positive, awareness of religion amongst European populations – the more so amongst those who assumed that more public welfare necessarily meant less public religion. This was a zero sum game. Precisely the same people, interestingly, have assumed a similar displacement in global terms: namely, that a growing understanding of democracy and human rights would eclipse the need for religion worldwide.

Such assumptions, whether national or global, are now increasingly being questioned. Both in Europe and beyond, religious institutions are not only becoming partners in the delivery of care, but also bearers of values that – from time to time at least – challenge and critique both global and national systems. It is these shifts in perspective that are central to the WREP enquiry.

Among other things, they have led to revised historical understandings regarding the place of religion – more precisely of religious traditions – in the development of welfare in Europe. Indeed, a key point to emerge from recent research in this field concerns the significance of the churches' social teaching for the development of different welfare regimes across the continent. That awareness led, in turn, to new questions concerning the privatization of religion (regarding both its scope and its inevitability), at precisely the same moment as scholars of religion were revising their ideas about secularization as a necessary feature of modernization. Europe, it is true, reveals a relatively strong relationship between the two, but for particularly European reasons (Davie 2000; 2002). Such connections cannot, however, simply be taken for granted: quite different things have happened in other parts of the developed and developing world, most obviously in the United States. It is this combination of factors that has led us to reconsider the place of religion in our own societies, including the continuing – or perhaps growing – significance of religion in matters of welfare.

In order to examine these points empirically, WREP has found its focus in a detailed examination of the social economy of a single locality in eight European countries: Sweden, Norway, Finland, Germany, England, France, Italy and Greece. The goals were straightforward enough: to map the place of both welfare and religion in the locality in question; to note the similarities and differences across Europe regarding the responses of the state (in its local forms), the churches,[1] and a range of voluntary organizations to the current situation; and to ask what this information told us about the nature of European societies, which are clearly facing similar issues. How, then, do these principal actors respond, and what resources do they have at their disposal? To what extent do these resources depend on the fact that the modern welfare state has developed differently in different parts of Europe – developments which leave distinctive 'spaces' not only for the churches to contribute, but for their role to adjust as circumstances require? And how, finally, might this situation evolve? These are the central questions which have driven the WREP enquiry.

---

[1] In the Welfare and Religion in Europe (WaVE) project, WREP's successor, a wide range of religious and other minorities have been studied. In WREP itself, however, the emphasis lies on the *majority* churches, and includes both their contributions to welfare, and their 'prophetic' role (that is, their role as social commentators). WaVE is introduced in the concluding section of this chapter. See also http://www.waveproject.org/

The Building-Blocks of WREP

It is now time to turn to the nuts and bolts of the project: how was it constructed, and what were the key concepts embedded in our thinking? The distinctive welfare traditions that exist in modern Europe are the obvious starting point.

Welfare Traditions in Europe

The modern welfare state is, above all, a national project. As we have seen, its beginnings are best understood as a response to the upheavals taking place as Europe both industrialized and urbanized. Specifically, the foundations of the welfare state as we know it were laid in Germany under the directions of Bismarck, and took the form of a rudimentary system of social insurance (Leis 2004a). Bit by bit, other European nations followed suit, both adopting and adapting the German institutions – ideas that developed strongly after 1945. A good example of post-war initiatives can be found in the Beveridge plan, introduced in England in 1948. In *Full Employment in a Free Society* (1944), Beveridge declared war on poverty, ill-health and ignorance, insisting at the same time that the idea of citizenship formed the core of the welfare system. Interestingly, it is this principle that the Nordic countries – rather than Britain – have developed to the fullest extent. As a result, welfare grounded in citizenship became a characteristic of much of northern Europe. Further south, a 'continental' model emerged, based not simply on citizenship but on the notion of social rights – noting that these are not simply given but, in one way or another, have to be earned (Blomqvist 2003b: 10).

Esping-Andersen's analysis of the different welfare regimes in Europe has become a touchstone text in the welfare debate (Esping-Andersen 1990). In this, he distinguishes between three dominant models, which are outlined briefly below.

The Liberal Model   This model is typical of Anglo-Saxon countries, such as England, the United States, Australia and New Zealand. Here responsibility is taken by the state for basic social issues such as health, education and social care, although independent agencies are also given considerable scope.

The Conservative Model   This is found mainly in continental Europe – for example, in Germany, France, Austria and Belgium. In this model, the state has responsibility for the social welfare framework, while voluntary bodies of various kinds (including large numbers of paid professionals) play a defining role. A sub-division of this model is sometimes included. Termed the *Weak Conservative or Rudimentary Model*, it is found in countries in southern and eastern Europe, which are also linked to the conservative model, but where the family is more important than the state in the delivery of welfare. This model predominates in Italy, Spain, Portugal, Greece, Croatia and Romania.

The Social Democratic Model   This is typical of the Nordic countries – Sweden, Norway, Finland, Denmark, Iceland and, to some extent, the Netherlands. It gives the state overall responsibility for general social welfare, while voluntary organisations provide only complementary services.

The advantages and disadvantages of Esping-Andersen's initial analysis, his critics and his subsequent revisions will be discussed in detail in Chapter 2. Equally important will be the applicability of these approaches to the work of WREP. At this stage, however, the crucial point to grasp is that all of the variations outlined above are represented in the project: the liberal model in England; the social democratic model in Sweden, Norway and Finland; the conservative model in Germany and France; and the weak conservative or rudimentary model in Italy and Greece.

Church Traditions in Europe

WREP also includes the major Christian traditions which exist in Europe: Anglican, Lutheran/Protestant, Catholic and Orthodox.[2] Indeed, an important starting point for the study as a whole lies in the fact that the majority churches of Europe – as theologically-motivated carriers of values – are related to the different welfare models that have emerged across the continent. Specific theologies quite clearly lead in different directions, bearing in mind the multiplicity of factors that must be taken into account in these evidently complex processes. In England, for example, the Church of England has very largely withdrawn from the provision of welfare as such, but retains a critical voice. Here the welfare system relies extensively on unpaid volunteers, whose contributions are often under-valued.[3] In the Nordic countries, the Lutheran folk-churches have embraced the doctrine of the 'two kingdoms' – a body of teaching which ascribes much more positively a particular role to the state in the organization of welfare. In Italy, and to some extent in Germany and France, Catholic social teaching has been influential in a different way, this time through the concept of subsidiarity – a notion which implies that welfare, just like everything else, should be delivered at the lowest effective level of society. The further south one goes, the more evident this concept becomes, a point that will resonate repeatedly. Orthodoxy, finally, maintained a distance from 'society' well into the twentieth century. Currently, however, it is possible to see a shift towards greater social involvement – an evolution that is well-exemplified in the Greek case study. In Greece, the church has become increasingly observant of social issues through a renewed understanding of the church as *diakonia*.[4]

---

[2]   Regrettably, there is no Reformed or Calvinist case study as such.

[3]   See, for example, Davis et al. (2008). This report – published shortly before this book went to press – was researched and written by representatives of the von Hügel Institute in Cambridge. It reveals both the extent of welfare undertaken by the churches and the lack of awareness on the part of government regarding such activities.

[4]   See, for example, the Conferences on Orthodox *Diakonia* that took place in Greece (Crete) in 1978 and in Finland in 2004.

The point to grasp here is the interconnectedness of theological traditions and welfare regimes, a relationship that is possible to examine in different ways. Taking notice of religion, however, is not something that comes easily to experts in social policy, whether past or present. It is true that the religious factor was recognized in work that related to the Christian-Democrat parties of continental Europe – parties that have been dominant in Italy, Austria, Germany, Holland and Belgium. The approach, however, was largely negative. With some justification, the churches in these countries have been seen primarily as a constraining factor – that is, as institutions that opposed the initiatives of the state as it attempted to establish elements of care for the populations for which it was responsible. This is especially true in Catholic countries (see below). More recent research has taken a more positive view. This can be seen, for example, in the European Identity, Welfare State and Religion(s) project, funded by the European Commission and completed in 2001. The existence of this project is significant in itself, let alone its insistence on a growing third sector in all its case studies – a 'space' which included religious institutions.

Even more pertinent to WREP, however, are the publications of Manow (2004), Kahl (2005) and van Kersbergen and Manow (2009), who have opened up new areas of debate – highlighting amongst other things the significance of religious ideas in the formative period of the welfare state from the nineteenth century onwards. These authors demonstrate convincingly that the Lutheran countries of Northern Europe, including Germany, were the first to develop systems of welfare and social insurance. Catholic and Reformed countries adopted these ideas somewhat later. The explanation for the differences in timing can, moreover, be found in the religious factor. Driven by the notion of 'two kingdoms', the Lutheran churches welcomed the welfare state, or – at the very least – offered little resistance to its creation and development. The Catholic Church, conversely, actively hindered the intrusion of the state into the aspects of society which had long been regarded as central to its own identity. Hence the state–church cleavage that can still be felt in much of southern Europe, where the welfare system remains rudimentary. Unsurprisingly, it is in these parts of Europe that the family – supported by the churches – has retained control of many areas of welfare, especially those where family values predominate (like the care of children and elderly people). Much less predictably, rather similar hesitations can be found in countries influenced by Reformed as opposed to Lutheran theology (the Netherlands, Switzerland and, to some extent, England), but for rather different reasons – a point developed in detail by Manow (2004). Once again, there was resistance to state welfare, but this time in the name of theological as well as political individualism. Self-reliance, rather than social care, became the supreme virtue.

In short, religion is important as an independent, as well as dependent, variable in the evolution of welfare in Europe. It is true that certain forms of religion resist certain forms of welfare. Equally important, however, are the positive consequences of theological traditions – those that actively encourage secular alternatives. Both must be taken into account. Grasping the continuing significance of religion in the debates about welfare right across Europe is central to the work of WREP. Exactly what roles the churches play, however, and in which directions they are likely to move, must be the subject of careful empirical enquiry. None of these things can be assumed at the outset.

The Significance of Gender

Embedded in WREP are three cross-cutting themes. The first two have already been introduced: these are the sociological (the different patterns of welfare in Europe) and the theological (the formative role of the churches' social teaching in the development of welfare regimes). The third theme concerns gender, and for a very good reason: an extremely large proportion of the care that is delivered in Europe is, and always has been, dispensed by women. An awareness that this is done in different ways in different countries does not detract from the significance of gender overall; it simply contextualizes the debate. In large parts of northern Europe, for example, disproportionate numbers of women are employed by the state to take care of vulnerable groups of people; further south, families – or more accurately, women in families – play a vital role in countries where comprehensive care by the state remains an aspiration. Both will be explored in the case studies in this book and in the developed discussion of gender in its partner volume.

Significantly, differences of gender are equally present in the religious life of modern Europe, as indeed they are throughout the Christian west. Somewhat belatedly, scholars from many disciplines have begun to recognize the dominance of gender as an explanatory variable in the understanding of religion. This is so much the case, in fact, that the current generation of students finds it difficult to grasp the absence of such focus in the past. Happily, the work is now catching up with reality. Quite apart from this, it is the gender variable more than any other that provides an obvious link between the different strands that come together in WREP. This is true in more ways than one. If women are noticeably present as actors in the day-to-day delivery of both welfare and religion, they are correspondingly absent at the senior levels of both institutions. Both elements – presence and absence – will require our attention.

One final point is important: why is it that so few commentators have noticed the very marked similarities between welfare and religion, and why is it that so many respondents – when challenged – simply regarded the dominance of women in both spheres as 'natural'? From Finland to Greece, the answer was always the same: women do the caring because they are better at it, just as women do the praying – on behalf of everyone else. Our case studies seek both to unpick and explain these widespread and very dominant assumptions.

Concepts and Definitions

The following section concerns the key concepts of the WREP project: welfare, well-being, civil society and the social economy. The discussion of welfare and well-being will be followed by a clarification of the current 'challenges' to the welfare state: what exactly are these, and why have they come about? The material on civil society and the social economy – the local context – comes next. The section will conclude with some remarks about the European context and the pressures that come from the European Union itself.

Before embarking on this discussion, one further preliminary requires attention: WREP is a comparative project involving eight different countries and eight different languages. Questions of translation – not least of key concepts – were central to our deliberations, the more so in that the existence or not of a particular word or technical term in any given language revealed crucially important differences between our case studies. There is not space in this chapter to develop this point in detail; we have, however, included a briefing paper on this issue in Appendix 2. The paper was prepared by one of our researchers; it makes clear that what was initially perceived as a problem became, in the course of our deliberations, an additional tool of analysis. 'Words' were not simply labels – their presence or absence helped us to unpack the cultural values that lay beneath the surface of our different cases.

Welfare and Well-Being

Almost all commentators agree that welfare begins with the basics: economic and social security, adequate housing, medical care at the point of need and education for all. European citizens expect these things, and they assume that they will be provided by the state – funded either by taxation or by systems of social insurance. In addition to this economic, or 'external' idea of welfare, however, rather more subjective ideas have emerged – those, for example, which relate not simply to basic securities, but to what has become known as 'quality of life' (Furniss 1990: 8). The Nordic scholar Erik Allardt, in a well-known exposition on the subject, goes further still, recognizing three aspects of welfare: welfare in an economic or material sense, associated with 'having'; welfare connected with skills, profession or identity, associated with 'being'; and welfare as something human and qualitative, associated with 'loving' (Allardt 1975). Several of the case studies that follow utilize this framework – an approach which makes it abundantly clear that questions about welfare cannot simply be answered on the basis of one dimension; essentially subjective perceptions form a central part of the discussion (Kommittén Välfärdsbokslut 2000a: 12). If this is the case, we need to examine the resources or opportunities that individuals or populations might have in order to fulfil their ambitions, *whatever these might be*.

A subjective element in welfare leads inevitably to the related notion of well-being, appreciating that the line between the two ideas is necessarily blurred.

But wherever we establish the boundary, it is important to include a value dimension. One way of doing so is to note the widely-recognized shift away from *material* values, which are associated first and foremost with security, to *post-material* values, associated above all with freedom. Amongst other places, such a shift emerges from the work in Ronald Inglehart and his colleagues in the World Values Survey (WVS), housed at the University of Michigan in the United States.[5] Assembling enormous data sets from over 80 countries, the WVS team have established patterns of change across the world (Inglehart 1997; 2007). Their work has generated a lively discussion, for not everyone agrees with their conclusions. It is plausible, nevertheless, to suggest that developed societies – among which European countries are leading the way – are undergoing a significant shift in emphasis away from purely material comfort (now taken for granted by significant sections of the population) towards post-material aspirations. Putting the same point in political parlance, 'freedoms from' (want or insecurity) have increasingly given way to 'freedoms to' (explore new and different life-styles).

Important consequences follow from this. At an individual level, there is an ever-greater emphasis on choice. Everything – from welfare services to worldviews – becomes a matter of personal discovery. Heelas and Woodhead (2005) explore this notion in some detail, noting in particular the subjectivization of western culture – in other words, a growing emphasis on the self as a project in its own right, at the expense of the objective material world (Heelas 2006). The debt to Charles Taylor's work is evident (Taylor 1989). There are similar shifts in perspective at a societal level. The notion of solidarity, for instance, increasingly involves questions of risk rather than poverty – indeed, for commentators such as Beck (Beck and Ritter 1992), the management of risk becomes a defining feature of modernity. Zygmunt Bauman's analysis employs a different terminology: a consumer society is framed by an expanding range of individual choices, in which notions of solidarity, health and security become ever more 'liquid'. In this perspective, welfare and well-being are seen in terms of assets, readily available to the majority of the population, but not to all. As we saw in the introduction to this chapter, those who fall outside these limits find themselves excluded from mainstream society and – simply because of this – are defined as poor (Bauman 1998; 2002; 2006).

The churches are part and parcel of these discussions. Their contribution (both real and potential) is best expressed in a series of questions. How, for example, is welfare defined or described in different theological traditions? What do the churches do to promote these goals? How do they respond to the 'failures' of society to meet the expectations of its citizens? And what, finally, are the expectations of these citizens regarding the religious organizations themselves? Such questions are central to the work of WREP and, once again, relate closely to the debate about privatization. Regarding the latter, the discussion is not only

---

[5]   See http://www.worldvaluessurvey.org/ for more information on the WVS, including a detailed list of publications.

empirical (what happens on a daily basis all over Europe), but normative, and connects very directly to the growing visibility of religion in almost all European societies. On the one hand are those who view the majority churches as primarily spiritual entities operating for the most part in the private sphere. On the other are those – both inside and outside the churches – who resist these trends. Which of these, thirdly, is the 'correct' option? The point is hotly contested in a discussion which engages not only the religious institutions of modern Europe but the constitutional arrangements of the societies of which they are part (Casanova 1994; 2006). It resonates repeatedly in the interviews undertaken in each of the WREP case studies.

The Challenge to the Welfare State

Taking all these things into account, it is clear that European populations have common understandings of welfare. Despite the differences in welfare regimes and in the vocabularies associated with them, it is possible to talk about a 'European social model' (Hettne 1997), the more so if this is contrasted to the much more individualistic approach that can be found in the United States (Magnusson 2000: 100). It is, moreover, the European model which is currently exposed to strain – a widely recognized factor, albeit one which takes different forms in different parts of Europe.

How, then, should we understand this 'challenge'? A whole range of factors need to be taken into account – some internal and some external. Many of the internal pressures, paradoxically, are the direct consequence of successful social care. Precisely this, for example, accounts both for rising expectations and for Europe's changing demographic profile. Populations which are well looked-after expect not only to be fit and well, but to live longer, and will therefore require more care – a never-ending spiral that places increasing burdens on the health and welfare services. The problem, moreover, is exacerbated in the sense that the proportion of the population in employment continues to diminish, relatively speaking – European populations now not only live longer, but also have fewer children, many of whom remain in full-time education until their mid-twenties. All three factors erode the size of the workforce. How, then, is adequate care to be provided, and who is going to pay for it? How, in other words can the expectations of European populations continue to be met? This is one aspect of the 'challenge'.

Another can be found in the pressures that come from outside. Whether Europeans like it or not, they live in a world in which economic forces lie beyond the control of even the most successful nation-state. To start with the most obvious example, the downturn in the global economy following the oil crisis of the 1970s had a profound effect on the economic health of all industrialized nations, including European ones. In many ways, this was a wake-up call to the west, the moment when the optimism of the 1960s gave way to a much less confident decade. No longer could the advanced economies of the world assume the levels of growth to which they had become accustomed in the early post-war decades – which had, amongst other things, provided a sound financial basis for the modern welfare state. Like it or not, all European societies were, in one way or another, subject to radical change – dislocations in which there were undoubtedly winners, but also large numbers of losers, as declining industrial enterprises shed large sections of their labour force or relocated them to different parts of the world. Post-war securities, including full employment, very rapidly became a thing of the past. Those who remain in work, moreover, are obliged to function in different ways, which in themselves challenge a system based not only on traditional forms of labour, but on a relatively stable model of family life – a nuclear family with a male bread-winner and female carer.

It is these necessarily interrelated questions that confront European governments in the early years of the twenty-first century, not to mention the populations for which they are responsible. Among the latter, expectations alter: even the relatively successful middle class no longer believe unproblematically in the state's ability to sustain a real sense of security (Rothstein 2003). Despite the growth in the economic indicators of much of modern Europe, the old certainties have gone – and gone, many people think, forever, as one economic recession has followed another first in the 1990s and again in 2008. It follows that the 'challenge' to the welfare state is as much subjective as it is objective.

Civil Society, the Voluntary Sector and the Social Economy

The notion of 'civil society' – that is, the multitude of activities that take place between the state and the individual or family – has been the focus of extensive research in recent years (Trägårdh 2007: 1). Almost all commentators are agreed on certain things: first, that the growth of civil society has to do with the decreasing authority of the nation-state, and second, that the social movements that emerged in most European societies in the nineteenth century no longer carry the authority that they used to (Eisenstadt 2000).

Particularly vulnerable, in this respect, are the social movements most closely bound to the state. In the Nordic countries, such movements include the trade unions and, interestingly for WREP, the state churches themselves. Both enjoyed not only a close relationship to the state, but considerable support from it – links that made their role increasingly untenable as time went on. Both, it follows, have been obliged to respond to the shifts that began in the 1960s and accelerated rapidly as the twentieth century drew to a close. Post-industrial structures began to assert themselves alongside post-material values. Unsurprisingly, more individualistic expressions of solidarity began to replace the collective mass movements of previous decades – challenging some long-standing vested interests (Rothstein 2003: 136). Indeed, many of the newer groups that have emerged have become, extraordinarily quickly, the folk movements of our time: those, for instance, concerned with the environment, gender equality, different kinds of discrimination (ethnic, racial, sexual and so on), innovative forms of democracy and an acute awareness of global inequalities. The final point is important: in many ways, these movements constitute a response to the previously unanticipated *global* pressures already mentioned (Held and McGrew 2002: 77).

Religious organizations figure strongly in these changes, a shift that is closely related to the growing visibility of religion in global terms. Here, in fact, is a place where the global and the local are brought together, sometimes at the expense of both nation-state and national church. This connection is captured in the idea of 'glocalization'. At one and the same time, the more enterprising elements within the churches establish strong links in the local community, creating thereby reserves of social capital, whilst also engaging themselves in international debates by means of their transnational organizations (for example, the World Council of Churches, the Lutheran World Federation and the Anglican Communion). The Catholic Church is, of course, a central player in this field, given its pre-eminence as a global institution – a tendency that grows almost by the day as its constituency, like those of Christianity more generally, migrates to the global south (Casanova 2001; Jenkins 2002).[6] It follows that the pressures on the *national* churches come from two directions: from articulate minorities at home, who make links with like-minded people in other parts of the world. Paradoxically, it is often the conservative groups who do this most effectively.[7]

Civil society involves the 'voluntary sector' in every understanding of the term. It includes – indeed it is made up of – the myriad organizations that belong neither to the state nor to the market, but which employ significant sections of the population. It also includes – though in different proportions in different places – the armies of unpaid volunteers who give their services freely to a multitude of different organizations (Wijkström and Einarsson 2006). Such people can be found in religious, social, humanitarian and cultural associations, all of which engage the loyalties of the individual, linking him or her to the wider society. Such groups become thereby a central aspect of a modern democracy (Amnå 1995; 2005). Once again, the terminology differs from place to place. Equally varied are the activities undertaken and the precise locations of the groups in question – some, for instance, are closer to the state than others (Herbert 2003). The voluntary sector remains, nonetheless, an essential feature of modern European societies, not least in the field of welfare. It is central to the work of WREP.

A third and final metaphor can be found in the idea of a 'social economy'. Here the emphasis lies on the generation of social rather than economic goals, and on activities that have value in themselves rather than being a means to an end. Good examples can be found in the day school run by parents, or in consumer or service co-operatives. A widely-recognized feature of such initiatives is that they offer

---

[6]   Exactly the same trend can be found in the transformations of some secular or non-governmental organizations, such as the Red Cross, which have become increasingly international rather than national in their concerns (Thörn 2002: 154).

[7]   The most obvious example can be found in the difficult debate about homosexuality in the Anglican Communion. Conservative groups in the North exploit the much greater number of people who share their views in the global South.

rich resources of social capital quite apart from the delivery of a specific product (Putnam 2000). A definition proposed by the Swedish Ministry of Culture nicely captures this combination of factors:

> By social economy is meant organized activities which have primarily social goals, which are democratic in character and organizationally independent of the public sector. These social and economic activities are mainly carried out in associations, co-operatives, foundations and similar organized groups of people. Activities in the social economy have a general value or a value for members as their main driving force, not profit. (Kulturdepartementet, 1999: 37)

Once again, local church organizations are one of several actors within the social economy, the more so given the non-material nature of their aims, some of which relate to the delivery of welfare in both the immediate and broader (added-value) sense of the term (Engvall 2002: 4). The prophetic as well as organizational role of the churches will be examined in detail in the case studies that follow.

The European Union and the Social Dimension

All the countries involved in WREP, apart from Norway, are members of the European Union. It is important therefore to take firm note of the welfare policies of the Union itself. It is not always recognized that, from the 1990s onwards, the European Union has made strenuous efforts in the direction of a common welfare policy – more specifically to strengthen the social rights of the citizen (such as the right to work or to social care), and, wherever possible, to eliminate poverty and social marginalization within its boundaries. Such aspirations can be seen, for example, in the Open Method of Co-ordination (OMC) agreed in Lisbon in 2000.[8]

The way of working outlined in the Lisbon agreements recognizes, however, that legislation in the field of social care is the responsibility of the member states, not of the European Union as such (Scharpf and Schmidt 2000). In this way, it is possible to retain very different national policies alongside genuinely European objectives, both internally and externally. Regarding the former, increasing mobilities have become an important factor – not only with regard to education and employment, but to social rights as well. If European populations are to move about during the course of their working lives, how does this affect their concomitant benefits – not least their pensions? Anyone with responsibility for a European project will know that finding an answer to these questions is easier said than done.[9]

Rather different, but equally important, are the European regulations regarding competitive tendering. Not only do these challenge official monopolies regarding

---

[8]   See http://ec.europa.eu/invest-in-research/coordination/coordination01_en.htm for more details.

[9]   For example, a number of the researchers in WREP lived in one country and worked in another. Their social security arrangements were complicated to say the least.

school, health care and the provision of care, but they also influence the ways in which a wide variety of groups, including church groups, bid for contracts in the welfare system. How, then, should more traditional institutions operate? How, in other words, should they engage in a system in which competition and for-profit actors have become increasingly present, and in which the norms of the market are beginning bit by bit to outweigh purely social considerations (Scharpf 2003: 74)?

It is unlikely that the churches will resist policies that are designed to combat poverty and to eliminate exclusion. The growing competitiveness in the provision of care, however, is a different matter. Here the churches are faced with a dilemma: should they participate in the process, recognizing that an important goal for those who will make the decisions is the reduction of costs overall (Thidevall 2003)? Or should they abandon the system altogether, resisting on principle the intrusions of the market into the provision of care? WREP has examined these questions in detail, highlighting a very obvious tension between the practical and prophetic functions of the churches. The dilemma is particularly apparent in the German case, where the diaconal institutions have long enjoyed a privileged situation, but are now exposed to more open competition (see Leis 2004a; Schmidt 2005; and Chapter 6 in this volume). Such competition, moreover, is increasingly involving commercial (even transnational) companies, especially in the care of elderly people – a rapidly growing field. An additional question follows from this. Does this transnational activity in itself imply a growing coherence between the European welfare regimes or will the very different goals and structures of national regimes endure despite everything? Whatever the case, increasing mobilities require increased flexibility, across as well as within national boundaries (Scharpf 2003: 78). The European situation, just like a European project, is not only complex but full of internal contradictions, to which solutions must, sooner or later, be found.

Uppsala's Centre for the Study of Religion and Society

WREP is the second of three major projects to have emerged from the Centre for the Study of Religion and Society at the University of Uppsala in Sweden[10] – an institution whose evolution is closely related to both the form and content of the projects themselves. Both the Centre and its offspring must now be introduced.

The story begins in 1996, when the Faculty of Theology in Uppsala launched a research programme concerned with religious and social change, in which the constitutional status of the Church of Sweden became a central theme. At the same time, a diaconal foundation known as Samariterhemmet, also in Uppsala,[11] took a decision to support research in the field of social and diaconal studies – an interest inscribed in its statutes. A third, and crucially important, piece of the jigsaw can

---

[10]   See http://www.impactofreligion.uu.se/ for more details.

[11]   More information about Samariterhemmet can be found at http://www. svenskakyrkan.se/samariterhemmet/

be found in a research initiative funded by the national Swedish Research Council under the title 'The State and the Individual: Swedish Society in the Process of Change' (1996). The aim was to examine closely the changing nature of Swedish society at the turn of the millennium, bringing together a variety of projects under a single theme. An application entitled 'From State Church to Free Folk Church' was made to this programme; the proposal was accepted and became a major part of the initiative (Bäckström 1999a). Its principal goal was to document the constitutional changes that took place in Sweden in 2000 – the moment when the Church of Sweden ceased to be a state church and became instead a free folk church – and to examine the implications of this change for Swedish society. It was the success of this application, together with a growing interest from the Foundation Samariterhemmet and the support from the Faculty of Theology, that enabled the inauguration of the Uppsala Institute for Diaconal and Social Studies (DVI) in 1999.

The programme of research that emerged from the state church project was ambitious. The core can be found in an extensive overview of the debate surrounding the disestablishment of the state church in Sweden, paying particular attention to the relationship between the discussion itself and the nature of the society in which it took place. Each influenced the other, and both were set in a long-term historical perspective. What emerged is a typically Nordic picture: Swedish society is becoming increasingly secular – there can be no doubt about that – but the place of the churches (both official and semi-official) remains important, a fact that is recognized by the vast majority of Swedish people. Roughly 75 per cent of the population continue to belong to the Swedish church, which is characterized by high rates of participation in the occasional offices (of birth, marriage and death), alongside very low levels of regular church-going, and relatively low levels of belief in God in an orthodox sense (Bäckström et al. 2004). Such characteristics remain intact, despite the change in constitutional status.

In total, the state church project included 15 researchers and resulted in 14 publications. These are listed in Appendix 3. In terms of content, particular themes within the project relate very directly to WREP. Indeed, they functioned almost as pilot studies, in the sense that they analysed the changing nature of Swedish society following the recession of the 1990s, an adjustment that included some initial steps towards the privatization of welfare. These themes include:

- An account of the relationship between the local church and the services provided by the local authority, which reveals that the Church of Sweden is expected to organize welfare services of high quality which are complementary to those provided by the state (Bäckström 2001).
- An outline of the social welfare provided by religious organizations in one Swedish locality; this study shows that there is considerable uncertainty concerning the nature of the complementarity suggested in the previous point (Jeppsson Grassman 2001).

- A comparison of the diaconal work carried out in Sweden and Germany, which highlights both the similarities and differences in the organization of church-based welfare in the two cases (Leis 2004a).

One further factor is important in terms of WREP. The state church project was supported by an international research group, representing a variety of countries and academic institutions. This group met annually, meetings which permitted the initial discussion of WREP and the formation of a new proposal. The next step followed naturally: the support group of the state church project became the core of the network necessary for the work on welfare and religion.

WREP, it is clear, has Nordic roots – it has grown out of a specifically Swedish project, is housed in a Swedish institution, and is financed by Nordic money. The advantages and disadvantages of this situation will be addressed briefly in the concluding section of this chapter. At this stage it is sufficient to note that both the state church project and WREP itself build onto established traditions of research, and onto studies that deal both with the place of religion in late modern societies and, more specifically, with the role of the churches as active voluntary organizations both in the Nordic countries and elsewhere.

Methodological Questions

WREP is an empirical study concerned with the place of majority churches in the delivery of welfare in eight European societies. It was, from the start, a comparative project in the sense that it was looking for commonalities as well as differences across the case studies. What, then, was the best way to do this, bearing in mind that WREP had, by its very nature, to be an exploratory project given that it was a pioneer in the field?

In the initial project meetings, well before the official 2003 start date, the team discussed these questions in detail – including the possibility that the emphasis might lie on quantitative rather than qualitative data, drawn from questionnaires directed to a representative sample of the population in the eight European countries. The advantages of such an approach were evident: an overview of religious and social attitudes or values would emerge across countries with markedly different welfare regimes and church traditions. Given the standard nature of the data, the possibilities for comparison would increase, bearing in mind the difficulties that inevitably arise when questionnaires are translated into different languages (see Appendix 2). We were aware, however, that this kind of data already existed – at least to some extent – generated by the European Values Study (the precursor of the World Values Survey), the International Social Survey programme, and the European Social Survey. The WVS in particular is a comprehensive study with a broad spectrum of questions and a wide geographical coverage (Esmer and Pettersson 2007: 2).[12]

The uncertainty which characterizes the present situation urged us, however, to go in a different direction. Instead of collecting statistical data on a national level, we decided instead to dig deep into one medium-sized town in each country, using qualitative rather than quantitative methods. The great advantage of working in this way has been a much more profound understanding of the welfare regime in a particular locality, including the place of the majority churches. It has also been possible to observe at first-hand the contributions of women in both spheres. Conversely, it was much more difficult to foresee exactly what would happen in the course of the research: what welfare needs would we find, and in what ways were the churches involved? For this reason, it was important to allow space for an initial mapping of the organizations in question, and then to construct a way of working that was sufficiently flexible to accommodate the unexpected.

The first step was to decide on the specific localities. The process was thoroughly discussed by the research team as a whole, before the choices were made by the senior advisor in each country. Some prior knowledge of both the local welfare situation and the churches was essential; equally important were practical issues such as accessibility and appropriate contacts. After considerable thought, the following towns were selected:

- Sweden: Gävle (population circa 90,000, located north of Stockholm)
- Norway: Drammen (population circa 55,000, located close to Oslo)
- Finland: Lahti (population circa 98,000, located north of Helsinki)
- Germany: Reutlingen (population circa 110,000, located south of Stuttgart)[13]
- England: Darlington (population circa 98,000, located south of Newcastle)
- France: Evreux (population circa 100,000, located north-west of Paris)
- Italy: Vicenza (population circa 110,000, located close to Padua)
- Greece: Thiva and Livadeia (combined population circa 43,000, located north of Athens).

More information about each of these can be found on the project website (http://web.archive.org/web/20071107195737/http:/www.student.teolineuu.se/wrep/), in the project description, and in the case studies brought together in the working papers of the project (see below) and in this book. The precise location of each town can be seen in Figure 1.1.

---

[12] Details of these projects can be found at http://www.europeanvalues.nl/; http://www.issp.org/; and http://www.europeansocialsurvey.org/

[13] A second (Catholic) case study in Germany, located in Schweinfurt, had to be put on hold due to lack of resources. It was included in the WaVE project.

Figure 1.1   Map of Case Study Locations

Despite the emphasis on the local, it was also necessary to master the national contours – in other words, to gain a thorough knowledge of the welfare system of each country together with its dominant religious tradition(s). Careful attention was also paid to the different understandings of gender across Europe, and the literature available on these questions. Each researcher was given time to do this before embarking on the fieldwork as such. Setting the empirical data into the appropriate national context has been central to our work – enabling, we maintain, sensitive and well-informed comparisons. We are, however, mindful of the limits of our way of working: the data that have emerged are manifestly rich, but not all of this material lends itself to immediate comparison.

That said, WREP has aimed to collect the following types of data in each of the eight towns:

- Data (of all kinds) which document the ongoing co-operation at a local level between the local authorities and church organizations.
- Data (interviews) which document how representatives of the local authorities view the role of the churches as social welfare providers and how local churches view the organization and development of social welfare.
- Data (interviews and focus groups) which document the attitudes of a sample of the population towards the function of churches as welfare providers.
- Data (documents, minutes, the local press) which document the theological position of the local church and its representatives, in so far as these are expressed in words and action.
- Data which document the importance of gender within all the areas listed above.

Each case study began by compiling an extensive dossier concerning the delivery of welfare in the locality in question and the place of the churches within this. The researchers were encouraged to use the widest possible range of resources: 'official' materials of all kinds (secular as well as religious), newspapers, informal interviews, observation and study visits. Bit by bit a more complete picture emerged, which provided a solid base for the subsequent interviews.

Regarding the latter, the first task was to select a strategic sample of local actors (that is, significant individuals in the field of welfare in both secular and religious organizations). These were the key players as far as WREP was concerned. Indeed, in some cases, these people turned out to be even more significant than we had anticipated – particular individuals could make a huge difference to the research process, not to mention to the welfare system as such. It was equally important, however, to discover the opinion of the general population – this time by means of focus groups as well as interviews, involving as wide a range of people as possible. Wherever possible, this stage of the research took place within existing communities – for example, among students, women's groups, retired people or unemployed individuals; in some cases, however, the researcher had to start from scratch. Quite clearly, and for a whole variety of reasons, the process was easier in some places than others. The results are nonetheless impressive: about 30 individual interviews have been completed in each town, together with 2–4 focus groups. Adding everything together, the WREP team have achieved approximately 250 interviews with individual Europeans, and 24 focus groups which between them gathered 200 or so individuals. All the interviews (individual and group) have been taped and transcribed.

In order to optimize the possibilities for effective comparison, seven common questions were asked in all individual and focus-group interviews. The remaining questions in the interview guide differed between the countries, depending on national and local context. All interview questions were 'open' questions – in other words, there were no fixed or coded answers. People could say what they liked. The common questions – exemplified by the Swedish case – were as follows:

1. In your opinion, what is welfare?
2. In your opinion, how well does the *Swedish* welfare system function in *Gävle*?
3. In your opinion, does the *Church of Sweden* have a role to play in the welfare and the well-being of people? – (If yes) How would you describe the role of the church?
4. In your opinion, should the *Church of Sweden* carry out practical social work? – (If yes) Of what type?
5. In your opinion, should the *Church of Sweden* contribute to the public debate on welfare issues? – (If yes) How should the church contribute?
6. In what ways do you think that the *Church of Sweden's* role in society has changed over the past ten years?
7. Is there anything you would like to change regarding the church's current role in society?

By and large these questions worked well and elicited the required information. That said, it is clear that many respondents had never thought about these issues until the moment of questioning – the taken-for-grantedness of the *status quo* was apparent in many cases.

The data that emerged were organized as follows. The first stage was to establish a 'map' of the local welfare system, looking in detail at both providers and recipients. Who did what for whom, and on what authority? The second task was to look at 'connections': in other words, the areas and activities in which co-operation – both formal and informal – existed between the local church and more secular providers, and the reasons for this. The absence of any such collaboration was also noted. Equally important were the views expressed regarding the pros and cons of the local system. At every stage close attention was paid to gender: where were both women and men located in the system and how did they – and indeed others – justify their presence? The researchers were also invited to think carefully about the specificities of the local case in relation to the country in which they were working: to what extent was this typical, or not, of the national situation? Given the extent of their knowledge, the team were then able not only to initiate the local analysis, but to offer valuable input into the comparative aspects of WREP, bearing in mind that the latter was first and foremost the responsibility of the co-ordinating group based in Uppsala.

It is the contributions of the researchers which are contained in this book – it is they (rather than the senior scholars) who have written the eight case studies that follow. They are primarily descriptive, but also contain the insights of their authors regarding the advantages and disadvantages of the systems they observed, their adequacy in fulfilling the goals for which they were designed and the possibilities for future development. Each researcher was encouraged to tell the 'story' as they saw it – not least to make the project 'live'. What emerges are real people who live and work in real places, many of whom engage with more or less intractable problems on a daily basis. The more analytical chapters – that is, the extended reflections from the point of view of sociology, gender and theology – can be found in the companion volume. Both have been facilitated by two sets of working papers produced by the co-ordinating group in Uppsala. The first contains the background material for each case study, including a careful description of the national as well the local case. The second (two-volume) set contains the principal findings from the empirical work. Both are referenced frequently in the chapters that follow and will be necessary for readers who require a more detailed knowledge of any or all of the case studies.[14] All the texts delivered have been in English, which has been the official language of the project.

A project as diverse as this one has required very clear direction, but at the same time, a degree of flexibility. It was essential to maintain sufficient control to permit the comparative work whilst allowing space for the individuality of each case. Broadly speaking, the former was achieved by means of careful administration in Uppsala and the regular meetings of the WREP team (which were annual for the whole group and bi-annual for the junior researchers), whilst the latter was left to the skills and experience of the senior scholar. At each stage of the project very careful instruction was given, which was thoroughly discussed at a project meeting, before the local researchers returned to the field. In general the system worked well, but the research process was by no means problem-free; the problems, however, were openly confronted. Almost immediately, for example, it became clear that sources of information available to Nordic scholars simply did not exist in southern Europe, and in the French case there was explicit hostility to a project that included a religious factor. It was unreasonable, therefore, to expect the researchers in these countries to produce exactly the same materials as their Nordic colleagues – a 'fact' that has enriched our thinking about the European situation. Additional examples of the research negotiation can be found in many of the case studies that follow.

Conclusion

WREP has set out to examine the main welfare models in Europe, together with the major theological traditions. To a large extent, it has succeeded – there are, however, some gaps. Conspicuously absent, for example, is an example of a pillarized society (either the Netherlands or Belgium) and a representative from the Iberian peninsula. Both are regrettable. Nor does WREP pay direct attention to the many religious minorities now present in Europe – a lacuna which has been

---

[14]   See Edgardh Beckman (2004), and Yeung et al. (2006).

filled by the research undertaken in WREP's successor. This is known as WaVE – the acronym for a project on Welfare and Values in Europe.[15]

It seems appropriate, therefore, to conclude this introduction with a word or two about the work with which the Centre for the Study of Religion and Society in Uppsala is currently engaged – in terms of both projects and programmes. Regarding the former, WaVE strictly speaking began before WREP had finished. As the data collection within WREP drew to a close, the European Commission, through its Framework 6 programme, initiated a call for Europe-wide research in the field of religion and values. Given its experience in these questions, the WREP team was well placed to make an application: indeed, it felt a strong obligation to do so. The application was approved in the autumn of 2005 and the study was launched the following spring. It ended, officially, in March 2009. Both title and subtitle reveal the affinities with WREP. Some elements are clearly very similar (notably the attention paid to gender), but others are different. Most important are the two 'extensions' to the project: first to the religious minorities which now exist all over Europe, and second to the post-communist parts of the continent (specifically Latvia, Poland, Croatia and Romania). The team has been enlarged accordingly. Welfare, moreover, has become not so much the focus of the study as such, so much as the 'prism' through which core values are perceived – those, for example, of inclusion and exclusion.

It is important to note that the current books are first and foremost an account of WREP. It is inevitable, however, that the initial findings of its successor have coloured not only our general thinking but the more detailed analyses that came towards the end of the research process. That said, a full account of WaVE remains to be written. Of considerable interest, however, is the fact that two major funding bodies in Europe (one private and one public) have devoted substantial resources to the study of welfare and religion in different parts of Europe. That, in turn, relates to the gradual change in perspective that took place during the life of WREP itself. At the outset – for reasons that have already been outlined – WREP had a markedly Nordic perspective, a fact which also accounts for the disproportionately large number of case studies that come from that part of Europe and for the emphasis on the Nordic literature. As the project developed, however, the priorities began to change. Not only did it become clear that Europeans were increasingly concerned about their welfare systems, they were beginning to pay close attention to religion – noting its presence in public as well as private life. Indeed, it was a growing anxiety about the more negative aspects of religion which lay behind the European Commission's call for research in this field – an example which others have followed.[16] In this sense WREP, without entirely shedding its origins, has not only become less Nordic and more European in its outlook, but has

---

[15]   See http://www.waveproject.org/

[16]   See, for example, the NORFACE projects on the re-emergence of religion as a social force in Europe: http://www.norface.org/norface/publisher/index.jsp?&1nID=93&pI D=94&nID=215 and the 'Tolerance and Diversity' and the 'Religion and Secularism across

become increasingly part of the agenda that it was created to address. It has been a pioneer in every sense of the term.

An additional step in the life of the Centre for the Study of Religion and Society took place in the summer of 2008: it concerns the establishment of a Centre of Excellence in Uppsala, hosted by the Centre, under the title 'The Impact of Religion: Challenges for Society, Law and Religion'.[17] This is an ambitious ten-year research programme funded jointly by the Swedish Research Council and the University and includes within it two streams relating to welfare and well-being. The work on religion and welfare, therefore, is not only ongoing, but increasingly recognized as a central field in the inter-disciplinary study of religion and society.

Two final points are important. For those engaged in WREP (as indeed in its successors), there are no preconceptions about religion. The latter can, it is true, create tensions; it can also offer solutions. Both situations can be found in the case studies brought together in WREP. A careful perusal of the accounts that follow, however, will reveal that large sections of the welfare system in Europe would simply collapse without the contributions of the churches, which remain – despite everything – key players in the field. The second point concerns timing: most of the case studies in WREP took place between 2004 and 2005. They capture, therefore a particular moment in the evolution of each of the societies of which they were part. Some updating has taken place – mostly in terms of more recent publications. The profiles (in terms of statistics, current debates and key personnel), however, remain as they were at the time of the research – they form an integral part of each account. The delay in publication is regrettable. A principal reason for this can be seen in the preceding paragraphs: it lies in the constant pressure to take on new research in what is clearly an expanding field. The topicality of our work, however, grows daily.

Before embarking on the case studies in detail, it is important to complete the background material. The following chapter has been written by a specialist in the field of welfare, and builds very directly onto the ideas set out thus far.

Europe' streams within the European Commission's Seventh Framework Programme, Area 3.3. Cultural interactions in an international perspective (2009).

[17]   See http://www.impactofreligion.uu.se

Chapter 2
Welfare in Western Europe:
Existing Regimes and Patterns of Change

Eva Jeppsson Grassman

Introduction

Few questions have attracted more attention during the past 15 years than those surrounding the welfare state – in particular, its 'crisis' and its chances of surviving in the late modern era given current economic pressures. 'Welfare states in transition' has become a key phrase in a rhetoric which suggests that welfare regimes in advanced western societies face important challenges. These include the need to adapt to the pressures of globalization, the current demographic situation (with its ageing populations and low fertility rates), and the changing role of women. Such challenges, in other words, relate to the foundations of the welfare state itself (Esping-Andersen 1996). Whatever welfare solutions were eventually chosen – and they vary in the different European countries – the fact remains that the welfare models in most western European countries were created in a historical context with preconditions which no longer exist. In the last two decades, for example, several western European countries have seen cuts in public expenditure or the enforcement of stricter priorities as a response to current pressures on the welfare system. As a result, new geographies of vulnerability have replaced or been added to old ones.

The 'welfare state in transition' discourse, furthermore, not only concerns the financing of the welfare state, and degrees of coverage, but also its organization and the provision of services, both of which have seen important changes. The decentralization and deregularization of welfare often go hand in hand. In several of the case studies reported in this book, for instance, more or less far-reaching decentralization has been coupled with new arrangements for welfare provision, notably the increasing prominence of both non-profit and for-profit welfare providers. Though different in each case, such shifts can be seen in France, England and Sweden, all three of which are represented in WREP (see also Archambault 1997; Billis 2001; Jeppsson Grassman 1999; Trydegård 2003).

The concept of privatization implies that services which were formerly provided by the public sector have now been taken over by the market – that is, by for-profit actors. Trends of privatization in this sense can be seen in various forms in different European countries, and mostly date from the 1990s. Usually these are the result of market-influenced changes in organization, inspired by what has been termed the 'new public management' introduced in the public sector (Almquist 2004; Pollitt 1995; Wollmann 2004). The concept of privatization is, however, ambiguous. In principle, it can include an increased focus on contributions from all agencies or actors that are not in the public sector – that is to say, not only for-profit companies, but also the voluntary sector, the church and the family. These very varied actors have had different levels of importance in the welfare regimes of Europe. It follows that the patterns of change currently taking place emerge from very different starting points: the institutional heritage, in welfare as in so much else, is extremely varied.

Alongside the trends and patterns that have already been described, a new element in the rhetoric about welfare states in transition has appeared in international debate. In the 1990s, the notion of the four sectors of society was introduced, concerning in particular the respective roles of the various sectors in welfare provision (Anheier and Salamon 1994; Pestoff 1991). In connection with this notion, which has its roots in the historical development of the welfare state (see van Kersbergen and Manow 2009), a key issue has to do with debates about 'complementarity and substitution' and the relevance of these concepts for understanding the changes in the welfare state (Dahlberg 2005). From this perspective, the voluntary sector is the sphere of society that is not the state, the market or the family. It has often been overlooked in scholarly research. More recently, however, the voluntary sector has been 'made visible', and the boundaries between the four sectors of society have been more carefully articulated, highlighting in new ways the division of responsibilities (Jeppsson Grassman 1999). At the same time, certain patterns of paid and unpaid work in welfare service provision have attracted attention: notably unpaid volunteer work in a wide variety of organizations (Gaskin and Davis Smith 1995; Jeppsson Grassman and Svedberg 1996) and the informal care by families of elderly and frail relatives (Parker and Lawton 1994; Szebehely 1999; Twigg 1993). In sum, during the 1990s, questions about who should finance, who should organize and who should provide welfare – which have always been central in welfare discourse – were brought to the fore in a new way.

The church does not go untouched by these changes in welfare provision. Whether it has a well-established role as the provider of welfare services, as in some continental and southern European countries, or a more complementary role, as in the Nordic countries, it seems that new demands and new welfare situations entail an increased focus on the church as a welfare agent, sometimes implying an innovative role (Edgardh Beckman 2004; Fix and Fix 2002). At the same time, some churches are beginning to develop their own discourse, in an attempt to explore their role in welfare in more detail (Jeppsson Grassman and Whitaker 2006). An important question follows from this: in what sector should the church be placed – in the state or the voluntary sector? The fact that there is no single or comprehensive answer to this question in the European context is one reason for the neglect of the church's role in welfare on the part of academics, despite the boom in research into the voluntary sector which has taken place in the last 15 years in Europe.[1] Indeed, a glance at the principal publications concerned with 'typical' research on the welfare state in Europe in the same period reveals that the church has seldom been regarded as a welfare actor at all. A welcome exception, however, can be found in the work of van Kersbergen and Manow, in which the multi-faceted links between religion, religious cleavages and the shaping of European welfare states are thoroughly explored. The case studies collected in this book are similarly focused.

More precisely, the picture of 'welfare states in transition' offers a point of departure for the WREP project which – as was made clear in the previous chapter – aims at analysing the function of the majority churches as agents of social welfare in a comparative European perspective. This chapter presents a detailed review of the current literature, in order to provide a frame of reference and some conceptual tools for the case studies that follow.

Welfare and the Welfare State

Welfare is about the good society and the lives of citizens. In the Scandinavian tradition, welfare is often defined as 'the individual resources by means of which members of society can control and consciously steer the direction of their own lives' (Palme et al. 2002: 17). It has, therefore, to do with conditions of life in relation to the economy, healthcare, employment, social relations, housing, security and political resources. These areas are considered central to welfare, whether they are thought of as resources or as the fulfilment of needs (Fritzell and Lundberg 2000). It follows that welfare systems are concerned with issues such as coverage and eligibility – who qualifies for what, and to what extent the individual is compensated for the risks to which he or she is exposed within the areas referenced above.

The concept of welfare, however, is not always clear, and it is used with different connotations in different situations. Here it is important to refer to Allardt's famous typology (see Chapter 1), which is based on three categories: having, loving and being. The latter two categories reflect the subjective dimensions of welfare or 'quality of life', a concept which is often used to complement, or even to contrast with, material conditions (Allardt 1975). These subjective dimensions refer both to social relations (love), and to existential dimensions (a sense of wholeness and meaning, and the possibility of achieving existential goals). With such a wide definition, it is inevitable that we depart from what are usually considered to be the core areas of the welfare state. Putting the same point more positively, it has been argued – notably in the Nordic countries – that the concept of welfare in late-modern, post-materialist societies takes on new meanings as circumstances alter

---

[1]   When compared to American research the contrast is, of course, striking: research on faith-based welfare provision is extensive in the United States (Chaves and Tsitsos 2001; Cnaan 2002; Cnaan et al. 2006).

(Pettersson 1992). In other words, it should not simply be interpreted from a state perspective. From the point of view of WREP, it is clear that a wider definition of welfare is essential if we are to understand the welfare provided by churches and voluntary organizations in many European countries (Jeppsson Grassman 2001; Yeung 2004). It is equally clear that these subtler dimensions of welfare are not usually addressed in comparative studies of the welfare state as such.

The concept of the 'welfare state' is strongly related to the post-war history of many European countries, but its foundations date from the end of the nineteenth century. Important and crucial breakthroughs followed in the early decades of the twentieth century. Exactly what is meant by 'welfare state', however, is not always evident. Esping-Andersen argues that the welfare state must mean something more, and something other, than whatever menu of social benefits a state happens to offer. Furthermore, the welfare state as we understand it must be viewed as 'a unique historical construction, an explicit redefinition of what the state is all about' (Esping-Andersen 1999: 33). This specific historical construction had its strongest phase of development in many European countries between 1930 and 1960. Thereafter, it was refined and elaborated. Indeed in some countries, the years between 1950 and 1970 have been referred to as the golden age of the welfare state[2] – a point with obvious implications for the current discussion. Welfare states were built on assumptions about the state, the market and the family which may in many respects now be obsolete.

Welfare Regimes in Europe

A common point of departure for research about welfare systems in western countries can be found in Esping-Andersen's typology (Baldock 1999; Gilbert 2002; Kautto 1999; Sainsbury 1999). Basically, this is a 'three worlds' typology, of welfare regimes which are neither equal to welfare states nor to particular social policies. According to Esping-Andersen, 'regimes' refers to the way in which welfare production is allocated between state, market and households in a variety of European countries. They may be seen as ideal types. The real world is likely to exhibit hybrid forms. As we saw in Chapter 1, three principal regimes are identified: the liberal, the conservative and the social-democratic.

This typology has been criticized on many points: for being too static (Esping-Andersen 1996); for using the wrong criteria (Kautto et al. 2001); for having theoretical shortcomings (Baldwin 1996); for omitting a fourth, Mediterranean regime-type (Ferrera 1997; Leibfried 1992); for failing to explain differences between countries within a regime-type (van Kersbergen and Manow 2009); for being too focused on income maintenance and paid work (Sainsbury 1999); for neglecting gender issues (Lewis 1992; 1997); and for neglecting aspects of social

---

[2]　　Other countries, however, moved more slowly. This is true, for instance, for some of the southern European countries.

care (Anttonen and Sipilä 1996) and the voluntary sector (Kuhnle and Selle 1992). The typology developed by Esping-Andersen is nevertheless considered to have both sensitizing and clarifying power. It has had, and indeed still has, a great impact on welfare state research.[3] It is the obvious frame of reference within which the welfare arrangements of the countries participating in WREP can be understood.

The Liberal Welfare Regime

Liberal welfare-regime countries are those where socialist or Christian democrat movements were weak or absent. Typically, these are the Anglo-Saxon countries: the United States, Australia, New Zealand and Canada. Among the European countries, it is the United Kingdom which comes closest to fitting this regime-type. Although there are differences between them, these countries display common characteristics: the welfare regime is residual in the sense that it adopts a very narrow definition of risk, of eligibility and of what is considered 'social'. Liberal social policy favours means-tested social assistance. Targeted social assistance is a major element of the total social protection package in these countries. Insurance schemes are often quite modest, although it is important to underline that the United Kingdom has a universal health service. A pertinent characteristic of this regime-type is its encouragement of market solutions in welfare – in health, pensions and so on. Nowhere in Europe was such encouragement more pronounced than during the Thatcher era in Britain. The liberal model, then, can be summarized in terms of residualism, relatively few rights and modest levels of de-commodification.[4]

Esping-Andersen initially presented his typology in *The Three Worlds of Welfare Capitalism* (1990). In one of his more recent works (1999) he explores and discusses the robustness of the typology from a comparative perspective. One problem, he argues, is that the typology emerges from a particular point in time and does not account for change. A good example of this problem can be found in the United Kingdom. Had the comparison been made in the immediate post-war period, Esping-Andersen argues, the United Kingdom and Scandinavia would probably have been in the same cluster: both were built on universal, flat-rate benefits, national health care and a vocational commitment to full employment. Since then, a gradual privatization and residualization has taken place in the United Kingdom, which has veered more and more towards the liberal model. Precisely this point can be seen very clearly if we compare the English and the Swedish case studies in the WREP project.

---

[3] For an overview of the debate concerning Esping-Andersen's typology, see Arts and Gelissen (2002).

[4] De-commodification is the degree to which welfare states weaken the cash nexus by granting entitlements independent of market participation (Offe and Keane 1984; Esping-Andersen 1990).

The Conservative Welfare Regime

The conservative regime-type, in Esping-Andersen's typology, groups together a wide range of countries with different institutional responses to welfare needs. A common denominator can be found, however, in their affinity with conservative political ideas and actions, often encouraged by religious cleavages and conflicts between church and state (van Kersbergen and Manow 2009). In continental Europe, the beginnings of social policy were frequently inspired by monarchical 'etatism', by traditional corporatism and by Catholic social teaching – the more so in countries with a Catholic majority. For the most part, post-war developments continue to be guided by Christian Democrat or conservative coalitions (bearing in mind a fascist interregnum in some cases). The very varied countries in this regime-type include France, Germany, Austria, Belgium and the Netherlands.[5] Italy is also placed in this category, but Greece (though present in WREP) is not included (Esping-Andersen 1990; 1999).

The essence of the conservative regime-type lies in its blend of status segmentation and familialism. Early social insurance schemes did not build on to egalitarian ideals, with the result that far-reaching status differentials have been preserved in many of the insurance programmes in these countries. The 'etatist' legacy remains strong in the privileged treatment of public civil servants, especially in Germany, France, Italy and Austria (Esping-Andersen 1990; 1999). Despite attempts to consolidate the myriad of occupational schemes that exist in these places, corporate status divisions continue to characterize the systems of social security. Only the Netherlands constitutes an exception to this pattern, particularly with regard to the pension scheme. In most of these countries, private or market solutions generally play a marginal role. Non-state solutions to welfare issues mean, instead, the involvement of non-profit, voluntary organizations, often affiliated to the church or 'pillared' along denominational or language lines (as, for example, in the Netherlands and Belgium).

Familialism and subsidiarity are important, and closely interrelated, attributes of this regime-type, the more so in southern Europe (Esping-Andersen 1999; Leibfried 1992). Familialism is defined as a combination of the male-bread-winner bias of social protection, and the centrality of the family as care-giver, which – following the principle of subsidiarity – is ultimately responsible for its members' welfare. At the same time, there is a residual pattern in the conservative welfare regime, but in this case it does not reflect market failure as it does in the liberal model. Conservative residualism, rather, is a response to *family* failure: state provision in the form of targeted services is only introduced when the family and/or civil society are unable to respond adequately. It is also clear that both

---

[5]   This is the case in spite of the high degree of de-commodification in the Netherlands. In fact, this seems to be one of the most difficult countries to place: Esping-Andersen first assigned the Netherlands to the social-democratic regime-type, but later placed it in the conservative regime-type.

principles – familialism and subsidiarity – are more present in some places than in others. Both, for example, are strong in Germany, the Netherlands and the southern European countries. Familialism is, however, a much less pertinent attribute in France and Belgium (Morgan 2009). Indeed, in some respects, it is problematic to place France in this regime-type at all (Esping-Andersen 1999; Manow and Palier 2009; Martin 1997).

A number of scholars have argued that there are grounds for including an additional regime-type, which must be introduced at this point. The countries in question would be Italy, Spain and Portugal which, the authors claim, have regional characteristics and similarities that make them distinctive (Ferrera 1997; Leibfried 1992; Trifiletti 1999). These are countries where the welfare state is weak. A characteristic trait in the systems that do exist is the dominance of transfer payments, and extreme status segmentation in the systems of income maintenance (Ferrera 1997). Family benefits and support are underdeveloped – as, indeed are services, including social care. Conversely, the role of the family – not least in social aid – is stronger than in the conservative welfare regimes further north. The chapters on Italy and Greece in this volume will develop these themes further. Interestingly, Esping-Andersen refutes the argument that there are grounds for a further sub-division of regime-types. With their strong focus on status segmentation in social insurance and their high degree of familialism, he argues that the southern European welfare systems are simply a variant of the conservative model already described.

The Social-Democratic Welfare Regime

The principles of universalism, comprehensive risk coverage, generous benefit levels, egalitarianism and full employment are characteristics of the social-democratic regime-type, the cornerstones of which were laid with the advent of social democracy prior to World War 2. This regime-type, which is usually considered the 'political child' of decades of social democratic rule, is virtually synonymous with the Nordic countries, despite the differences in their precise welfare arrangements and in their trajectories of change. Sweden, Finland and Norway are the three Nordic countries involved in WREP.

Universalism in this model is coupled to citizens' rights; that is, social entitlements are attached to individuals, and based on citizenship rather than on a demonstrated need or employment relationship. This means that citizens have a basic right to a broad range of services and benefits regardless of income and position in the labour market. High income replacement rates diminish the importance of the market in this regime-type, and the degree of de-commodification is, from a comparative perspective, also considered high. According to Esping-Andersen (1999), the social-democratic model is also distinct in terms of its active efforts to abolish dependency on private welfare.

A second attribute of this regime-type is (or has been at least) the political commitment to full employment even at times of economic recession (Stephens

1996). This is not unique to the Nordic countries. However, active employment policies have been pushed further in these countries, which have extremely high aims in this respect, exploiting the Nordic principle of productivism. Finally, the social-democratic regime-type is characterized by a high degree of de-familialization. This concept, introduced earlier by Lister (1995), is used by Esping-Andersen (1999) to denote policies that reduce the dependence of the individual on the family, and that maximize the ability of each individual to command economic resources independent of familial or conjugal reciprocities. Such policies can be seen, for instance, in the range of state subsidies for childcare, for elderly or disabled people and for other care services.

Variations in the 'Women-Friendliness' of Welfare Regimes

De-familialization as a concept seems gender-neutral at first glance. Other authors, however, prefer to speak about the degree of 'women-friendliness' of a welfare regime or state. The Nordic countries have commonly been viewed as women-friendly states (Hernes 1987). This means that they encourage self-help through work or welfare transfers, thus freeing women from economic dependence on their husbands (Kjelstad 2001; Lewis 1997).

In more recent work on his regime typology, Esping-Andersen (1999) has looked into variations in de-familialization between regime-types. He discovered that the variations were as great as they were for de-commodification, concluding that the Nordic states remain the only place where social policy is explicitly designed to maximize a woman's economic independence. Specifically, he found that the social-democratic regime-type ranked highest on all the following indicators of de-familialization: commitment to services in general, subsidies to families with children, public day-care for small children and the percentage of those aged 65 and over receiving care in their own home. The conservative regime-type came second, apart from the southern European countries which ranked very low.

That said, marked variations exist within each regime-types. For example, both France and Belgium scored high on public child-care and education, which are women-friendly issues (Morgan 2009). Critics maintain, moreover, that the 'women-friendliness' of a regime-type is a complex issue and that there is a risk of Scandinavian normativity in the way this phenomenon is measured (Kjelstad 2001). It is equally important to remember that the five Nordic welfare states represent five rather different gender profiles, yet they are all considered women-friendly (Siim and Borchorst 2005).

Systems of Social Care Provision

A dominant critique of the welfare regime typology developed by Esping-Andersen argues that, in both theoretical conceptualization and empirical analysis, it is focused almost entirely on income maintenance, social insurance, the labour market and paid work. It does not address the issue of social care as such, nor in any specific sense the provision of welfare services.[6] The same goes for the more tangible aspects of welfare organization and the role of the family in care provision. All that can be said is that the regime-type conceptualization offers a context from which some inference about organization, provision and welfare agents can be made. To a great extent, however, these aspects are invisible. Indeed, comparative analysis of care and other welfare provision in the different countries of Europe sometimes reveal patterns contrary to those associated with alleged regime-types (Anttonen and Sipilä 1996; Kautto 2002). There may even be reasons to make a division between the social insurance state, which is 'cash-heavy' and the social service state, which is 'service-heavy' (Sipilä 1997).

Daly and Lewis (2000) argue that it is not possible to understand contemporary welfare states at all without addressing the care issue. Provision of care has increasing weight in welfare state policies in Europe. Social care arrangements are an integral part of society, and are of growing importance in countries with ageing populations and those in need of day-care for children. A typology of social care regimes would focus not only on the given care rationale, but on the agency, the recipient and the carer (Anttonen et al. 2003). Agency has to do with the four sectors of society: state, market, family and the voluntary sector. The research tradition that focuses on different agents and sources of welfare provision uses concepts such as 'welfare mix'. Szebehely (1999), for instance, argues for the need to be specific in distinguishing between paid and unpaid work in relation to each agency. Social care research has also drawn attention to the need to explore the character of 'the product': what is care and what is it that recipients get? What is the relationship between the carer and the recipient (Waerness 2005)? And who is the recipient?

In this research tradition, childcare and the care of elderly people are often treated separately (with the partial exception of some Scandinavian research). One reason for this may be that arrangements for children and elderly people often follow different welfare regime-paths even within one country. Precisely this was shown by Anttonen and Sipilä (1996), who made an attempt to classify European social care services into different models. Taking this particular fact as their point of departure, Daly and Lewis (2000) attempted to categorize European countries into care regimes, based on a framework of variations in care arrangements and agency. Only the Scandinavian countries form a distinct group in this regard, with their public, formal care arrangements both in childcare and in care for elderly people. The continental and the Mediterranean welfare states all seem to favour 'privatized' solutions in care, but there is considerable variation as to the nature of privatization. In the Mediterranean welfare states, for example, care tends to take place in families, whereas in Germany it is seen primarily as the domain of

---

[6] The more recent work on de-familialization by Esping-Andersen does not, on the whole, change this overall critique (Arts and Gelissen 2002).

voluntary service providers. In France a clear distinction is made between care for children and care for elderly people, with a strong public sector and a high degree of universalism in the former, but an emphasis on the voluntary sector and the family in the latter. In Britain and Ireland it is the other way around: childcare is constructed as a 'state-free zone', whilst care for elderly people is still for the most part the responsibility of the public sector (although increasingly becoming privatized). The reasons for these differences are historical and, as argued by Morgan (2009), are largely explained by the balance between religious and secular political forces at crucial moments in the history of each country.

It is not only the welfare mix in the provision of social care that varies between countries. They have also undergone organizational changes in the past decade; such changes differ from place to place but more often than not they imply a more rigorous division between the enabling agent and the provider role according to reforms inspired by new public management (Wollmann 2004). Decentralization patterns are equally diverse. What may in one country be the responsibility of regional government may in another be the responsibility of a local authority. It is for these reasons that comparative studies of social care are complicated – a point underlined by Rostgaard and Lehto (2001), who studied formal social care for elderly people on a comparative basis. They found complex combinations regarding structures of responsibility, the agency of care and the direction of change in their different cases. That said, the care of elderly people is generally regarded as one of the fields most touched by privatization. Even in the Nordic countries, where the public sector is still, by far, the most important provider, it is possible to see a marked privatization in the care of older people since the beginning of the 1990s, notably in Finland and in Sweden. Contracted care carried out by private, mainly for-profit providers, quadrupled during the 1990s in Sweden (Trydegård 2003). The privatization of this field is an even more striking feature in the United Kingdom where care for elderly people is increasingly provided by private, for-profit contracted actors in addition to voluntary organizations (Rostgaard and Lehto 2001). Even in countries of the conservative regime-type, where the main providers of care are often non-profit voluntary organizations, market-oriented changes are becoming increasingly visible (Bahle 2003). A German example was given in the previous chapter. Finally, the growth of an informal market through which migrant workers are privately employed is a significant trend of the past decade in some countries, not least in Italy. Here, the presence of large numbers of migrants has encouraged a growing informal economy, notably in the provision of care (Lyon and Glucksmann 2008).

In addition, a de-institutionalization of formal care for old people has taken place in recent decades in many European countries. This implies that formal social care is often given in the form of 'home help', meaning that old, frequently frail, people can remain in their 'natural surroundings'. While 'ageing in situ' has become an important welfare goal in most western countries, it is interesting to note that in two Nordic countries – Sweden and Finland, in which comprehensive home-based care has been offered for many years – a reduction in home-help provision has occurred since 1990 (Szebehely 2005). Priorities have been enforced more strictly. At the same time, in Sweden at least, institution-based care has also decreased, to a point where 'the right to age in situ' has been replaced by 'the right to residential care' in contemporary Swedish care discourse.

Making Informal Care and Volunteering More Visible

The idea of a welfare mix also includes unpaid work in welfare and care. Characteristic of the welfare discourse in European countries in the past 15 years has been an increased interest on the part of politicians and administrators in unpaid care carried out by citizens. The background to this shift is ideological on the one hand, and financial on the other (driven by budget deficits). For both reasons, unpaid welfare work not only fulfils a complementary role, it also becomes in many situations the only care available. Indeed, unpaid informal care – provided by the family for frail parents, spouses or relatives – is likely to account for the major part of all social care for these groups, no matter what the regime-type (Johansson 1991).

It is generally assumed, given their high degree of familialism, that informal care is particularly extensive in the southern European countries. It has also been argued that it is more characteristic of conservative and liberal regime countries than it is of the socio-democratic type countries (Anttonen and Sipilä 1996; Rostgaard and Lehto 2001). Recent research in Sweden revealed, however, that informal care was surprisingly extensive and of increasing importance even here – perhaps in response to changed policies and greater prioritization in more formal systems of provision (Jeppsson Grassman 2003; Szebehely 2005). In fact, a recent Eurobarometer which compared levels of informal care in a range of European countries indicated very varied patterns, which cut right across welfare regime-types (Alber and Köhler 2004).

Clearly, changing patterns of care must be interpreted in light of the contexts in which they occur. Taking this into account, however, there is a common observation that informal care is of increasing importance, understanding this as a response to a retrenchment in the welfare state. Families are obliged to substitute for formal care. Using Esping-Andersen's concept as point of departure, there may therefore be reasons to speak about a 're-familialization' of the welfare state with respect to care, at least in some countries. Here systems of support for informal carers have become important ingredients in the welfare panorama (Jegermalm 2005; Lamura 2003).

Volunteering

The new welfare situation of the 1990s has spurred research on the voluntary sector in many countries, notably concerning its role in welfare (Harris et al. 2001; Jeppsson Grassman and Svedberg 2007). A central feature in this (comparative) work is the attention paid to the extent and character of unpaid work in voluntary organizations – that is, to volunteering itself (Gaskin and Davis Smith 1995). Curtis et al. (2001) used data from the 1993 World Values Survey to make cross-national comparisons of volunteering, once again using Esping-Anderson's three regime-types. They found that countries of the social-democratic regime-type take the lead in volunteer work, followed, or equalled by, countries of the liberal type. Countries of the conservative type – with the exception of the Netherlands – had lower scores. Countries in southern Europe, with their high degree of familialism, often seemed to rank very low with respect to volunteering. As for volunteering specifically in voluntary organizations for social care and welfare, Gaskin and Davis Smith (1995) found a somewhat different pattern, implying that volunteering in this type of organization might be more developed in Anglo-Saxon countries, together with some examples of the conservative regime-type, than in the Nordic countries. Whatever the case, volunteer work in social care and welfare organizations appears to have increased in the past ten years in a number of countries, notably in Sweden, perhaps in response to the current situation of the welfare state (Jeppsson Grassman and Svedberg 2007).

Difference and Convergence

Are the welfare states of Europe converging in response to common problems and external pressures of economic, demographic or political nature, or not? Are they, in other words, becoming more alike? If so, which welfare regime should converge with which – given that they appear to differ with regard to their resistance to current pressures? Convergence is sometimes defined simply as a process of movement towards a European average, or even a European minimum. If this were the case, convergence from a Nordic perspective would mean a 'Europeanization' of Nordic welfare states, whilst countries in southern Europe would be seen as 'catching-up' with the European average. In the 1990s, for instance, cutbacks in welfare, restricted eligibility and more market-oriented solutions prompted some Swedish scholars to speak about 'the flight from universalism' and a trend towards more liberal solutions (Sunesson et al. 1998). Rather more positively, the social policies of one country may function as an inspiration for new solutions in another country. A recent illustration of the latter can be found in the German reform concerning parental leave allowance, which is quite clearly modelled on the Swedish parental leave system.[7]

Empirically, however, most commentators seem to agree that there are few clear signs of real regime convergence across Europe (Bouget and Palier 1999; Kautto et al 2001). Castles (2004), for example, argues that there is no distinct pattern leading towards a 'European model'. Rather, what can be observed is a consolidation of the 'family of nations pattern', the four families being the

---

[7]   This reform came into force on 1 January 2007.

different European welfare regime-types (including a southern European model). These families remain diverse, he concludes, and do not all face exactly the same challenges; nor are they likely to address common and contemporary problems in the same way.

This debate, which is not new, also revolves around the issue of European integration: that is to say, the effect of the latter on the social policies of the member states. Here there is an interesting contrast between globalization and other external pressures, and Europeanization per se. If the former are assumed to impact on welfare states mainly through unintended consequences, the latter – European integration – is more a question of intentional effects in order to achieve 'harmonization' between countries. There seems, however, to be little consensus regarding how and to what extent, or if at all, this 'harmonization' will be realized.

Concluding Remarks

The short overview presented in this chapter has aimed to draw attention to the various welfare contexts within which the majority churches of each case study exist and act, and to present some key concepts pertinent to the welfare field. The goal has been to provide a frame of reference through which the country-specific patterns presented in the coming chapters can be read, and to offer some tools for further understanding. The focus has been on European welfare regime-types, their characteristics and the differences between them. Most scholars maintain that these diverse regimes have a considerable degree of robustness and that differences between them will remain. With all its alleged imperfections, the welfare regime typology developed by Esping-Andersen seems nonetheless to be a useful tool when it comes to understanding the diverse welfare geographies of which the majority churches are part. At the same time the similarities in discourses, as well as in welfare problems and challenges, have been briefly explored.

In short, there is ample evidence that changes in welfare organization, provision and levels of responsibility are happening all over Europe. Policy-making, however, varies widely in all these fields. It is clear that differences in historical and institutional structures continue to account for path-dependence in welfare patterns. It is these precisely these issues – the similarities and differences – that the following chapters will explore in more detail.

Chapter 3

The Church of Sweden: A Church for All, Especially the Most Vulnerable

Ninna Edgardh and Per Pettersson[1]

Introduction

'Swedish welfare means security from the cradle to the grave. From the moment you are born until you are laid to rest you are taken care of by the public authorities if you can't manage on your own' (m).[2] This quotation from a focus group interview with representatives of the population in the town of Gävle illustrates the character of the Swedish welfare system. The social security system is expected to serve as a life-long safety-net for all citizens. The twentieth-century image of Swedish society was that of a big family, 'the home of the people' (*folkhemmet*). The welfare model developed to suit this home was characterized by homogeneity, universality and equal access for all people, regardless of social position or financial opportunities. Interestingly, the same is true of the church. Having experienced a gradual marginalization from its dominant position in an agricultural society, the Church of Sweden found a new role in the *folkhemmet* as 'the people's church' (*folkkyrkan*), expected to serve the religious needs of all citizens.

Since the 1980s the Swedish welfare model has, however, been challenged by demands for reduced public costs alongside the emergence of new forms of poverty and exclusion. The public welfare and state church system were deregulated simultaneously. Since 2000, the Church of Sweden has become a free agent in relation to the state, and expectations of its role both as a direct provider of welfare services and as a defender of the values of solidarity and care have moved on. The Swedish case shows therefore signs of an emerging new role for the church in society – as a social agent distinct from the state.

The Swedish Case: Gävle

The Swedish case study was conducted in Gävle, a town situated on the coast, two hours' drive north of Stockholm. From the 1950s onwards, this old industrial

---

[1]   The study on which this chapter is based was carried out with the help of Thomas Ekstrand (Edgardh Beckman et al. 2006).

[2]   In what follows (f) stands for a female and (m) for a male interviewee.

town has gradually transformed itself into part of the new service economy. As in Sweden generally, the labour movement and the Social Democrats have dominated politically. From a religious point of view, the Church of Sweden is the dominant agent. Approximately 80 per cent of the town's population belongs to the church and pays an annual fee of roughly one per cent of its income to it. Some 92,000 people live in the municipality, 75 per cent in the urban area. The present case study is focused on urban Gävle. It is based on studies of documents concerning the welfare situation and the role of the church, as well as on interviews with employed and elected representatives from the public authorities and Church of Sweden parishes. In addition, group interviews have been conducted with representatives from the population at large.

Welfare in the Swedish Context

Välfärd in Swedish covers the meanings of both 'welfare' and 'well-being'. It implies the satisfaction of basic material needs, and the availability of help when in need, as in cases of illness. The interviewees in the Swedish case study take it for granted that the public welfare system will ensure the material welfare of every individual. They point out that 'when you become unemployed, when you become ill or when you are handicapped by accident or illness or whatever, there is a security system that takes care of you. You are not put out on the street' (f). In addition, *välfärd* also has non-material aspects. One church informant expresses it thus: 'To have a roof over your head and food for the day, but also a meaningful life, to be part of a meaningful setting. You cannot live only for food and housing, you ought to have something more, and that I think is included in welfare' (m). Good welfare includes a sense of meaning, the fulfilling of spiritual needs, social relationships and a sense of security; it means 'that a human being has a good life, from the perspective of his or her conditions ... not only at a material level, but also at a spiritual level' (m).

From Poverty to Abundance

International comparisons now rank Sweden amongst the highest in terms of public welfare provision (Vogel 2003). This is a relatively recent achievement. As little as 150 years ago, poverty threatened large parts of the Swedish population, and the gap between the rich and the poor was enormous. The improvements in health care, education and social care are strongly related to decades of struggle against poverty and social exclusion on the part of the labour movement. Among the older generation which was part of this struggle and has witnessed the remarkable economic growth after World War 2, 'welfare' is a highly value-laden word. Basic material welfare is not taken for granted, but considered something to be proud of. Members of the younger generations, however, tend to take the system for granted and to notice its disadvantages, in the form of high taxes and a presupposition of homogeneity discordant with the growing emphasis on individual choice in society. Such critical opinions played a major role in the autumn 2006 Swedish general election, when the ruling Social Democrats were defeated by an alliance of more liberal and conservative parties. Nonetheless, there remains in Sweden a broad consensus between all political parties on the basic character of the Swedish welfare model.

The principle of universality undergirds the system. Basic social benefits and services are provided for all citizens, who are, in their turn, expected loyally to share responsibility through taxation according to income (Rothstein 1994). Significantly, the development of the welfare system has been closely connected with the introduction of individual, rather than family rights, which has in turn been part of a wider policy of gender equality. Welfare services are generally uniform, and directed towards the individual from birth to death. They start at infancy with public maternity care centres, continuing with day-care centres and preschools. Schooling is totally free and tax-financed, even at college and university level. Generous state-financed loans are offered to all students so that people of every social class can afford to study. The health insurance system guarantees all inhabitants virtually free health care and subsidized medicine and dental care. Care for elderly people is also almost entirely financed by the public sector: there is a basic public pension as well as an income-based supplementary pension. The Swedish state has publicly-financed systems of housing allowances, unemployment benefits, sick pay, child allowances, parental insurance and social assistance. The intention of the social security net is that all Swedes, regardless of ability or circumstances, should always be able to rely on the public sector to provide for at least their most basic needs.

Historically, the church has played an important role in welfare provision in Sweden. Until the middle of the nineteenth century, the church was closely integrated with the state, and shouldered much of the formal responsibility for social welfare (Enochsson 1949; Gellerstam 1971; Selander 1986). The first major step away from this system was taken in 1862, when the local authorities were divided into a civil and an ecclesiastical section (Bexell 2003). During the first half of the twentieth century, social responsibilities were gradually transferred from family and voluntary organizations to the public sector. A number of institutions were separated from the church. By the end of the nineteenth century, this transition had already taken place in the areas of education and care for poor people. Health and social care were transferred during the first decades of the twentieth century. Later, voluntary care provided by the church's diakonal institutions was incorporated into the public welfare system in a similar way (Leis 2004a and b). As part of this development, the Church of Sweden's role as a 'folk church' was integrated into the framework of the Swedish welfare model (Wrede 1966, 1992; Ekstrand 2002). The church became a provider of public welfare in the spiritual sphere, with clear and legally-defined boundaries in relation to the social welfare responsibility of the state.

The Deregulation of Welfare and Church

Recent changes have affected this set-up. The Swedish model has been challenged from a variety of perspectives, ranging from demographic change to the emergence of new transnational financial and political agents. During the 1980s, the economy grew rapidly and continuously, and new ideas of decentralization (inspired by European ideas on subsidiarity and the influence of neo-liberalism) emerged (Hort 1990). A number of reforms were implemented which meant a decentralization of public administration. The dominant role of the state was criticized more frequently in political and economic debate, even within the Social Democratic party. The centrally-governed welfare state was reformed, and many former state monopolies (such as telecommunications, the postal service and railways) were deregulated and subjected to commercialization and competition. The decision to deregulate the Swedish state church in 2000 took place against the backdrop of these societal reforms. The separation of church and state is thus part of a larger process of change.

During the financial recession of the 1990s, discussion of decentralization and the privatization of public welfare services intensified. The potentially complementary role of the family and voluntary organizations as resources in medical and social care, as well as in schools, began to be recognized (Kulturdepartementet 1999). Private companies as well as voluntary organizations were suggested as possible welfare entrepreneurs.

Subsequently, a consensus has gradually emerged among the political parties concerning the value of allowing other agents to complement the state and municipality in the field of welfare. Today relatives are expected to take much more responsibility for their close kin than they did in the early 1990s. Within medical and social care services a number of commercial companies have been established, running their own hospitals, social care institutions and staff distribution agencies. In many localities, voluntary organizations and co-operatives have established nurseries and schools with financial support from public authorities. The emerging role of the Church of Sweden must be seen in this context (Bäckström 2001; Jeppsson Grassman 2001).

The Welfare Situation in Gävle

In Gävle the welfare state is organized at the local level by the local and regional authorities, which are also the largest employers in the municipality. As the major residential area in Gävleborg County, Gävle has a large hospital and many other regional public services. Another public institution in the town is the University of Gävle with 13,500 students. It is one of many recently-established centres for higher education in Sweden.

The challenges faced by the Swedish welfare system are clearly visible in Gävle. Many of them are linked to the fact that the system is based on the ideal of full employment for both women and men from the time they leave school or university until retirement. This ideal is confronting a reality where the proportion of citizens active in the labour market is shrinking as the numbers in need of support grow. Due to unemployment and higher levels of general education, young people are entering the labour market later and later. During the 1960s and 1970s immigrants were welcomed into the labour market, but today many of them have great difficulties finding a job. The number of pensioners is also increasing due to a general lengthening of life-span. Increasing chronic illness and uptake of early retirement reduces the size of the labour force yet further. In Gävle the financial problems of the welfare system are demonstrated by the fact that income from taxes is outstripped by welfare costs for schools and the care of elderly people. Unemployment in Gävle is slightly higher than the national average, at 10 per cent compared to 6 per cent (Regionfakta 2005; Statistics Sweden 2005). As in the rest of Sweden, sick days, compensated by social insurance, have increased rapidly and are most frequent among middle-aged women. This is causing extra strain on a welfare sector largely founded on the work of women.

These threats to universal welfare are generally seen as more problematic by the representatives of the church and general population interviewed in Gävle, than by representatives of the public authorities as such. The latter tend to see the local welfare situation as moderately good and under control, whereas representatives of the church and the population at large think it has deteriorated. They willingly give examples of particular things which, in their opinion, do not work well. Health and social care are frequently mentioned, alongside the loneliness of many people, and the growing gap between rich and poor. A church representative says:

> The welfare system is about to crack … here in Gävle … there are people with nowhere to live, those with drug problems, but also people with mental illnesses, often a combination of both … yes, and then I also think of the lack of integration of those who come here from other countries. (f)

Representatives of the population stress the difficulties that individuals in need encounter when accessing welfare services. Some give examples from their own family experience of how the gap between individuals and the public welfare organization has widened in recent years. A pensioner says, 'The way that things are handled has deteriorated … it is as though there should be a barbed wire that you have to get over before you can get help' (f). Like the church representatives, they observe a decline in ambition on the part of the public authorities.

Representatives of the public authorities tend to stress the positive development of the welfare state from a longer-term perspective. From this point of view, problems are isolated, and linked to shortcomings concerning the provision of welfare for certain groups and individuals within the population. The problems are not primarily related to the public welfare system per se, but rather to the way individual citizens use welfare services. Some representatives of the public authorities see a growing egoism in society as a problem. A woman in a managerial position in a local authority, for example, summarizes her perception of what is going on:

> I feel sad over how the basic ideas of those who built this have developed . . . . We have got a very egoistic perspective, where the point is for the individual to get as much out of the system as possible. Sometimes I wonder where it is going to go. Will private initiatives be able to replace the common welfare construction? How will our common values develop? (f)

The Church in Gävle as an Agent of Welfare

What, then, is the role of the Church of Sweden parishes for the welfare of the population in Gävle? The public authorities have approximately 15,000 people employed in administration and services in the municipality. The five parishes in Gävle have 150 employees between them (Statistics Sweden 2005; *Gävle kyrkliga samfällighet* 2003). Although the figures are not completely comparable, they give an indication of the relative size of the two agents. In addition to the employees, there are church volunteers. However, there are few volunteers in the Church of Sweden as compared to other churches (both within Sweden and internationally), simply because the former has thus far been relatively wealthy and able to employ people to perform its major duties. The role of the church in welfare cannot, therefore, be more than complementary. This chimes with the ideal role of the church envisaged by public authority, church and population representatives in Gävle. That said, the contribution of the church to welfare, although limited, is regarded as essential.

The church, for example, is expected to engage with social issues, preferably in co-operation with the public authorities, as the public welfare system is seen as foundational. Such involvement is seen as natural and a consequence of the church's mission. This is, to a large extent, the practice in Gävle. One priest says: 'I think that we in the church must work together with others; the local and regional authorities and other organizations. I think that is the best, and that is much the way we do it in Gävle' (f).

An overview of the social activities of the parishes in Gävle is provided in Table 3.1, within which they are categorized according to how they relate to the basic services provided by the public authorities.

As Table 3.1 shows, most church activities are financed by the church and performed on its own premises. Worship is, according to the church's constitution, part of the basic task of every parish (Kyrkoordning 1999). Gatherings for worship, which – with their primarily religious aim – fit well with the church's role as 'religious specialist', are often accompanied by a social gathering, normally over a cup of coffee. Indeed, the function of the church in the establishment of social networks and social trust should not be underestimated, given that a large majority of the population belongs to the church and regularly actualizes this relationship by, for

Table 3.1   Different Types of Organizational and Financial Relationships in Church and Public Authorities

Church-based activities	*Church presence/activities within the public sector*
Social gatherings related to worship	University church
Peace-of-mind-services	Teaching, crisis groups, anti-harassment
Choirs	groups in schools
Sewing circles	Presence in the hospital, prison and health
Groups for children and young people	care centre
Cafés, soup kitchens, town walks, international gatherings	Worship, visits and guidance for personnel in geriatric institutions
Counselling groups for the bereaved	
Financial assistance through the Diakonal Council	
Individual counselling	
Home visits	
Family guidance	

Publicly-financed activities run by the church

Preschools
Youth centre
Hostel for homeless people

Joint ventures between the church, the public sector and other organizations

Emergency counselling
Emergency group in case of accidents
     (POSOM)
Family centre

Other forms of co-operation

Presence in the private sector
Financial contributions

example, taking part in a baptism, attending a concert or sending teenage children to confirmation classes. Linked to acts of worship are church choirs, involving altogether more than 100,000 Swedes. Choirs constitute important social groups in every parish in Sweden. A rather different new type of worship, closely connected to the social mission of the church, is the so-called 'peace of mind service'. This was developed with inspiration from the 'Minnesota' therapy model for drug-rehabilitation (also named the 12-step programme), famously practised by the Alcoholics Anonymous organization (AA). These services have become popular within the wider population and are spontaneously mentioned by representatives of all three categories of interviewees.

Apart from worship, there are many other opportunities for community building in the parishes in Gävle. The types of regular group activities which reach most people are the activities for children and young people, including preparation for confirmation. In total, approximately 1,500 children are engaged in different parish group activities. A traditional twentieth-century type of gathering, today attracting mostly elderly women, is the sewing circle (Gävle kyrkliga samfällighet 2003). There are also cafés, soup kitchens and organized walks. Many of these activities, such as gatherings for elderly men and meetings where Swedish and immigrant women can mix, are aimed at groups of people who lack strong social networks of their own. Other activities are targeted at people in temporary crises, for example counselling groups for the bereaved.

Much of the parishes' welfare work is oriented towards individuals. Priests and deacons offer individual counselling. Deacons and volunteers visit the elderly and sick in their homes. The parishes, in co-operation with professionals, offer family guidance. Direct financial assistance has traditionally been part of the social work of the church, as a complement to the support given by the authorities. Previously, the parishes were unable to use church taxes collected for this type of diakonal work, because of the legal restrictions upon their activities, and such financial assistance was regarded as the responsibility of the public authorities. In Gävle, the parishes solved this problem by creating an independent foundation. The Diakonal Council (*Heliga Trefaldighets Diakoniförening*) was formed in 1919, and now deals with about 1,500 requests for help each year. The Diakonal Council aspires not only to meet immediate needs, but to strengthen the ability of the individual to support him or herself and to contribute to a better general social situation for the individual. To this end, an initiative has recently been taken to create a preventative Centre for Financial Advice providing information to individuals.

These activities constitute complementary welfare functions, organized separately from the public authorities. There is, however, another category of parish activity, integrated within the public sector and complementing it in basic ways. The Church of Sweden has a long tradition of being present within major public institutions such as the military, schools, prisons and hospitals (Levenskog 1997), deriving from the period when church and state were united and the church was the basic authority at the local level. In Gävle, some parishes remain very active within schools. Throughout the nine-year compulsory school period, parishes contribute through teaching and dialogue about the Christian tradition, ethics and values, and special activities are organized at Easter and Christmas.

At the hospital, a Church of Sweden priest serves in close collaboration with pastors from the free churches. The 'hospital church' (*sjukhuskyrkan*) is an integral part of the hospital, but is financed and administered by the church. At one of the health care centres in the town a priest is present one day a week and all parishes are, in differing ways, present in geriatric institutions. One priest has special responsibility for the prison. Another example of recently established social involvement is a parish priest serving as a chaplain within one of the town's major industries. The service is funded by the parish, but assigned to the staff manager as a resource for the 'spiritual aspect' of the preventative health measures of the company.

During recent years it has become common for the public sector to contract out some of its services to the church. One such venture in Gävle has been the shelter for homeless people, which was run for several years by a local ecumenical organization, the Council of Christian Churches in Gävle (*Gävle kristna råd*), with financial support from the local authorities. Other examples of activities run by the church, but partly financed by the public sector, include preschools and a youth centre. The latter is run together with the youth organization of the Mission Covenant Church.

The public sector, church and, sometimes, other actors, also co-operate directly on specific projects. The *Samtalsakuten* ('emergency counselling') is perhaps the best example of this form of co-operation. This is a centre for counselling related to so-called 'healthy life crises' caused by accidents, unemployment or other incidents which may cause a temporary loss of balance. The so-called POSOM groups, which are part of the emergency organization of the local authorities, are another example of this direct co-operation. POSOM stands for 'Psychological and social care in the case of major accidents or disasters'. These groups are responsible for co-ordinating emergency activities, and build on local networks consisting of public institutions like schools, primary health care and social services, in co-operation with voluntary organizations. The Church of Sweden in Gävle is a POSOM partner, as it is in most localities. A recent initiative in Gävle, based on direct co-operation between the church, local and regional authorities, is the Family Centre, which aims to offer preventative support to families through co-operation between public services and civil society.

Seven Areas of Consensus

The most striking result of the interviews with people in Gävle is the general level of consensus concerning the welfare system as such as well as the role of the church. We will summarize this consensus in seven points:

1. Representatives of public authorities and the church, as well as the population generally, tend to agree that it is the obligation of the public authorities to provide basic welfare for all people.
2. There is general agreement that involvement in social issues is a natural consequence of the church's mission, although the church is not expected to take over responsibility for practical social work from the public authorities. A church representative expresses it like this: 'I think the churches ought to be there and support, but they should not take over what society cannot handle. The situation can arise that the churches take over when society is in a bad financial situation, and that I think is totally wrong' (f).

3. There is a consensus concerning the complementary role that the church should and does fulfil within the field of welfare, preferably in co-operation with the public welfare system. Most interviewees think that providing society and individuals with good values, and a sense of meaning and belonging, is the church's most basic welfare function. This role is realized through, for example, church membership, the life rites used by almost everyone (such as baptisms and funerals), and through the church's work with children and young people. A population representative says: 'I think it is of great importance … it is also a tradition and a sense of belonging … I believe that we human beings need someone to hold our hand, who … we can talk to in times of difficulty' (f). Public authority representatives see the contributions of the church as especially important within the area of crisis and disaster management, individual crisis support and the defence of what are identified as weak groups (like homeless people and those in need of individual counselling). People can turn to the church confident of being treated with respect. The church is regarded as having an advantage in not being subject to as much regulation as the public authorities, allowing it more room to act. Through its financial support the church can add 'that little extra' (m). The complementary role of the church in welfare is regarded as important and sometimes even crucial. One public authority representative says explicitly that he is 'convinced that the church has saved many human lives' (m).

4. Respondents recognized that the relationship between church and society has changed. The representatives of the public authorities see a more open attitude from the church, downplaying old hierarchies and paternalism. Representatives from the church in turn perceive a more open attitude from the public authorities regarding co-operation with the church: '[A] typical example is to look at the schools coming to church, which was not possible at all for a time. Today it is a matter of course to come to Christmas services, coming to Easter gatherings and such things' (m). Several informants mention the growing role of the church in the handling of major disasters and crises as a crucial factor in these changed relations. A turning point mentioned by several people was a major bus accident in Norway in 1988 in which several children from Kista, a suburb of Stockholm, were killed. The local church in Kista came to play a key role for the families of these children, as well as for the municipality as a whole, and this work attracted a lot of media attention. Since then, the role of the church in such situations has been recognized in a new way (Pettersson 2003). This has had an effect even in other social areas: 'One has somehow discovered the need for the knowledge that exists in the Church of Sweden. And I think this has happened in connection with crises, all since this bus in Kista' (f).

5. There is also consensus regarding the role of the church in public debate on welfare issues. The church is welcomed, and even expected to take part in such debate, as long as it does not interfere with party politics. A female

local politician and public authority representative says: 'I would be very disappointed if the church was to keep silent and avoid social issues of various kinds' (f). It is seen as especially important that the church defends the most vulnerable groups in society. This function is sometimes seen as a major reason to remain a church member: 'I am a member of the Church of Sweden, but I have thought of withdrawing. But then I think that I want to stay on, because I want to contribute in my way to the activities of the church, because they have good activities, also protecting these weak groups in society. So it is much because of that that I am still there, not so much because I exactly have the faith' (f).

6. There is a general opinion that the Church of Sweden is, and should be, a church for the whole population. The open and broad character of the church is stressed and defended, sometimes in comparison to more 'closed' denominational settings.

7. The final area of consensus concerns equality between women and men. This value is taken as a given. Even church interviewees tend to refer to gender equality as a common value in society rather than one which is theologically motivated.

The high degree of agreement shown in the interviews illustrates the prevailing homogeneity of Swedish welfare society. The Swedish welfare model, the idea of society as the 'home of the people', has enduringly strong support. There are also strong expectations that the 'folk-church' will keep pace with developments in society and there is much good will amongst church staff and leaders to respond positively to these expectations. In sum, this demonstrates that there is a high degree of unity around the basic values of the welfare system in Gävle and the role of the church. The tensions shown in the responses often have to do with conflicts between these ideals and a reality which is more complicated. These tensions will now be discussed in more depth from three perspectives: the church as a theologically motivated agent, the church as a highly gendered agent, and the church as a social agent in Swedish society.

The Church as a Theologically Motivated Agent

The theological basis for the engagement of the parishes in Gävle in social welfare is broadly speaking in keeping with contemporary Church of Sweden 'folk-church' theology: that is, the idea of a church that is of, for, and with the people. This ecclesiological concept has shown a remarkable capacity to survive and adapt as a comprehensive theological idea for different groups and in different periods since it was developed during the first decades of the twentieth century. This is illustrated by the fact that the concept is still used in the present versions of the Church Law and the Church Order for the Church of Sweden (Ekstrand 2002). In this context, the folk church concept is used to stress that the church has an open character and is there for all people without reservation. It also emphasizes that the church has a caring responsibility for all those who live in Sweden. Its constitution ensures a democratic organization working together with the ordained ministry.

The Church of Sweden does not have a tradition of publishing authoritative theological texts. Nonetheless, the task of the church is summarized in a recent publication entitled 'Communication Platform for the Church of Sweden', which was accepted by the Board of the national church as the theological basis for the public profile of the church. This document states that the church 'makes room' for the presence of God in all phases of life, by organizing worship in the form of Sunday services, together with baptisms, weddings, confirmation and funeral services, thereby offering support for life in Swedish society. The church aims at being an open folk church and a bearer of hope: 'The Church wants to contribute to the possibility for everyone to experience their lives as meaningful.' The textual expression of the theology of the parishes in Gävle is very much in keeping with this summary.

The constitution of the Church of Sweden requires every parish to develop a pastoral programme, which has to be approved by the diocesan chapter (Kyrkoordning 1999). These pastoral programmes can be used to understand the theological motives for church social work. The programmes for the parishes in Gävle mention the task of meeting people in crisis or distress according to their needs. This is to be done 'without reservation' and 'disregarding individual factors'. The parish is to give 'voice to the weak' (Gävle Heliga Trefaldighets församling 2001: 2), and be 'a critical voice in society' (Gävle Maria församling 2001: 2). Theological themes motivating the church's activities within the field of welfare can be inferred from these programmes and recur in the interviews with church employees. These themes are: the imitation of Christ or the love of Christ; a necessary practical expression of Christian faith; and respect for human dignity. A church representative explains that social work is essential, as 'it is simply a part of the Gospel, in the Christian message, to help one's neighbour, so it goes without saying for Christians to contribute' (m). Directly or indirectly, many of the informants refer to the words of Jesus in Matthew 25:40: 'Just as you did it to one of the least of these who are members of my family, you did it to me.'[3] This passage seems to be the most important text when informants refer to the Bible in relation to the church's welfare activities.

Representatives from the church stress, in various ways, that the church's most important task in the context of welfare is to give hope and faith for the future and to emphasize the value of every human being – that is, to contribute a spiritual dimension, and be seen to be doing so. Consequently, one function of the church is seen as enhancing the quality of welfare. Mission and social work are viewed as closely related, although the church assists everyone, regardless of personal belief. With regard to whether the church has a particular responsibility for certain groups of people, several of the interviewees respond by pointing out that Christians and

---

[3]   Bible quotations are taken from the New Revised Standard Version here and throughout.

the church have a special responsibility to acknowledge and help the weak and neglected. Some note, however, that it might not be easy to determine who is in fact weak. As one priest says:

> There is a task that one ought to care for the weak. And then it becomes necessary to identify what is meant by being weak. Today I believe that what have traditionally been considered to be weak groups might not be the weak groups at all. So then you have to analyse what you mean by weak and then you have to see: where are the weak groups today? (f)

The pastoral programmes all state that the church's social action should preferably be carried out in co-operation with local and state authorities and other voluntary organizations. In this way, the attitude is collaborative, with no indication of a view of the church as an alternative or contrasting society in open or tacit opposition to the world. That said, most interviewees from the church think that the church should take part in public debate on welfare issues as well as carrying out practical social work. Here there is a tension between the church as a prophetic and critical voice defending the weak and vulnerable, and a more collaborative attitude expressed elsewhere. Yet only a few examples of this more critical voice in the media have been identified through the case study. Church personnel suggest that it is mainly clergy who take on the role of expressing the voice of the church in the media. If this is the case, our findings may be affected by the fact that two very media-active clergy left their positions in Gävle at the beginning of the research period. An interesting example of the church as a prophetic voice did, however, appear towards the end when a deacon was interviewed in a local newspaper under the headline 'The Poor in Gävle ask the Church for Money' (*Arbetarbladet*, 4 December 2004). The article was the result of an initiative from Church of Sweden deacons, in co-operation with other voluntary agents, focusing on emerging and new forms of poverty.

Our sources clearly indicate that there is a real tension between the folk-church situation on the one hand and the expectation that the church be a defender of contested values on the other. How should the church combine being both a free agent and a critical voice, whilst simultaneously being a church that represents the majority of the population? A church representative says 'We have this problem with the type of church we have, that it makes it difficult to find someone who can represent the church. We have the privilege or the problem that almost all people can say they represent the church' (m).

Another church informant provides an opposing view, stressing that the church is an interest group, a bearer of values and ideology, and an active opinion former: '[O]pinion forming is important. I don't believe that the church needs to do everything. It does not need to be the one that carries out everything, because we will never ever manage to do that' (m). He means that the church should defend the public welfare system and argue for a high level of public welfare rather than become a welfare entrepreneur itself. Several interviewees also point to the difficulty in drawing the line between a religiously motivated prophetic role, and being directly involved in party politics, which none of the church representatives seems to think would be appropriate.

The Church as a Gendered Agent

As mentioned above, a high degree of female participation in the labour market is characteristic of the Swedish welfare model. Another side of the gender question in the labour market can be found, however, in professional (horizontal) gender segregation, with a high percentage of women in salaried caring work. Around 90 per cent of the personnel employed in health and social care in Gävle are women (Statistics Sweden 2005). There is also hierarchical (vertical) gender segregation, meaning that there is a higher percentage of men in decision-making positions and with higher salaries, whereas a larger percentage of women work part-time, in lower-paid positions and with less influence (Gonäs and Karlsson 2006).

This vertical and horizontal gender segregation creates hierarchies, privileging men and male activities (cf. Hirdman 1998). Such structures are also clearly visible within the Church of Sweden. In the first half of the twentieth century the church had very few female employees. During the second half of the century, however, the number of church employees rose, especially in new types of church work such as in social care, and with children and young people. Consequently, many more women were employed. This change is well exemplified in Gävle, where three out of four church employees are now women. Generally these new professions are lower paid and have a lower degree of formal influence than the traditional positions held by male priests. There are no statistics available on church volunteers, but clearly the majority are women. Yet men still dominate in higher positions. Every parish has a (senior) priest, who is responsible for overall supervision and co-ordination of the parish's work. Four of the five of these in Gävle are men, as is the highest-ranked administrator. The chain of decision-making in the Church of Sweden is divided between the ordained ministry and elected representatives. However, taking the democratic system into account does not radically change the gender relationships, because the majority of elected church councils in Gävle are headed by men.

The study in Gävle shows that women are also the major beneficiaries of church social work, though there are specific services, such as the shelter for homeless people, which are primarily used by men. Another tendency is for women to be positioned as representatives of the family in relation to the church, both when it comes to more traditional tasks such as baptism and in times of family crisis. This reflects analyses showing that patterns of secularization in Europe are gendered and affect women and men in different ways (Woodhead 2005). The gendered nature of many aspects of welfare organization and provision has been given much attention in international debate in recent years. Material and ideological processes tend to intersect in mechanisms constructing care as 'work with a woman's face' (Daly and Rake 2003: 49). Researchers highlight the relation between a social and economic devaluing of caring work and gender hierarchies devaluing women (Pfau-Effinger and Geissler 2005). From this perspective, the challenge facing Swedish welfare society, as well as most other western welfare systems, may be seen as a 'caring deficit' with close links to the differing values attributed to male and female work (Hochschild 1995). This deficit leads to an increasing gap between the demand for care and the resources available.

Against this background it is interesting to analyse how the gendered character of the social work of the church interacts with the gendered structures of the Swedish welfare system at large. At the level of empirical data, it seems that church-based welfare simply reflects the societal situation. Moreover, the attitudes of church representatives about the ideal of welfare seem to reflect common attitudes in society. There is unanimous support for the principles of gender equality. Yet this runs parallel with the tendency to 'naturalize' caring as women's work. As one church employee expresses it, 'the role of the mother is always there' (m). The clearest tension related to the church as a gendered social agent appears in the very different analyses regarding gender equality made by church representatives on the one hand and representatives of public authorities on the other. Several representatives of the latter, and also some of those interviewed in focus groups, refer to the struggle over the issue of the ordination of women as a problem for the church. This is noteworthy as it does not seem to be an issue in the parishes in Gävle, although it is in the church at large. Though it is now 50 years since women were first allowed to be priests in the Church of Sweden, there is active resistance against their ordination from some minority groups, especially of male priests. Some interviewees are quite explicit in arguing that the church has not overcome its negative history with regard to gender equality: 'I think of the games played against women priests. It does not feel satisfactory and for me it becomes a crisis for the credibility of the Church of Sweden' (m).

The problem most often observed by the church representatives with regard to gender equality, though, is quite different. It is sometimes formulated as the problem of 'female dominance'. The numerical dominance of women in different areas of church activity is, in this line of thought, reformulated as a problem of general female dominance, with several negative consequences. One frequently articulated concern is that women tend to recruit other women as personnel, volunteers and service users, which may result in even greater difficulties recruiting men. This in turn comes into conflict with an ideal of numerical gender balance, which is sometimes even given a divine legitimacy: 'If you imagine … that the human being reflects the divine, then both men and women are needed. Somehow this is what it is about' (m). A secondary negative consequence of the predominance of women, following from the first and stressed by one interviewee, is the lowering of salaries and status, which in turn makes the church less attractive to both women and men.

As the data from Gävle show, the gendered character of church social work has strong connections to the persisting conflicts in Swedish society at large concerning the prevalence of both vertical and horizontal gender segregation.

Of the relatively few negative comments against the church made by the general population and public authority representatives, some have to do with the church's position on gender equality. The lack of theological argumentation on these matters in parish documents as well as in interviews reveals, however, a lack of critical reflection within the church. In terms of its position on gender equality, it seems that the church has not yet proved its credibility in the eyes of Swedish society. A tension worth observing is that the church is expected on the one hand to act as a defender of values of solidarity and care for the weak in society. On the other hand, the church reflects to a high degree, in its own practice in the welfare arena, the devaluing of female care work that can be seen in society at large. These patterns make it difficult for the church to defend theologically and publicly the values it is expected to maintain.

Rediscovering the Church as a Social Agent

Following the separation between state and church in 2000, the Church of Sweden became the largest organization, apart from the state, in Swedish society. The social role of this organization is broad, and reaches out to almost all inhabitants (Pettersson 2000; Bäckström 2001). Most previous research on Swedish voluntary organizations has, however, neglected the activities of the Church of Sweden, since it has been regarded as part of the state (Amnå 1995; Lundström 1995; Lundström and Wijkström 1995; Wijkström and Lundström 2002). On the other hand, the church has also been excluded from studies of state welfare provision (Hort 1990; Rothstein 1994). The combination of both these factors means that the social role of the church has, to a large extent, remained hidden – under the umbrella of the state. There are, however, signs that the recognition given to the role of religion in Swedish society is undergoing major changes.

As the Gävle case shows, the Church of Sweden fulfils a wide range of welfare functions in Swedish society. Its welfare services can be categorized into two types of provision: material provision, such as running a shelter for homeless people or distributing extra financial support to individuals in need; and non-material provision, including both direct activities and more symbolic functions. Regarding the latter, direct activities – for example bereavement counselling and daytime activities for elderly people – meet different psychological and social needs. The indirect or more symbolic functions are harder to assess but include those which link individuals to a collective identity and those which provide a relationship to a transcendent sphere. As expressed in several interviews in the case study, as well as in other Swedish data, formal membership of the church is seen in itself as a welfare factor by many people. Belonging to the church has a symbolic function which offers a sense of security. The life rites, in particular baptisms and funerals, give people a sense of belonging and meaning (Reimers 1995; Pettersson 2000).

The case study also shows that the church is regarded as a bearer of the values of care and solidarity, especially for and with the underprivileged. Specifically, the church is seen as a critical voice defending values of human dignity and of solidarity. It is important that there is no incompatibility between the church's values, its explicit welfare activities and its implicit symbolic functions. Accordingly, the church's evocation of symbolic links to the transcendent is seen as adding a distinctive quality to its social activities (Pettersson 2000).

In this context, it is interesting to consider the social role of the church in relation to the commonly held view of Sweden as one of the world's most secularized societies. This description is, of course, dependent on the definition of secularization used (Dobbelaere 2002; Martin 2005). But whatever the case, the data from Gävle challenge the notion of secularization in terms of the declining position of the church in society as a whole; they reveal instead the complexity of the religious scene in Sweden (cf. Bäckström et al. 2004). At a more individual level, the case study reinforces the 'standard' Nordic position: that is, a high degree of personal affiliation with the church with regard to membership and the proportion of the population participating in life rites. When it comes to attendance at worship, however, the figures are very low. In this respect Gävle is a typical Swedish town.

At the organizational level of society, the image of ongoing secularization is also ambiguous. In public and political debate over the course of the twentieth century, the (then) future disestablishment of the church was often envisioned as a dramatic change (Bäckström et al. 2004). Paradoxically, after it happened, it seems that the church is, in a sense, perceived as more closely related to the public service sector (the state) than it was before. Gävle certainly shows this, in so far as co-operation between the Church of Sweden and the public authorities appears to increase alongside the church–state separation process. This apparently contradictory development has partly to do with the removal of legal restrictions on church social work that were part of the former division of labour between state and church. It also has to do with the implicit relationship at an individual level between almost all Swedes and the church, which sustains the institution as an integral part of the society and culture (Pettersson 2000).

The change in position, from being one legal authority among others to becoming the largest voluntary organization in the land, is as important for the church as it is for the state, not least with respect to its social role. Even if the new 'public' role of the church is mostly welcomed, there are aspects that are perceived as provocative. One such has to do with the fact that religion has largely been regarded as a private matter, belonging to the sphere of the individual and the family (Bäckström et al. 2004). Many people perceive it as embarrassing when this privacy is violated in a public or semi-public space. Interestingly, this became apparent in the process of collecting data for the case study. In the group interviews, for example, representatives from the population show marked levels of shyness in discussing their personal religious positions. Furthermore, for many interviewees the possibility that the church might have a role in welfare provision was an issue which they had never been confronted with before.

In sum, the Swedish case can be seen as a good example of the general societal process of functional differentiation, through which the role of the church has become limited, specializing in core religious and ethical issues (Dobbelaere 1981, 2002; Luhmann 1982). That, however, is not the whole story. In the face of a number of challenges to the Swedish welfare model, the competence of the church has been noticed and appreciated in new ways as a social resource for other organizations as well as for society at large (cf. Beyer 1994). Many Swedes refer to this changing perception of the church in relation to its obvious and important role in major crises and disasters (cf. Gustafsson 1995; Pettersson 2003).

What we have described is a new situation in the sense that the church now has to rely on the trust it has earned as an organization and the proven quality of its performance of services (in every sense), and not on a legal position as a state authority. A crucial issue in this respect is how the church will handle the growing encouragement from public authorities to co-operate with voluntary organizations in the provision of basic welfare services (Wijkström and Lundström 2002). With the increasing 'outsourcing' of welfare services to voluntary organizations, there is a risk that these organizations will become too dependent on the income they receive from their service production – a shift that might, in turn, make them more reluctant to be critical towards the state authorities and their management of welfare. The trend of 'outsourcing' has not yet affected the Church of Sweden in any radical way, but any further development in this direction might complicate the already problematic role of the folk-church as a critical voice in Swedish society (cf. Ekstrand 2002). Only time will tell.

Chapter 4

Sacred Welfare Agents in Secular Welfare Space: The Church of Norway in Drammen

Olav Helge Angell

Introduction

How meaningful is it to apply the term 'sacred' to a welfare agent? What are the boundaries of the sacred? The field of welfare provision is generally conceived as part of the secular, its operations based on professional, rational action in the Weberian sense, which characterizes modernity (Weber 1958). The sacred, on the other hand, is associated with religion and religious institutions, and the way 'religion' is ordinarily used in the sociology of religion. Religion as a concept in sociology too often restricts its focus to belief-systems;[1] as a consequence, welfare agency tends to fall outside the scope of sociologists of religion. This restriction has rightly been criticized (as in Swatos 2003).

Swatos has explored the dimensions of religion involved in the work of Max Weber, deriving two basic dimensions, one regarding social relationships and another related to ethical considerations. Based on this analysis he constructs what he calls a 'situational approach' to religion, in which three sets of considerations are included: that religions create action orientations, involve subjective experience and consist of systems of discourse (Swatos 2003: 50–51). However, like Weber, Swatos does not seem to include social actions in the form of social service in his framework.

The practical role of religion is an important part of many religious traditions, not least the so-called 'book religions', among them Christianity. In Christian theology, one way of viewing the Christian religion or the responsibility of the church is through the dimensions of *liturgia*, *martyria*, *diakonia* and *koinonia*.[2] To simplify a little, the first refers to the ritual dimension; the second to the witness dimension (that is, the belief-system and the way it is shared among the believers and communicated in society); the third to the human service aspect of religion, the social or welfare role of the church; and the fourth to the social community aspect. These dimensions may be related to the sociological distinctions drawn

---

[1] This seems to be the case in Berger (1969), Casanova (1994), Martin (2005) and Stark and Bainbridge (1987), to name but a few.

[2] See Heitink (1999). A recent reference is the first encyclical letter issued by Pope Benedict XVI, *Deus caritas est* (January 2006).

by Swatos from Weber. The ritual, witness and community dimensions can be associated with the Weberian social relationship dimension. *Diakonia*, as such, is more difficult to place. It might, however, be interpreted as referring to social relationships based on ethical considerations, and a form of action.

Diakonia refers to moral action systems involving subjective experience usually couched in a system of discourse, an example of which is the theological analysis of the Christian religion outlined above. The point that I want to make is that church-based social work, *diakonia*, may usefully be included within the sociology of religion's remit. This does not imply that the activities constituting *diakonia* in practical life necessarily distinguish themselves from other, non-church-based welfare activities. Most important here is their cultural embeddedness. In this way we may consider it fruitful to speak about sacred agents in a generally secular space of social action, and thus include welfare action within the boundaries of the sacred.

Two possible roles of religion in welfare are the ideological role and the practical role. The ideological role can be seen when religious agents are active in the public discourse on welfare. This is what Ralph Kramer, in his analysis of the functions of voluntary organizations in the welfare state, has termed the *value guardian* role (Kramer 1981)[3] – a role that may indeed be fulfilled in both words and deeds. The practical role is captured in various forms of welfare provision, independently or in collaboration with the state or public sector at different levels.

In this chapter I describe and analyse the roles of the local church as related to welfare provision.[4] I pay special attention to one particular agent in order to illustrate the potential significance of the church in welfare at a local level. A *value guardian* function will be seen as significant in the social actions and activities organized and in the values espoused in the public discourse (Schein 1985). Such values may serve as resources in political processes, as well as in local identity formation. For the latter, I draw on Taylor's analysis of the quest for authenticity in modern society (Taylor 1991) in analysing the welfare functions of religiously-based agents. As an introduction to the presentation and analysis, the wider context of the Norwegian welfare system and the role of the church in welfare provision are outlined.

---

[3]   Kramer identifies four main functions of voluntary organizations in the welfare state: vanguard, improver, value guardian and service provider. In addition he distinguishes between different service provider roles.

[4]   The most important data for this chapter were gathered through interviews with representatives of the local church and the public sector in Drammen, and from the local newspaper, *Drammens Tidende*.

The Norwegian Welfare System and the Role of the Church of Norway in Welfare[5]

The Concept of Welfare

The concept of welfare is central to this research. It is most productively understood as a multidimensional concept. In Chapters 1 and 2, the Finnish sociologist Erik Allardt's conception of welfare was elaborated.[6] Simplifying somewhat, the way that the church defines its mission in society – to preach and to help others – ideally covers all three of Allardt's dimensions of welfare: 'having', 'being' and 'loving'. The present study focuses on all these functions, which comprise the social welfare aspect, the practical activities undertaken to 'care for fellow human beings' and to develop community spirit, and services particularly directed at people 'in need', to use the words of the Church of Norway's official definition of *diakonia* (Comprehensive Diaconal Programme for the Church of Norway 1997). The study also includes a political dimension of welfare, referring to the role of the church in the public discourse on welfare. Normatively it may be related to the struggle for social justice.

The Norwegian Welfare System

Religious and political history provides an important context for understanding today's welfare regime. Many typologies exist to characterize such regimes. As we have seen, in Gösta Esping-Andersen's typology (1990), the Scandinavian countries belong in the category of the social democratic welfare regime, characterized by a large public sector, a system of 'full employment' and a high rate of labour-market engagement for women. Against this background it is to be expected that church-based welfare activities, as part of the voluntary sector, will be of little importance – quantitatively speaking. In general terms, responsibilities and duties are divided across three tiers of government: the national, regional and local levels. The central authorities are responsible for national policy, for drawing up general guidelines, for advising and for ensuring that services offered comply with national goals. At the local level, the municipalities cover many domains including health promotion, primary health care, care for elderly people and those with physical or intellectual disabilities, kindergarten and primary school education, and social work.

One of the ideas behind the Norwegian, and Scandinavian, welfare model, with its universalistic orientation, is that it protects society's members against the social risks connected with everyday life. As long as members are active in the labour market, the national insurance system will protect the individual and the family against poverty. Active interventions in the labour market are therefore a central element of the total welfare policy system. Specifically, the goal of employment

---

[5]   The presentation in this section is based on Angell (2004).
[6]   See also Allardt (1975).

policy has been to stimulate the economy in such a way that the demand for labour will provide job opportunities for everybody, leading to full employment. The problem with this system, however, is that it does not provide well for those who are not integrated into the labour market. As a result, the source of income provided by the welfare state for those who are not directly or indirectly integrated in the labour market becomes needs-based residual social assistance – at this point the notion of citizenship-based rights is found wanting.

The National Insurance Scheme is the very core of the Norwegian welfare system. The primary aims of the scheme are:

- to provide financial security by ensuring income and compensating for certain costs during unemployment, pregnancy and childbirth, for single-parent childcare, care for elderly people and in the event of death;
- to help equalize incomes and living standards, during the lifetime of individuals and between groups of persons;
- to promote self-sufficiency for each individual.

The National Insurance Scheme provides short-term assistance for those of working age, assistance for a transitional period for those who are unemployed for a few years and permanent assistance for those who have finished their working careers.

The organizational structure of the Norwegian health care system is built on the principle of equal access to services. All inhabitants of the country should have the same access to services, independent of social status, location and income. To fulfil this aim, the organizational structure has three levels following the political tiers described above. The main responsibility for the actual provision of health care services lies with the regional health care enterprises and the 435 municipalities. The health care enterprises assume responsibility for the planning and operating of the hospital sector (including both general and psychiatric institutions) as well as other specialized medical services, such as targeted care for those addicted to alcohol and other drugs.

Social care in Norway includes social welfare services, care for elderly people, disabled and psychiatric patients, and alcoholics and drug addicts. Since the late 1990s, municipalities have had increasing responsibility for providing health and social care services. This expansion, however, has not reduced the amount of care, in terms of time, provided by family members. The state defines national goals, draws up the framework for social care services, and provides guidelines and advice. There is no system of taxes or charges being earmarked for particular services. Generally, transfers from the government to the municipalities are block grants. The allocation of resources to different public goods (like health and social services) is mainly a political matter in the parliament, in the counties and in the municipalities.

The Church of Norway and its Role in Welfare Provision

The Norwegian Constitution confirms that the Norwegian state maintains the Evangelical-Lutheran religion as the official state religion, and that the King (later broadened to encompass the government) has the right and duty to structure and finance the life of the church in terms of the work of the pastors.[7] A General Synod was established in 1984, but the parliament still decides the laws and the financial framework for the church, and the government appoints bishops. Thus, the Church of Norway can be defined as a state church with both an episcopal and a synodical structure. Freedom of religion is established by law, and every registered religious and philosophical community has approximately the same financial support from the state, in proportion to its membership. There is a Christian subject clause within the public school system, but the opportunity for religious preaching in schools is very restricted.

Some 86 per cent of Norwegians belong to the Church of Norway. Among the rest of the population, 4–5 per cent belong to other Christian communities, and 1–2 per cent belong to non-Christian religious communities (SSB 2008b; 2008c). The Church of Norway is responsible for services in a wide range of public institutions like hospitals, prisons and the military. There have, however, been calls for such services to be provided by others for people from differing religious or philosophical traditions.

So far, little systematic study has been done to explore the role of organized, church-based welfare in the Norwegian welfare state. With regard to gender there is even less documentation. On average, church-based activities make up about 10 per cent of the total institution-based activities in the health care and social services in Norway. The category of 'the church' in this case includes the majority church, the Church of Norway, and a plurality of minority churches. By sub-sectors there is one significant deviation from the average: with regard to substance abuse care, church-based activities comprise as much as 50 per cent of the total in-patient capacity. To use Kramer's typology (Kramer 1981), the church has a *vanguard* role in this respect. It functions as a pioneer in Norway in institution-based substance abuse rehabilitation. In its *service-provider* role the church is, in many respects, the primary provider of such services.

The church's involvement in the field of substance abuse rehabilitation can be explained historically. The state's reluctance to develop care for people who suffered from addiction to alcohol led to the largely religious temperance movement establishing the first in-patient facilities about a hundred years ago. Since then, the state has accepted this primary provider role, though the amount of public involvement has steadily increased. The stigmatization and low social status of people who are publicly identified as substance abusers, and the character of the social problem, the way it has been understood and classified (often within

---

[7]   The constitutional situation is currently under review. It is likely to change in the relatively near future.

a moral or religious framework) goes some way to account for the commitment of the church in this field.

The Welfare State and the Church from the Point of View of Gender

The participation of women in the Norwegian labour market is amongst the highest in Europe. According to figures from 2007, 77 per cent of all women aged 25–66 are in the workforce, compared to 84 per cent of men (SSB 2008a). Women have been in the majority in higher education since the 1980s. On the other hand, the labour market in Norway is one of the most segregated along gender lines in the western world. More than half of all female employees work in the public sector, and women comprise 68.9 per cent of all employees in this sector. In the health and social sector, which is primarily public, 83 per cent of employees are women. In typical private sector professions such as construction and entrepreneurial activity, only 9 per cent of employees are female (Statistics Norway 2006: 68). The general absence of women in decision-making positions in both the private and the public sectors is a matter of national concern.

The welfare state has been important for the labour market participation of women. Economic growth and expansion of the public sector meant that care for elderly people, education, social service offices, kindergartens and public administration were organized and expanded across the country. Many of the jobs this expansion created were typically 'women's jobs' involving care work. This new paid work within the local community was offered to women, who had in turn, in order to take it on, to pass on their own domestic responsibility for housework and care for children and elderly family members to kindergartens and other care institutions.

A Gender Equality Act was adopted in 1978. The Act prohibits all discrimination on the grounds of gender, and is applicable to all areas of society, including education, employment and cultural matters. Pursuant to the Gender Equality Act, it is the responsibility of the public authorities to promote gender equality in all areas of society. One of the most important elements of the Act was the establishment of a Gender Equality Ombud as an independent body responsible for enforcing the Act. A government-funded Gender Equality Centre has been established to monitor and promote gender equality and equal opportunity measures in all areas of society. The principle of gender mainstreaming has been integrated into Norwegian government budget policy.

Norway is reputed to be one of the best countries in the world for women. One of the reasons may be 'state feminism', the particular form of policy of gender equality in the Scandinavian countries which has 'the women-friendly state' as a precondition. The policy implies that a women-friendly society would be the result of public policies, family and social policies, and an explicit gender-equality policy. However, special benefits for women have tended to focus on women as mothers, something which may maintain the traditional view of women (of child-bearing age) as unstable labour, with consequences for the return of their 'investment' in the labour market: that is, lower wages and fewer chances of promotion. On this basis the 'women-friendly welfare state' has been criticized for emphasizing the differences between men and women, and not what they have in common. In this respect the welfare state is 'gender conservative', as women are primarily defined by their family ties and not as individuals.

In the Church of Norway the issue of gender has first and foremost been articulated at the central level of the church. At the Church of Norway General Synod in 1990, a resolution was adopted saying that all councils and committees at the level of the congregation, the diocese and the National Council of the Church of Norway should work towards ensuring that neither sex has less than 40 per cent representation. Since then, equality has been expressed as a matter of both quantity and mentality, with a view to its becoming a natural part of church life. This view has been contested, as has the conclusion that it should be the aim of the church to fully realize the intentions of the Gender Equality Act. A critical examination of the gender equality process in the church has concluded that many people within the church regard men and women as of equal worth. Despite this belief, however, they still hesitate to implement full equality (see Eriksen 2004).

In the field of religion, the Gender Equality Act must be seen in relation to the freedom of religion provided for in the constitution. In the Act, exception is made for 'the internal affairs of religious communities'. Consequently, where structures and processes in the Church of Norway are at odds with the requirements in the Gender Equality Act, church representatives have defended the position of the church by referring to the provisions in the constitution and the exceptions in the Equality Act.

The Town of Drammen

Drammen[8] is an old port, industrial town and commercial centre in the south-eastern part of Norway, only 40 km south of the capital, Oslo, and has about 57,000 inhabitants. Drammen has undergone significant structural change over the last 20 to 30 years and has become a regional service centre. Together with Oslo, Drammen is the Norwegian town with the largest proportion of non-western ethnic groups in its population. Social Democrats have, traditionally, held a majority in the town, but this is now changing. The local parishes and the voluntary organizations of the Church of Norway have a long history of engaging in social work.

Drammen hosts a plethora of Christian and non-Christian religious and philosophical groups and communities. The Church of Norway is the largest, comprising 77 per cent of the population. Other religious groups and traditions represented are Muslim, Buddhist, Jehovah's Witness, Hindu and Sikh. The largest religious group after the Church of Norway is Muslim, reflecting the significant

---

[8]   The source of the information presented in this paragraph is Angell and Wyller (2006).

immigration of ethnic minority groups. The Pentecostal movement is the second largest Christian group. This position of Muslims and Pentecostals in Drammen corresponds to the relative strength of the two groups at the national level.

The Local Church as a Welfare Agent

There are two main types of collective agents acting as church-based providers of welfare services in Drammen. These are the parishes, and the organizations and associations not formally linked to the parishes. On the basis of how the parishes describe their own welfare activities, their orientation may be characterized as traditional. The activities most frequently mentioned are directed towards children, young people and the elderly. The parishes, through their organized activities, provide welfare. This provision is delivered especially through the engagement of volunteers in social activities: bringing people together, and arranging for opportunities for people to meet and share. It is worth noting that several of the parishes also engage in musical activities, both as a vehicle for community and as a way of communicating aesthetic values. The parishes appear less involved in sustained welfare activities requiring professionally trained staff. In Drammen these kinds of activities are the domain of the church-based voluntary organizations.

A high-ranking public official expresses some critical views about the priorities of the church with regard to who, exactly, was the focus of its care activities. The interviewee characterizes the target groups of parish social care as the 'nice guys' and asks for a commitment to, say, people with intellectual disabilities. The criticism may be interpreted as a wish to see a public commitment on the part of the church to groups who do not have their own public voice. This brings us to the second aspect of the role of the church in welfare provision: its role as a contributor to the public discourse on welfare.

The public authority representatives interviewed generally perceive the local church to be relatively invisible in the public discourse, and church representatives (especially parish priests) to be sceptical about taking this kind of public role, even though it is desired. The reasons given by the interviewees for their views tend to be related to the idea of participatory, political democracy. A typical view is: 'The more participants holding an opinion [on matters of welfare], the better for society. A public debate is important' (f). Some public employees state the view that such voices may serve as a corrective to the public welfare system in which officially employed professionals may well be limited by their participation in an authority structure which requires obedience and strict adherence to regulations.

The Significance of Gender

Aspects of gender within the church were explicitly focused on only in the interviews with church representatives. The gender dimension appeared mainly in two ways in these encounters: in the question of the distribution of men and women in various formal positions in the church, and in the structure of the roles, activities and tasks related to church work and practical *diakonia*. Most of the interviewees who comment on gender questions agree that the majority of volunteers in the church are women. Yet they are also aware that the proportion of women is lower in higher-ranked positions. Some (women) consider this situation a challenge. Others (men) do not consider it a problem. Interviewees agree that gender equality is an important issue, but opinions vary as to its urgency.

In some of the parishes separate activities are arranged for men and women. This implies that men's groups and women's groups are different in content. This difference is based on a presupposition that, for some purposes, it will be easier for men and women to relate to persons of the same gender.

Some types of activities organized by the parishes seem to be gender-biased by their names, even though they are in principle gender-neutral. For example, gatherings for parents (fathers included) and young children are frequently referred to as gatherings for mothers and young children (*mor-barn-treff*). This is understandable as, in practice, it is usually mothers who take care of very young children.[9] In some of the parishes, however, these types of arrangements are termed 'baby gatherings' to make them more gender-neutral.

Several interviewees consider many of the traditional forms of voluntary welfare activities organized by parishes, such as groups for the bereaved, visiting services and other traditional household-oriented activities, to appeal more to female volunteers. However, gender roles are changing, and more men participate in such activities today than was the case previously. One of the church representatives puts it this way:

> I am impressed when I have seen that males and females are not very specific about what kinds of tasks they engage in. They do what they are told, and males engage themselves in all kinds of tasks ... It has become more natural for males to participate in more traditional household oriented activities ... But females still make up the majority. (f)

A male interviewee expresses a contrasting view:

> I don't think it has been the tradition to ask people what they would like to do and what their abilities are, and adapt [their tasks] accordingly. [To a greater extent than men,] women are brought up to be obedient, to do what they are told,

---

9   In the Scandinavian countries paid, wage-related parental leave has been introduced as an extension of paid maternity leave. In this way, preconditions have been established for both parents to be involved in the care of infants. Fathers, however, have turned out to be more reluctant than mothers to take parental leave. In response, a certain period of (non-transferable) leave has been reserved for fathers. This 'daddy leave' has proved popular among fathers, and has gradually established a new norm for being a good father (Leira 2002).

> to take responsibility and to feel a sense of duty. It has been easier for them [than
> for men] to adapt to what has been worked out for them in advance. (m)

The statements cited above point to some structural aspects of traditional types of welfare activities in the parishes and the roles of volunteers, relating these to more or less traditional gender roles. To some extent there seems to be a mismatch between parish activities and the traditional male role. Implicitly at least, however, interviewees notice that changes are taking place with regard to gender roles. That said, it is less evident that the structure of voluntary work and its organization is changing in the direction of adapting tasks increasingly to the preferences of the volunteers as indicated in the preceding quotation (see Byrådet i Oslo 2002; Wollebæk et al. 2000).

Co-operation between the Public Sector and the Church

Generally the interviewees representing the church and the public sector do not report much systematic or regular co-operation. The interviews provide a somewhat unclear picture; in many cases the situation seems to be that the church has contacts at several public care facilities through their visiting services, but without any real exchange in the relationship. Only in the field of substance abuse care and rehabilitation are church-based activities integrated in public schemes and co-operation institutionalized.

There are various reasons for this situation. One reason seems to be a lack of knowledge of the work of the parishes on the part of public authorities. This is mentioned by several interviewees, both representing the church and the municipality. One of the public employees says: 'You feel that the church is a bit invisible ... We know it's there, but you don't know what it has to offer if you have no knowledge of it' (m). The day-to-day situation of the staff and managers of public welfare may leave them too busy to sit down and think about possible partners and resources beyond the public sector. In such a situation, it would be left to church agencies to initiate contact and convey information about possible issues of common interest.

This implies that co-operation between the church and the public sector generally seems to be of little importance for the overall provision of welfare services in Drammen, but politicians' statements emphasizing the centrality of the church's role might indicate otherwise. One of the politicians states: 'This [the role of the public sector, the voluntary sector, and the church] is a strongly interlocked relationship. The public sector cannot function well without the voluntary sector, including the church' (m). As a characterization of the current situation, this seems to be an overstatement. It may be interpreted more as an ideal or a prediction.

Expectations of the Church as a Welfare Service Provider

In Drammen there seem to be few expectations of the church in terms of contribution to the provision of welfare, both on the part of representatives themselves and in the opinion of the general public as mediated by the public authority representatives. The following statement by a local politician is indicative of the views presented in the interviews:

> I do not think the people have expectations that the church should contribute. I think that when you actually see how the church contributes, you are positively surprised. In principle, the state is supposed to take care of you from cradle to grave. At least, that is the way I have perceived that people think about these things. (m)

This statement summarizes the responses given to a direct question on this point.

The church, and, more generally, the voluntary sector, fulfils a *complementary function* (Kramer 1981). This function is related to the church's command of volunteers and the significance of this resource in care for elderly people, for children and for substance abusers. This care is qualitatively different in kind from services provided by the public sector. In most of the interviews the impression is given that the whole issue of the role of the church as a welfare provider has not been raised with interviewees before, and that they are not well prepared to answer questions about this role. Generally respondents convey no strong opinions on how the church should contribute to welfare and well-being in the community. This may reflect the fairly marginal role of the church in welfare provision today. Among the resources associated with the church, committed volunteers are probably the most frequently mentioned. A possible interpretation is the following: that the comprehensive role of the public sector in welfare provision is taken for granted and the church's main contribution is to complement the public sector where it cannot provide the resources necessary to fulfil the demands for welfare services. This interpretation would be in line with other statements made by representatives of the public system. A centrally-placed public employee, for example, criticizes the church for being too oriented towards implementing its own ideas and too little interested in viewing its work in relation to that of the public sector.

Among the church representatives there is less ambiguity over the question of whether or not the church has a role to play in the welfare and well-being of people in the local community. What this role should be, though, is expressed in different ways. Several interviewees mention the *vanguard role* (Kramer 1981) as a traditional role of the church, which is still relevant in today's welfare situation:

> I think that the role of the local church is related to traditional church activities. To me it seems more important to improve the public welfare system. The church may serve as a vanguard. This ... would be the calling of the church. Then the public authorities may take over at a later stage. (m)

The *value guardian role* is also emphasized, and in different ways. The church has a role to play as a watchdog to make sure no one is marginalized:

> The church should be a prophetic voice in society. The church in Drammen is a bit toothless … The church should speak up when priorities by the public authorities contribute to offending individuals. I attend Sunday services, but I feel the church should focus more on the public sphere. (m)

The *service provider role* was touched upon earlier in the description of the church's contributions to current welfare provision in Drammen: 'In situations when the [public] welfare system does not function optimally the church may show that it cares and attend to those who are being forgotten. This means a complementary role.' (f)

Doubts about the role of the church are not explicitly voiced among the church representatives, but answers imply that its role should not be taken for granted. As a service provider, the church may fulfil various needs of its users. One of the interviewees puts it this way: 'I think that the most important contribution of the church in Drammen is to provide people with meaning and belonging' (m). These functions are fulfilled by the church in its role as a service provider, but they may also be related to its mission in the world more generally.

Only one of the interviewees reflects critically on the role of the church and the voluntary sector in the welfare state. A representative of the church comments, in his answer to the question about how to understand 'welfare' and the welfare state, that welfare is connected to citizens' rights. But, he says:

> There is, nevertheless, a discrepancy between theory and practice. As a church-based actor we live on the brink. We run the risk of ending up as nothing but operators compensating for society's betrayal [of the poor]. Therefore, we need to have two legs to stand on; we are obliged to help people in need, at the same time we must be outspoken about injustice. (m)

The Particular Role of the Church City Mission

In the interviews with representatives of the church and the public authorities, one particular church-based organization is repeatedly referenced as an example of the role (to be) taken by the church in the area of welfare: it is the Church City Mission (CCM). In eight out of a total of 11 interviews with representatives of the public authorities, the CCM and various aspects of its role in welfare provision are spontaneously mentioned. We may take this as an indication of the organization's central position in the minds of the interviewees when the subject is the role of the church in welfare provision in Drammen. Consequently, the rest of this chapter will be dedicated to describing and reflecting on the role of the CCM in Drammen. One point is clear from the outset: the public authority representatives interviewed perceive the CCM, with regard to its engagement in the welfare of substance abusers, as unambiguously positive. There are no critical comments of the work of the organization. On the contrary, the CCM is unanimously praised for its performance.

The CCM runs a café and an activity centre, staffed by a few paid workers and some 30 volunteers. This represents much less activity than that which comprises the diakonal work of several of the parishes. The CCM's primary target is people who struggle, or have struggled, with substance abuse. Its stated goal is to 'make everyday life a little better for people in a difficult life situation'. About 45 per cent of the running expenses are covered through grants from the municipality (*Drammens Tidende*, 22 November 2003). Other sources are private grants, donations, private foundations, and associations.

Quantitatively, the activities of the CCM are rather limited. Qualitatively, they are of considerable significance, since little is done to serve the needs of substance abusers besides what the CCM organizes. A sign of the trust and appreciation that the organization enjoys in the local community is that the local bank, which provided the loan needed to finance the premises in which the organization runs its activities, decided to relieve the organization of its debt (€210,000) (*Drammens Tidende*, 24 March 2004).

The CCM is seen as fulfilling a *vanguard role*. Certain statements by public authority representatives may be interpreted in this way: 'The Church City Mission has taken on work that no one else would do' (f); 'The Church City Mission takes care of those that fall outside every [public arrangement]' (f); 'What I can say, is that the Church City Mission shows the way ... People say it's so good that someone does, that someone demonstrates [in action] models of how things can be done' (m). These statements may, at the same time, be indicative of the organization's *value guardian role*. The organization demonstrates in its activities its solidarity with those at the bottom of society, and speaks up for those at the margins through its role in the public discourse on welfare. No other church-based agent, agency or activity is described and evaluated as favourably as the CCM.[10] One can interpret the statements of the interviewees as an expression of the organization's symbolic function in the town. The role the leader of the CCM plays in the local news media may be taken as support for such an interpretation.

The Role of the CCM as a Contributor in the Public Discourse on Welfare

Analyses of local newspapers reveal that the director[11] of the CCM is the only person affiliated with the church who has taken the opportunity to act politically, in the sense of trying to influence public opinion and political decision-making.

---

[10]   The organization that came closest to the CCM in its positive reputation in the field of welfare work was the Salvation Army.

[11]   'Director' here should not be interpreted as a formal title, but the individual in question was responsible for managing himself and a group of volunteers.

From the statements presented in the newspapers, an important part of his public message demands that people and the political system acknowledge the dignity of all those who live in the community, be they 'straight' citizens or substance abusers. The responsibility of the municipality or the public sector to secure the basic welfare of all its citizens is often underscored. The director voices his message in various public contexts, and the newspaper seems to serve as a willing channel.

Developing a point made earlier, the role the church should take in forming public opinion may be exemplified in the following quotation from the director of the CCM:

> [W]e need to have two legs to stand on; we are obliged to help people in need; at the same time we must be outspoken about injustice. I am a columnist in the local paper every fourth week. We must confront the authorities. We must use the media and our political contacts. (m)

Cases where the director has been contacted by public authority employees and provided with information to be used in the public debate on welfare issues in Drammen are mentioned in interviews. In such situations there may be a danger that the 'messenger' is used as a pawn in a power game within the public sector. Also, to be offered and to take the role of messenger demands mutual confidence and a mutual feeling of shared values in the field of welfare. For (the leader of) the organization to be entrusted with such a mission, the organization has to have a strong record of performance in word and deed; such a role demands visibility.

It seems that the director's letter to *Drammens Tidende*'s editor concerning the plans for the town square kick-started this process. In an editorial in the local newspaper in 2002 on the topic of the reconstruction and future use of the town square the editor wrote:

> To make [the development of the town square] a success – to make parents dare to send their children and youth to the [town] centre in the afternoon and at night – a thorough housecleaning is required. In plain English addicts, pushers, beggars, graffiti artists, troublemakers and other rabble must be chased away from the 'town parlour'. (Editorial, *Drammens Tidende,* 30 July 2002)

The director of the CCM responded to this, and another editorial with similar content, saying:

> To call somebody 'rabble' is nothing but destructive … If we choose to call people by that term it only reinforces an experience of powerlessness. It strengthens their hatred against society and 'straight people' in Drammen. 'If I am a shit all I can do is just shit'. I have seen the opposite. I have seen narcotic addicts taking responsibility when met with trust. Of course, I have been cheated and had my moments of dejection. Nevertheless, I have seen people grow and

become confident in themselves and their personal resources when praised for
their good choices and the way they act [in life]. For rabble there is little hope.
(Letter to the Editor, *Drammens Tidende,* 22 August 2002)

This public expression of the values of the CCM and its reassertion in other
contexts attracted the attention of the local newspaper (despite the clash between
the editor and CCM director's views).

The voice of the CCM may be perceived as trustworthy and authoritative
because the activities organized by the CCM, as they were evaluated by the
interviewees in this study, are congruent with the words. This is in line with the
director's definition of *diakonia*:

It is easy to resort to the phrase 'the body language of the church'. To me
diakonia is to make the love of Christ visible. The *diakonia* of the church must
be visible. *Diakonia* is underestimated as a way of preaching. To be loved is
more important than verbal preaching. (m)

The church may have taken over some of the critical function which the labour
movement traditionally had in the public debate on welfare.[12] In this context it is
interesting to note that a recent study of power élites in Norway concludes that
the church élite appears to be the most radical in Norwegian society (Gulbrandsen
2002). This assessment is based, among other things, on the values espoused by
the church's prominent members. The radical profile of leaders may have to do
with the value tradition of the church, its social background and possibly its lack
of power in society (Repstad 2004). In such a context, with few vested interests
related to a position of power, it is easier to maintain radical principles. Analogous
reasoning may be applied to the position of the CCM in Drammen. The CCM is
without strong ties to the public sector, but has robust links to the national CCM
family and its ideology and values. In addition, the public role of the organization
has made it popular with the public. As the director expresses it:

The politicians would be afraid to do something to [harm] us. One of the things
that has been said [among public authorities] is that 'one of the things we could
do is to withdraw our support to the Church City Mission. But they are so
popular, that [a withdrawal of financial support] would create big noise'. (m)

---

[12]   This function may be associated with Casanova's analysis of public religion in
modern society (Casanova 1994). For obvious reasons, the role of the church and the CCM
in welfare may also be related to the wider question of the role of religion in contemporary
society. This aspect of the role of the CCM will not be pursued in this chapter.

Reflections

The information collected and presented above leaves an impression of the church contributing to some extent to welfare and well-being in Drammen through its organized activities. Yet the church (with one noticeable exception) keeps a low profile in the public sphere and is viewed as relatively invisible in the local welfare arena by the public authorities. The public authority representatives seem to have little knowledge of the welfare activities organized by the church – a fact that may, at least partly, explain the rather low expectations of the church in the field of welfare on the part of public authorities. Conversely, those who do have such knowledge are very appreciative of the work of the church; at least among politicians, both the church and other voluntary efforts are considered important to the local provision of welfare.

A more significant explanation may be that the public authorities take their dominant position for granted. This would be in accordance with what is to be expected in a welfare state like the Norwegian one. Even the representatives of the church share this taken-for-granted attitude. In this way, the church may be said to contribute to the legitimacy of a strong welfare state. This may even apply when we consider the role of the church in the public discourse on welfare. In other words, the lack of participation – though such participation is asked for by the public authorities – may be seen as tacit support of the welfare state. The critical role of the director of the CCM can be interpreted similarly. Taken in context, the role as a public conscience, a voice of the voiceless, is most reasonably interpreted as a way of pointing to deficiencies – that is, not undermining the basic structure of the welfare system, but modifying the operation of the system in order to improve it for the benefit of the neediest.

Ideologically, this stance would be in accordance with classical Lutheran theology, which emphasizes welfare, health and social security as the domain of the state. The fact that the Church of Norway is a state church means inevitably close relationships between the state and the church at different levels. The strong support for the welfare state among the church representatives mirrors the strong position the state enjoys as a welfare provider in the minds of the population at large. This is unsurprising in a Lutheran context, since Lutheran ideology or theology has in many respects contributed to institutional secularization. The doctrine of the 'two kingdoms', through which the state (and science as well as other institutions) was granted autonomy from the church, leads to religion becoming privatized and consequently threatened with marginalization despite the church's established status (Casanova 1994).

The generally acknowledged contrast between the public-sphere agency of the CCM on the one hand, and the much more muted role of the parishes on the other, could be a potential source of tension within the local church. However, no such tension was observed or felt: all interviewees who know about it seem to appreciate the CCM, and the public authorities at least seem to be less appreciative of the (lack of) agency of the parishes. The reaction of the representatives of the parishes to the requests for a more active church in the public sphere is somewhat hesitant. A simplified and straightforward interpretation of their responses may be that they appreciate the CCM and consider it their representative both in the service it organizes for people with substance-abuse problems and in its presence in the public debate.[13] The contrast between the two types of agents in their public sphere engagement may be figured, at least in part, as a division of roles.

Further analysis of how the church is perceived as an organization requires a more nuanced description. The extent to which the church is described as similar to or different from other organizations in society with respect to its welfare functions seems to depend on the position of the interviewee and function in question. The representatives of the church generally think of the church and its functions both in secular and religious terms. The basic ideas and values of the church may endow it with a special role. On the other hand, the voice of the church in the public space is approved of by many interviewees, with no distinction drawn between the significance of the potential contributions of the church and those of other organizations. With regard to the role of the church in welfare service provision, the same ambiguity is expressed; on the one hand, the church is grouped together with other voluntary organizations, but on the other, the religious character of the church implies a special role. This nuance is also mentioned by interviewees representing the public authorities.

From the perspectives of both the general public and church representatives, the CCM differs from other church-based agents. Like the specific contributions of the parishes, the CCM's contribution to welfare in Drammen may be characterized as complementary. In this case, however, the tendency is to see the CCM as an organization performing a unique and important role, both from an ecclesiological and a sociological perspective. According to the interviewees, the CCM does something which the welfare municipality does not do, and perhaps would not, even if it could. The work is performed in such a way that one sees the 'truer church'. Yet in addition to providing a complementary service to the welfare community, the CCM criticizes the municipality, and at the same time, the church.

The position of the CCM and its director in Drammen, as mediated through the local newspaper, calls for further analysis.[14] The extensive use of the director as a voice in matters of morals and ethics related to the *diakonia* of the church and the welfare state, as a kind of local moral authority in such matters, may be interpreted as an expression of a felt need for a social ethics in welfare policy – a need that the labour movement, and to a lesser extent the church, once fulfilled. Recent trends in political and ideological thinking about the welfare state, represented by new

---

[13] Further reasons for, and a development of this interpretation is provided in Angell and Wyller (2006).

[14] An analysis of this form of mediation, drawing upon modern media theory, is provided in Angell (2008).

public management,[15] with an increased emphasis on efficiency and economic aspects of government (perhaps at the expense of an emphasis on the ethical dimension of welfare management), may have left a void in the public discourse on welfare policy.

The voice of the CCM in Drammen may contribute to filling this void, not only through the words spoken, but through the deeds which form a basis for the significance of the words. This function may be related to Charles Taylor's analysis of the 'malaise of modernity' or 'the ethics of authenticity' (Taylor 1991). An authorized, shared and taken-for-granted set of norms and values is, by and large, missing from modern society. A demand to fulfil oneself is placed on the individual, based on the moral ideal of authenticity, or being true to oneself. This moral ideal of constructing one's own personal identity is not something that can be done by the individual in isolation. 'The making and sustaining of our identity ... remain dialogical throughout our lives' (Taylor 1991: 35). This line of reasoning is congruent with Anthony Giddens's theory about identity formation in modernity as a reflexive process (Giddens 1991). In this process we need partners, either through a genuine dialogue or someone to relate to indirectly – for example, through the mass media. The director of the CCM, through his visibility in the media, may be perceived as such a dialogue partner.

In an era of individualization, also characterized by an ethics of authenticity, to use Taylor's expression, the ideal of authenticity may be easily compatible with the idea that individual human beings are responsible for their own life-choices and life situations. On the other hand, from a structural point of view, there are those who do not command sufficient resources to choose and live the lives they would want to. Their life situations should not be seen only as the result of personal choices, for they are displaced to the margins of society. However, when each individual is regarded as essentially responsible for his or her own life, he or she is also blamed in the case of failure and made to accept the consequences of that failure (Beck and Hviid Nielsen 1997). The actions of the CCM and its director are a protest against this way of reasoning, and serve as a reinforcement of the traditional value of collective solidarity. In this case, the position of the CCM in the local media may be taken as an indication that the public appreciates a voice speaking in favour of those living on the margins of society; that the idea of an inclusive 'we' is stronger than an immediate urge to exclude.

The question of the extent to which local, organized *diakonia* may be considered gendered in its structure is not easily answered by the interviews. On the one hand, it is agreed that many activities concern what is traditionally the domain of women, either in the domestic sphere or in the fulfilment of more affective functions

---

[15] New public management implies transferring business and market principles and management techniques from the private to the public sector. It is based on neo-liberal understandings of state and economy, and may be seen as a response to criticism of the effectiveness and efficiency of the public sector which has grown since the mid-1980s. See Barzelay (2001); Ferlie et al. (2002).

such as visiting services. In this way, there has, to some extent, been a mismatch between the distribution of men and women in the parishes and the structure of the voluntary activities open to parishioners to engage in. On the other hand, changing gender roles in society have implied that men and women should share familial domestic chores more equally. In society as a whole, men now spend more time on household activities than before whilst women spend less. Church interviewees claim that men increasingly take part in activities traditionally associated with the household and with women. In this way corresponding change processes seem to be going on in society and church.

In conclusion, it can be seen from this presentation of the Drammen case study that welfare is a significant aspect of church work and that the church plays a small but important role in local welfare provision in a Norwegian town. Welfare services constitute a site where the sacred and secular interact, and are consequently a proper object of study for the sociology of religion.

Chapter 5

The Church as a Place of Encounter: Communality and the Good Life in Finland

Anne Birgitta Pessi

Welfare and the Good Life Today

Individuals need welfare in order to be content, satisfied and happy, and in order to have a more or less stable 'good life'. But – given the very complex intersections of dependence and independence in today's world – who or what constructs these things? Many observers, including individuals who are writing from their own experience, may simply conclude 'It is up to you; it is your choice!' Hence the novelty of looking again at the role of traditional institutions, not least majority churches, in the construction of welfare and the good life today.

First, however, we must tackle the primary question: what is welfare? As we have seen, Allardt uses the concept sociologically (Allardt 1976, 1989): welfare is a state in which it is possible for an individual to satisfy his or her basic needs. Both material and non-material needs have, however, to be considered – hence the division into three categories. 'Having' refers to material conditions and impersonal needs seen in a broad perspective; 'loving' represents the need to relate to other people and to form identities; and 'being' denotes the need for personal growth, through integration into society and living in harmony with nature. An intriguing question follows from this: is there a role for the church in any or all of these three?

This theme will be developed at some length in a chapter which focuses on the role of the Evangelical Lutheran Church of Finland as an agent of welfare and the good life. The data for this inquiry were collected in the Finnish town of Lahti. With its population of approximately 100,000, Lahti is a regional capital and a 'young' city of entrepreneurship. The recession of the early 1990s had a substantial impact on the industrial life of Lahti. At the height of the recession, for example, more than one in four inhabitants was unemployed (Lahden työttömyysaste 1990–2004). With its enduring economic issues, Lahti poses an interesting and challenging case study for research into welfare.

The National Situation

Welfare and its Recent Challenges

Industrialization came late to Finland; it was not until the 1960s that the country experienced a radical leap in modernization. Along with this came unprecedented economic prosperity. It was only then that universal welfare provision finally superseded poor relief and Finland caught up with the other Nordic countries (Julkunen 2003). Today, the Finnish system of social protection follows the principles of the Nordic welfare model: universality (the right of all to social protection regardless of where they live, their profession or economic position); a strong public sector; tax funding based on the legislative rights of citizens or residents; and equal treatment. Economic, social and educational rights are guaranteed by the state and the municipal authorities in Finland.

The Finnish Constitution affirms that all those unable to provide for themselves are entitled to basic income and care. The provision of certain services is considered so important that the resulting legislation gives to the individual what is known as a 'subjective right' to specific services. These include day-care for children, certain statutory services for people with disabilities and the right to emergency medical care. Municipalities are required to reserve adequate funds for the provision of these services in all circumstances. However, much social welfare and health care provision is subject to budget constraints. Thus, services may be targeted at those who need them most, particularly in poorer municipalities.

Finance for social expenditure in Finland comes mainly from central government, municipalities and employers. The contributions made by the insured are far lower in Finland than in other European Union countries. This is a characteristic feature of countries where benefits are based on the principle of universality. Municipal institutions provide statutory services; they can also purchase these obligatory services from the private sector or from other agents such as the church. In this sense, private services supplement public provision.

In the first decade of the twenty-first century, the economic development of Finland has been mainly positive. The only evidence remaining from the very harsh recession of the early 1990s is structural unemployment, which continues at a high level, and the relatively large national debt. New issues have, however, emerged in recent years: these include the growing disparities between different regions; the increase in income differentials; and, therefore, the risk of social exclusion (Kainulainen et al. 2001; Ministry of Social Affairs and Health 2002a, 2004). Finland is also one of Europe's fastest-ageing countries (Parjanne 2004); as a result, there have been significant changes in the age structure of the population.

Thus, it is not surprising that the public debate on welfare has focused recently on the care of elderly people and its costs. As women as well as men work full-time, the care of the elderly is both financed and organized by the public sector. The growing number of elderly people – together with financial cuts, and the difficulty of finding sufficient employees in the public sector – has led, however, to growing criticism. Care is considered inadequate or even poor in some places. In political debate, some have argued that the third sector should take on more responsibility – a shift interpreted by others as the return to unpaid care for elderly people by women. Increasing ageing is a central reason behind another welfare-related debate in Finland today: namely, the radical reorganization of the municipal service structure. Here there is a trend toward increasing co-operation between municipalities in welfare and health provision, and the possibility that smaller municipalities might merge (Kunta-ja palvelurakenneuudistus 2006).

Two further challenges must be noted. First, considerable changes have occurred in the Finnish operational environment and in the functioning of the health care system. The service system has become more and more oriented to out-patient care. Second, increasing long-term dependency on social assistance is a fact: if the number of social assistance recipients has, to some extent, fallen in recent years, costs have not decreased (Ministry of Social Affairs and Health 2002b). At the same time, it has been generally admitted that both support and services are inadequate for those with the greatest difficulties. Marginalization is a reality for many facing long-term unemployment or mental health problems. For example, fewer than half of the Finnish municipalities deemed it possible to provide high-quality social services with current resources, and 10 per cent admitted having serious difficulties (Sociobarometer 2006). Measures such as renewing the pension plan and the municipal service structure have been taken. Nevertheless, in the ensuing public debate the increasing responsibility of both the family and the third sector has been seen as unavoidable.

The Situation in Lahti

Similar challenges also affect the town which is the focus of this chapter, Lahti. The average age is rising, and thus the workforce is decreasing, relatively speaking. Unemployment remains high, and social services and health care have insufficient resources. More specifically, the income level of elderly people in Lahti is particularly low (*Lahden kaupungin tulevaisuuspaketti 2004* 2004; *Lahden kaupunki, talouden seurantaraportti* 2004; *Lahden kaupunki, talousarvio 2004 ja taloussuunnitelma 2004–2006* 2003; Liukko 2004). Lahti has tackled these challenges in a visionary manner. For example, one very interesting emphasis in the latest local documents on welfare and social and health care is the strategy of increasing mutual responsibility. The idea is that we do not need, or have sufficient money for, experts in every aspect of welfare and health. The local documents note,

> Cultural and value-related change ... aims to strengthen the willingness of local people to support and help each other when needed. Municipal social and health services will concentrate on their core functions in producing services that the local people will then complement with services they acquire themselves. (Toimintakertomus 2005: 1; Liukko 2004)

Against the background of the traditional Nordic rhetoric of strong public welfare services, this view is indeed quite radical. Specifically, it creates a fascinating context for studying welfare and the role of the majority church within it.

Introducing Gender

Plantenga writes, '[W]elfare states are not just a collection of laws and institutions, but are based on and contribute to norms and values of women's (and men's) proper roles' (Plantenga 1997: 97–98). She describes the social democratic welfare regime, among others, as a promoter of equality. Finland is a good example of such a state. Indeed, Finland was the European forerunner in gender equality in 1906. Finnish women were the first in Europe to receive the universal and equal franchise, and the first women in the world to become eligible for parliamentary elections (Sulkunen 2004; Manninen 1999).

Finnish women are highly educated, and their participation in the workforce is one of the highest in the world. However, Finland has been, and in many ways still is, more conservative than the other Nordic countries concerning a woman's rights regarding her body. For example, rape within marriage was criminalized as late as 1994, and family violence was made a matter for public prosecution only in 1995. There are also other signs of attitudinal patriarchy in Finland (Julkunen 2003). Similarly, some aspects of Finnish social security quite clearly privilege men. Nevertheless, women perceive the welfare state as a supportive partner rather than an oppressor. Individualized allowances and social insurance benefits have been a priority in Finland. Marriage in Finland is not associated with reduced labour-force participation for women. The Finnish social policy does not encourage women into part-time employment, as do other Nordic social democratic welfare states (Bryson et al. 1994: 123–124). That said, the history of Finnish social legislation quite clearly displays some tension and conflicts regarding the status of women. For instance, the legislation strives on the one hand to promote motherhood, but, on the other, to support women working outside the home (Manninen 1999).

In spite of Finland's egalitarian image, then, the position of women in the labour market is by no means equal to that of men. Even well-educated women earn on average 20 per cent less than men doing the same job (Julkunen 2003). Furthermore, pay differences between women and men have increased in Finland in the past years. Additionally, even if the quota provision in the Equality Act (since 1995) has increased women's participation in state administration decision-making, Finnish women still have a smaller role than men in decision-making for society (Equality Programme of the Finnish Government 1997). While both Finnish women and men work full-time, women are in fixed-term employment relationships, and work part-time, more frequently than men (Equality Programme of the Finnish Government 1997). This is especially true for younger cohorts

(Ministry of Social Affairs and Health 2003).[1] Women more often work in the public sector, whereas men are oriented to the private sector (Korvajärvi 2003.) For instance, a large majority (90 per cent) of church social workers is female. Furthermore, in many families women are still in charge of most domestic chores. Even though Nordic women participate both in politics and the labour market, they also retain the major responsibility for work in the household (Forsberg et al. 2000: 43). Thus, welfare work is gendered.

The recession did not mean the great setback for the welfare state and gender equality that some feared that it would, but the 1990s did leave a legacy. Finnish society as a whole is now tougher and more adversarial than ten years ago, and the state seems to be less women-friendly than it was at the start of the 1990s. The 1990s also brought about greater neutrality on the gender issue – it became less politicized and less talked about (Julkunen 2003). Unemployment today affects both men and women, though not quite to the same degree. After the recession, male unemployment fell faster, and female unemployment is now slightly higher.

Overall, however, there is no feminization of poverty, in the international sense of the word, in Finland. Indeed, evidence indicates that certain groups of men are, on average, more prone than other people to become marginalized and dependent on the safety-net provided by the welfare state (Equality Programme of the Finnish Government 1997; National Institute for Health and Welfare 2006). Still, one-third of households receiving minimum income security are single-parent households, and this usually means households headed by women.

The Church's Role in Welfare at the National and Local Level

The National Level

The Lutheran churches, in both Finland and the other Nordic countries, have played a vital role in shaping society. Not least, they have strongly supported the idea of caring for one's neighbour and of serving the community (Bäckström 2004; Helander 2005). By the second half of the nineteenth century, the status of the Evangelical Lutheran Church of Finland had already changed from that of a state church to a folk church. Nevertheless, both the Evangelical Lutheran and the Orthodox Churches retain duties that could be performed by either the state or the local government. For example, the parishes keep local population registers of their members, and even those who belong to other denominations or who are listed on the non-denominational population register are buried in the cemeteries

---

[1]   This is seen to be the consequence of women's more frequent use of parental and similar leaves, which brings costs to the employer. In 2001, nearly half (48 per cent) of women under 25 were employed short term. The number of men in short-term employment was 35 per cent. For 25 to 29-year-olds, the figure was 35 per cent of women and 19 per cent of men.

maintained by the parishes. For this reason, the church also has the right to collect taxes from commercial communities (companies). Taxes and membership fees (paid by members of the church) form the core of the church's finances.

Today the religious environment remains interestingly homogenous: no fewer than 83 per cent of Finns are members of the Evangelical Lutheran Church. It is also clear that Finland has relatively high levels of private religiosity (such as private prayer and belief in God), yet only a small minority are regular churchgoers, lower than in most European countries (Niemelä 2002). However, in addition to the main Sunday service, the parishes arrange a wide variety of other possibilities for worship. Religious television and radio broadcasts are watched or listened to by the majority of Finns. Furthermore, about half of Finns say they believe in God as taught by Christianity. This proportion increased significantly during the 1990s. Altogether, in recent decades, the trend in Finland has been towards declining public religiosity but continuing, even increasing, private religiosity, a clear illustration that institutional religious decline is not necessarily accompanied by decline in belief.

Church ceremonies enable the parishes to come into contact with almost the entire Finnish population on an annual basis: 87 per cent of all infants are baptized; only about 2 per cent of Finns are buried without a church service; and as many as 80 per cent of couples are married in church. Strikingly, approximately 90 per cent of all 15-year-olds have taken part in confirmation training (Church Research Institute 2004: 47). For Finns, the most important reason to belong to the Lutheran Church is church ceremonies. A clear majority also finds it important that the church assists elderly and infirm people, and teaches moral values to children and young people. Even for those who contemplate leaving the church, the rituals and the social work of the church are strong factors in favour of remaining a member. Thus, church ceremonies and welfare activities shape citizens' views of the church and their relationship to it.

From an international perspective, the Finnish system is interesting owing to its uniqueness. Social work in the church includes a large group of paid workers, and has a central position in church law and organization. Every parish must, by law, have at least one social work post. Activities range from food banks to counselling, from home visits to various camps, from financial assistance to support groups.[2] Church social workers are currently requesting more resources for family work

---

[2]   Today approximately 21,300 people work in the church, of whom 45 per cent do parish work and 9 per cent are diaconal workers. In 2000, the number of priests in the Finnish Lutheran Church was 2,162 and the number of church social workers as high as 1,462. The rest of the work is in administration, the care of cemeteries and so on. The number of diaconal workers increased by 21 per cent between 1999 and 2003. Some 70 per cent of all church employees and 91 per cent of diaconal workers are women. At the turn of the millennium, approximately 7 per cent of the population received help and counselling from parish diaconal workers. In 2004, church diaconal work involved 734,000 contacts, and parishes organized 11,000 occasions for distributing food in which 426,000 people

and preventative care. They see work with elderly people and children as particular challenges for the future (Kirkon tutkimuskeskus 2004). Church employee polls indicate that the majority considers parishes and church associations as having a continuing and central role to play in a variety of societal tasks. At the same time, the need for financial assistance and support for the unemployed is viewed as, or hoped to be, declining (Salonen et al. 2001).

Although the welfare budgets of the Church of Finland are only a fraction of the welfare budget of the Finnish state and municipalities, the visibility of the church's welfare actions is indeed important. This was particularly apparent during the recession of the early 1990s when the non-profit sector, voluntary work and Christian social work were recognized on a larger scale than before, and were seen as a means of filling the gaps in services created by budget cuts in the public sector. The church reacted quickly, setting up funds to help those in debt, providing meals, and organizing meeting-places and activities for unemployed people. Its employees supported mental-health patients who had been moved to out-patient care. Co-operation between the municipalities, congregations and associations also increased (Heino et al. 1997: 81; 154). Interestingly, the recession clearly caused a significant change in the nature of church social work, the emphasis shifting from work with elderly and disabled people to those of working age who were experiencing economic or psychological problems.

With its increasing social service provision during the recession, the church attained a very visible, public role in Finnish society. The rise in church social services was widely reported in the media. At the individual level this resulted in a more positive public image: whilst a third of Finns expressed confidence in the church in 1990, almost two-thirds (57 per cent) did so in 2000. Church social work is an essential factor in this trust, since more than 90 per cent of Finns consider the work of the church with elderly, disabled and young people as either important or very important (Salonen et al. 2001).[3] Recent figures also indicate that Finns are most dissatisfied with church activities among unemployed people,[4] meaning probably that they desire more rather than less church action. The positive image of the church among Finns has continued to increase since 2000: currently, 77 per cent of Finns view the church positively (*Gallup Ecclesiastica* 2003).

---

took part (Kääriäinen 2002; Salonen et al. 2001; Church Research Institute 2004; *Kirkon tilastollinen vuosikirja 2004* 2005).

[3]   Furthermore, most (82 per cent) Finnish church members consider church social work with elderly and disabled people an important reason for their church membership (*Gallup Ecclesiastica* 2003).

[4]   Those dissatisfied represent 23 per cent, and almost as many (18 per cent) are displeased with the church's public statements on ethical issues (*Gallup Ecclesiastica* 2003). The second group are more difficult to interpret, as they are probably divided between those who wish the church spoke more loudly in public debate and those who wish that it did not speak at all.

The church has also been active in its societal and ethical statements, especially during the 1990s. For instance, the Finnish bishops have published official statements concerning social ethics and their concern regarding the need for community-based responsibility (Hytönen 2003: 18). The church has also regularly offered statements on the initiatives of the Ministry of Social Affairs and Health. In contrast, when it comes to gender issues the Evangelical Lutheran Church of Finland has been relatively silent (Sulkunen 2004).

The Local Level

The Lahti parishes also have a long tradition of engaging in social work. Today social welfare work is strongly incorporated in the overall strategy of 'serving'. Parish documents summarize this role: '1) we help and support especially those in the deepest distress, and who are otherwise without help, 2) we carry our common responsibility for Christian welfare work in general, and 3) we promote rightness and participation in everything' (*Lahden seurakuntayhtymä* 2004: 5; 8–9). These aims are very much in line with the national-level documents on church social work. There is evidence of co-operation with the municipal social authorities at a number of levels, and in various contexts. For instance, the Lahti parish union provides the municipal afternoon clubs for schoolchildren (*Lahden seurakuntayhtymä* 2005). The parish union has also employed a church social worker focusing entirely on economic support – something very rare, even in Finland.[5]

Despite the fact that the overall number of clients has been steadily decreasing in recent years –though it increased again in 2004 – church social workers indicate that the problems of many of their clients have become increasingly complex. The main content of the client visits in Lahti has also altered: the importance of spiritual and faith-related topics as well as human relations has increased, while discussion about money has decreased (*Lahden seurakuntayhtymä* 2005). Altogether, the activities of Lahti church social workers may be considered a significant shaper of public opinion, particularly regarding the issues of altruism and welfare.

Varying Views on the Role of the Church at the Grassroots Level

The Views of Local Public Authorities

The local authorities clearly consider the church in Lahti as having a role to play in the construction of welfare, both in providing services and in reminding people of

---

[5]   Additionally, the fact that the social services of the Lahti parish union (as distinct from the parishes, which also have their separate social services such as care for disabled people) are located in the same premises may well increase public knowledge of the church's welfare services. This Service Centre (*palvelukeskus*) is centrally and very visibly located in central Lahti. It also incorporates the Mary's Chamber volunteer centre.

their responsibility for others' well-being. It is also thought that the welfare work of the church will be increasingly needed in the near future. Interestingly, contracts with the church are not really considered as outsourcing. This seems to reflect a certain 'state-church' image, which, according to law, is no longer the case.

That said, the provision of what are considered 'basic services' is clearly seen squarely as the responsibility of the local municipality. Conversely, the welfare role of the church concerns 'special welfare services', meaning primarily psychosocial services, crisis help and work with specific groups such as elderly people. Why exactly these fields of welfare? It seems that the public authorities consider church representatives to have special welfare know-how. In particular, it is felt that church representatives possess spirituality and values (especially the values of caring and communality), and the ability to relate to people better and more deeply than other agents. They also, it is felt, base their relationships on free will. Indeed, there seems to be a considerable idealism in the way that the welfare services of the church are portrayed: the church is seen as motivated by spirituality, love and free will. Such idealism is evident in interviewees' opinions about the municipality and church offering similar services (such as counselling): 'The church relates to individuals better.' Significantly, municipal representatives spontaneously offer an even more personal perspective: 'If I needed food money for my family, I think I would choose church social work over municipal agency … I feel they work there more based on neighbourly love' (f).

According to the municipal representatives, the church should adopt a clear stance in public welfare debates, even concerning municipal services, but should not 'patronize and preach': 'The church should keep up the voice of the weaker as well as the shared spirit of not leaving your pal who is in need behind' (m). They understand this public voice as promotion of welfare: maintaining the values of caring and spirit of solidarity. The church, in their view, is a special expert on this. However, the representatives also note that in close active co-operation with the state, the church may lose its distance and critical voice. Close co-operation, may, in this sense, thus be a double-edged sword.

What, then, all in all, is the relationship between the welfare and 'good life' activities of the municipality and the church? In those areas of well-being and welfare where the church's activities are strong, the resources of municipality social work can be reduced. Overlapping activities are viewed as unnecessary and avoidable. The fear of many of the church representatives that increased church involvement in welfare leads to decreased state responsibility thus seems to be understandable.

The Views of the Church Representatives

The church representatives conclude that the church indeed has a role to play in the welfare and well-being of the people, but views on this role vary. Some emphasize evangelism and spirituality and think that ideally the church should incorporate fewer welfare activities, or even none at all. Other people are more positive about welfare activities, but think the practical social work activities of the church should be temporary, not long term. Yet others emphasize that the church must incorporate both spiritual and social work, equally. A few even say that, in some instances, social work should be emphasized more than spiritual activities.

Overall, the church representatives agree that the church should have responsibility for those people whom no one else looks after – the 'weakest'. Many interviewees refer to the 'invisible misery which the society and municipal aid channels do not reach' (m). The church representatives, very much in line with the public authorities, also consider that it is the church's responsibility to remind people of their personal social responsibilities; the church is considered a promoter of the values of caring and communality. 'Encountering' is the core: 'When people are suffering illness and sickness and despair, they soon lose their participation and link with their parish. We should really reach out to them. This spirit should intimately inform our social work' (m).

Interestingly, however, views on the best way to encounter people vary greatly between representatives. Some think that the church should participate in everyday life as much as possible. This could involve taking part in market-place happenings, or participating in neighbourhood associations; or it could simply mean priests walking around their neighbourhoods and offering to assist in car repair, or church social workers offering cleaning assistance. However, some are of the opinion that the church should encounter people through spirituality or mental help; simply being close to people is not sufficient, and is perhaps even harmful. The church should not act as 'a show producer or stage manager' (m).

Similarly to the municipal authorities, church representatives see public debates on welfare and ethical issues as part of the church's social responsibility and welfare activities. However, a few are against public visibility, or at least further visibility. One vicar notes, 'People expect the church to be more obvious in ethical debates. But it is problematic. It may give the wrong impression of the core message of the church, which is only mercy' (m).

To conclude, the ideal seems to be that the church should act as a reactive, flexible societal actor providing resources for unexpected needs. Only then might it maintain its social work ideal of being 'a prophetic voice, a cry for help, a sort of provocative yell, an exclamation mark that speaks for the silent ones who do not have a voice' (m) in relation to other actors, specifically the local authorities.

The Views of the Local Population

The views of the local citizens on the church's welfare activities also vary. Some consider welfare activities integral to the church: 'Without welfare work the church would be like a barren cow. Sorry for this simile! But without social work the church could not produce spiritual fruits' (m). Others, however – in fact, the majority of the local people interviewed for this study – feel that the church's role is not, or should not have to be, in social work. Elderly people in particular think that social work belongs to the municipality: 'It means a secure future to know that our society and local municipality is prepared to take care of us entirely, once one's own strength is not enough' (m).

These views notwithstanding, local citizens all seem very positive about the fact that the church has, indeed, done something to help people in need by filling the welfare gaps. Areas within which the church is viewed as having a particular role are social networks and meeting places, overall psychological well-being and the needs of special groups. The majority consider the ideal role of the church as maintaining societal and individual morality, ethics and specifically the spirit of caring for one's neighbours. In this, the citizens are very much in line with the public representatives.

Contributing to the public welfare debate is seen, then, as the heart of the church's social welfare responsibility. In general, the interviewed citizens seem very satisfied with the church's recent nationwide statements as well as its public visibility and voice. In fact, at the local level, even more public statements and discussions on welfare are called for: 'The church must be the conscience of our society. It must dare to be in opposition. It should walk in the frontline and wave the flag. At the local level they should dare to oppose the clichés of the words and statements made by local authorities' (m).

In the long run, changes in the church have, according to the local people, been in the right direction. The church has become much closer to the grassroots level, everyday life concerns and the needs of citizens. The fact that the church today offers its services without asking about people's faith and level of religiousness is highly appreciated by the local people. The church aims, in their view, to assist all people in their experiences of good life. The church cares.

Church and the Construction of the Good Life

Let us return to the beginning of this chapter and the definition of welfare. How do the findings set out above relate to the elements of the good life – to having, loving and being?

The Church and Having: Various Ideals on the Role of the Church

Harris (1998: 156; 159) has written about the 'care catalyst' function of churches: being able to identify people in need of care and to spread information. This could be called, in Allardt's conception, a 'having catalyst'. As we have seen, 'having', in Allardt's analysis, refers to material conditions and impersonal needs, in a broad perspective. Should, then, the church offer material resources for living – or rather offer 'bread' only in the eucharistic sense? The diagram below (see Figure 5.1) is intended to capture the variety found in the three categories of Finnish data concerning the ideals projected onto the church.[6]

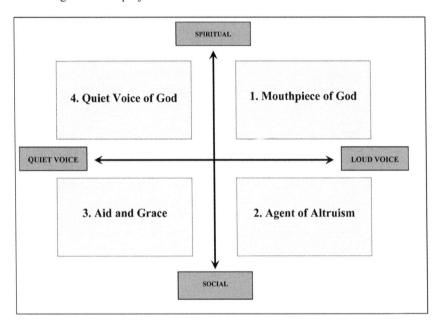

Figure 5.1   The Ideal of the Church

These dimensions do not exclude each other, but the four orientations illustrate differences in emphasis. All in all, social work is apparently a divisive issue, especially within the church. The two orientations 'mouthpiece of God' and 'quiet voice of God' describe some of the church representatives' views of the church's role in welfare and good life, and are particularly common among clergy. For instance, one individual notes, 'The main thing and the core must be in spiritual work. If my work and time and energy starts to go more into these practical matters … I have to sort of sit down and start to think whether am I in the right position and place' (f). The two orientations focusing more on helping and social assistance,

---

[6]   It is important to note that these dimensions do not exclude one another, but rather illustrate differences in primary emphasis. Most interviewees could easily be described using all four orientations; the municipal and citizens' viewpoints could be demonstrated by the model. It was harder, however, to apply the model to the church data. Nonetheless, I presented the model to a large group of church social workers in one of their training sessions in autumn 2004, and the feedback was positive and enthusiastic. A few noted that the model gave them good tools for thinking about their work environment and the teachings of the church. However, some noted that the dimensions are very interrelated – which is, of course, true. See also Yeung (2006).

'agent of altruism' and 'aid and grace', are most typical among the church social workers, as well as a few priests. As one man puts it, 'The helping activity of the church reminds us of the human values of justice and hope and equality. This is true counselling for everyday life!' (m). The church is pictured here as an expert in caring, and its welfare activities are legitimized by its being an expert in true human needs. Considering the viewpoints of the local official representatives, the picture is clear: they stress the orientation of 'agent of altruism' most strongly in their considerations of church institutions. Some of the local citizens very much agree, while others emphasize the orientation 'mouthpiece of God' far more.

Overall, this four-orientation model seems to coincide with the recent findings of a British study by Smith: faith-based organizations may have values and theologies which contradict values of social work and social inclusion, since an emphasis on evangelizing may be viewed as more important than focusing on social issues of whatever kind. There is an implicit dualism that separates the realms of the spiritual and material. Furthermore, some individuals may favour a spirituality that does not engage with politics and welfare (Smith 2004: 25). Interestingly, some of the citizens of Lahti seem to emphasize the welfare responsibility of the municipality (that is, 'the church should not be forced to do this much in actual welfare' type of thinking) more than Finnish citizens on average. This could be explained by the harsh economic challenges the town has recently struggled with.

The four orientations also capture well the theological variations in the data concerning the possible role of the church as a 'having catalyst'. Those representing the 'agent of altruism' orientation, in particular, appeal to the value of every individual: God has given us the task of reaching out to and assisting everyone. Precisely the same theological reason is used to legitimize the public voice of the church, public debates being one way of fulfilling God's teachings on charity. Words and deeds must come together. The theological motives for practical social work are based on the teachings of Christ about helping those in need, and, thus, Christian values. Values found in the present data correspond to those found in the British research mentioned above on faith-based urban regeneration: namely community, peace, love of one's neighbour, and social justice (Smith 2004: 25). My findings also seem to reflect the theological directives found in the welfare work of American churches: scriptural texts, response to God's love, and compassion. Also similar is the fact that political involvement is clearly not a preferred option (Cnaan 2002: 240–243); the church must do welfare work and fight for justice and people's good life, but it should not engage in party politics.

Conversely, those emphasizing the orientation 'mouthpiece of God' not only approve of church participation in ethical discussion, but encourage it. However, Luther's teaching on the 'two kingdoms' is used to explain why the church should not get involved in social work as such. Some people also use the same teaching to give theological legitimization to the church's contribution to public debate, since the church must remind the municipality of its welfare responsibility. Those representing the 'God's silent ones' attitude share this theological standpoint, while preferring that the church speak in the media only on spiritual issues. Furthermore, as one pastor indicates, an active media role might also be considered heretical, since the church must not teach that right actions bring people closer to God which the media voice of the church may be construed as conveying. The classical Lutheran position, distancing itself from the Roman Catholic tradition, is clearly reflected in these views.

There are no obvious gender differences in these four orientations. Overall, however, a few interviewees emphasize that there has been a trend toward altruism and social work in the church since women have been admitted as priests. One interviewee, a man, even notes in a highly visionary style, 'Men could go on arguing about power, they could keep the theology. Women could take over the diaconate and social work entirely. We could even have a separate national-level bishop for the diaconate! The voice of the whole of Finland!' Another illuminating and surprising viewpoint is offered by an elected official of the church: 'The time of church welfare has come! When we look at the entire Christian history, the first 500 years were the time of St Augustine, then in approximately AD 1000 Christianity and Islam separated. Then there was Luther in 1500. Now it has become the era of social welfare!' (f).

The Church and Loving: The Dilemma of Membership

'Loving' stands for the need to relate to other people and to form social identities. This is an individual need. However, in my view, different institutions play, both openly and more latently, a role in supporting this need and supplying resources to fill it. Institutions are also instrumental in creating and sustaining a societal atmosphere that either supports or weakens trust between individuals.

'Loving' plays what is perhaps the central role in the findings from the Finnish data. Indeed, if I had to capture the entire range of empirical findings of this case study in one expression, it would be 'encountering': an encountering church. In the data as a whole, there are clear illustrations that the church is different from, and not comparable to, other organizations. These elements relate, specifically, to the spirituality and value-basis of the church, its capacity to encounter people at a deeper and more holistic level, and to make itself heard in ethical statements and in the promotion of solidarity and altruism. To put it simply, if people receive welfare services from the municipality, they gain the benefit of professionalism, but if they receive welfare services from the church, they are both assisted and – primarily – encountered.

More than this, such expectations (concerning the values of solidarity, a spirit of altruism and the encountering of people) illustrate the social integration and trust-enhancement functions of the church. In a sociological sense, there is clearly a classical Durkheimian tone in these expectations. How, though, do these Durkheimian visions of communality, solidarity and altruism relate to the present-day, late-modern context? More precisely, a particular sociological challenge discovered in the Finnish data concerns the changing nature of membership. It is true that this question does not only relate to the church, but the church provides a fascinating context in which to explore it.

The church interviewees emphasize that future congregations must, indeed, face the question of what it means to be a member of a congregation. Recently, the membership rates of Finnish congregations have been the topic of vivid public discussions, due to the new and more flexible law on religious freedom (2003); it is now much easier for members to leave the church. This public debate has concerned Lahti in a particular way, since it had one of the highest rates of members leaving the church in 2004. Many interviewees ask, 'Has the local church worked so that people feel, even to some extent, that they are part of this community? What does the church mean to them?' (m). Conversely, a few interviewees point out that the fact that membership rates are still as high as they are is both surprising and positive in today's pluralistic society.

Concerning the sociological dilemma of late modern membership in relation to the welfare role of the church, three issues in particular arise from the data. First, the context evokes particular dilemmas. Quite often, church representatives note that welfare work today faces specific challenges in urban contexts. Some even ask whether there should be a clear division in the training of church social workers between urban and rural welfare work, since the work in urban contexts is so challenging. The municipal authorities also note that the need for the church to maintain communal values and a model of caring is more necessary than ever in an urban context, given that a sense of communality and social ties is clearly lacking. The same theme is underlined by citizens. One elderly man touchingly points out, 'We all should look now into a mirror and ask: is there watching a person who has a social conscience? Does our humanism sleep the hundred years' sleep of a princess? . . . The church should remind us of this.'

The second dilemma of late modern membership relates to the challenges of the church's paid staff. As seen above, church representatives do not share a unanimous picture of the ideal church, nor do they share a stance on whether church workers should be further involved in the everyday lives of church members. Some think that 'going into the field' (f) would clarify the role of church workers and encourage the membership and participation of citizens, while others think that this would be mere 'messing around' (f) – the specificity of the church would not be clearly expressed. The latter group explains this in terms of a personal need for anonymity, as well as on theological grounds: 'messing around' does not reflect the spiritual core of the church, and thus does not bring the church closer to its members. This debate, overall, reflects the social work-versus-spirituality dimensions in the model presented above.

The third membership-related welfare dilemma touches on the core question of what is understood as adequate membership by the church and what by the people. One theme here concerns church social work as a point of contact between members and congregations. Does social work constitute sufficient contact, or should these members have additional links to congregations? Not one of the church interviewees could offer a definitive answer. The citizens look at this question from quite a different viewpoint: today's society is, to very large extent, a service society. As noted above, people pay church taxes, and therefore they expect something in return.

What about gaining new souls and members through social welfare activities? Some church representatives, especially theologians, point out that while church social work does increase positive attitudes towards the church, thus enhancing its social status, it should not be used as an advertising gimmick. One interviewee, a vicar, even quotes the Bible: 'When your left hand is helping others, your right hand should not know about it' (m). One point is clear: just as in recent findings from research on American congregations and the provision of welfare (Cnaan 2002: 243), proselytizing does not really feature in the social actions of the church.

The Church and Being: Church as a Context of Volunteering

'Being', according to Allardt, denotes the need for personal growth: integration into society and living in harmony with nature. The positive side of 'being' may be characterized as personal growth, whereas the negative aspect refers to alienation. How do these ideas relate to my data? To start with, the previously mentioned elements of having and loving are, in my view, also elements of being: these are the ways in which the church promotes, and is expected to promote, an individual's potential to *be*, thus enabling him or her to live in harmony in society.

Quite apart from this, a rather different element of the church's 'being' activity arises directly from the data. This element is volunteer work. It is a crucial aspect of how the church encounters people, as well as how the church as an institution incorporates its members. Volunteering is also a central element in an individual's self-expression, potentially contributing to personal growth and the experience of a good life.

Volunteering in the local government context is viewed as very marginal, indeed practically non-existent. Conversely, third-sector associations and the church are considered to play a central role in maintaining both volunteering and citizen participation, in the sense of service delivery and – even more – of solidarity and cohesion. That said, the role of volunteering, and expectations surrounding it, relate to the church in particular ways. The data indicate that such activities are seen to some extent as the speciality of the church – something rather unique. One municipal authority notes:

> Even if most of our citizens do not even realize they are members of the church, it still is our common thing . . . this is enormous potential for the church. It does not have to invent its networks as we have to. The church could and should use its existing networks better, like for volunteering. (m)

Given that the representatives of the municipality have such high expectations of the church in this respect, how do the church representatives themselves view this? One of my Lahti church survey questions specifically concerned the place of volunteers in the church. The results clearly indicate that most respondents (60 per cent) think that the role of volunteering should be both broader and more central in the church. Many of these views are strongly expressed: 'Volunteering is the life line of the church!' (f). A clear majority of my interview data corroborates this viewpoint. The reasons are often related to theology: a true, living congregation involves each of its members in equal partnership.

Rather more surprising in the survey findings is the fact that quite a number of the parish union staff who work with children, and a few from other professional groups as well, had reservations – even negative views – concerning volunteers, and specifically, the possibility that their role might grow. More than two-thirds of children's workers shared this opinion: 'The quality of work will suffer if we start to have volunteers in everything . . . They let employed people go and explain that they have volunteers. Even safety suffers due to volunteers!' (f). These suspicions may well relate to constellations of power and to patterns of gender within the church. It follows that the status of those with the weakest educational background, often women, may be called into question.

Generally, however, the fact that the substantial majority of volunteers and paid employees in church welfare work are women is seen neither as a problem nor a challenge. Welfare work is considered a natural 'women's niche'. A few female church social workers emphasize, however, that they really are happy to have at least a few men working among them. In their view, the men bring versatility to the work, a little positive 'spark', and thereby encourage some clients to seek help. Such a 'spark' definitely seems to play a role in experiencing the good life.

Building Communality and the Good Life

The above analysis has indicated that the church's welfare activities indeed have many roles to play in the construction of the good life. In all the elements considered above (having, being and loving) the core message arising from the data concerns *communality*: in other words, the church can enhance people's welfare by encountering them.

This core finding illuminates something surely particular about the context, Finland. Even in the twenty-first century, Finns have strong memories of the much harder times that they have survived together: wars with their overbearing neighbour Russia, as well as the particularly harsh recession of the 1990s. In all these situations, it is the church that has fought for the people and their common identity. This shared cultural memory is related to the relatively recent modernization of the country – the communal values of the countryside still endure – and to cultural homogeneity. It is for this reason that a *lack* of communality and a shared spirit of altruism is considered one of the biggest welfare challenges for Finns, especially in urban areas.

The Finnish Church is clearly seen as an 'institution of authenticity'. Like my Norwegian colleague, I build here on the work of Charles Taylor (1991) who has written about the 'ethics of authenticity': as a shared set of norms and values is missing, there is an increasing demand to fulfil oneself and be true to oneself. With this in mind, I would like to ask whether the church's welfare actions are seen as a concrete example of an institution where words and deeds meet: that is, good words and good altruistic deeds. Particularly in a context of liberal social policy and more self-interested values, towards which Finland started to move during the recession of the early 1990s, there is a longing for a counter-weight. Today people are looking for 'institutions of authenticity' and larger frames of meaning. This is an intriguing sociological challenge that does not only concern Finland.

If the church continues to play an encountering role in the future, its welfare activities will contribute to communal well-being, or to what might be considered societal social capital. It is clear that the Finnish Church sustains the norms of altruism and mutual assistance even in a late-modern pluralist and somewhat secularized social context – indeed, paradoxically, even more so. As institutions become increasingly fragmented, fluid and porous, so the 'weight' of the social and welfare activities of the church in the eyes of citizens correspondingly increases.

Chapter 6
The German Dilemma:
Protestant Agents of Welfare in Reutlingen

Annette Leis-Peters

Introduction

The word 'crisis' arises frequently in contemporary debate about the German social state (Boll 2008; Butterwegge 2005; Metzler 2003).[1] It occurred repeatedly in the discussions and interviews conducted for the German case study. Remembering that in Germany both churches and church-related organizations play a more important role in welfare than in most European countries, such a 'crisis' places church-related welfare actors in an ambiguous situation.[2] On the one hand, many (both inside and outside the churches) have high expectations of their work. On the other, they are strongly affected by current developments. The problem is easily summarized. A major effect of the present 'crisis' is decreasing public funding; as a result, many interviewees hope that church-related bodies will fill at least some of the gaps in welfare. At the same time, church-related organizations are themselves forced to adapt. As membership continues to fall, both the shrinking revenues from church taxes and the decline in public funding narrow the room

---

[1]   One of the things learnt from participating in an international project such as WREP is to be more careful when using words such as 'crisis' when describing changes in a comparatively efficient system. Nevertheless, I use the term here, reflecting the views of my interviewees.

[2]   Mainly for practical reasons the study concentrates on the Protestant agents of welfare in Reutlingen, noting that there are important Catholic activities as well, though the Protestant ones are more numerous. At times, however, I use the term 'the churches' instead of 'the church'. Once again this corresponds to the language use of the interviewees who often refer to both churches when talking about welfare and religion. In every group, there are both Protestant and Catholic interviewees. Regarding the representatives of the public authorities, the population as a whole and the local politicians, it is sometimes difficult to know which of the two folk churches they are talking about. It does not seem to be important to distinguish between them. The term 'church' might be more intriguing in the German case study than in other case studies, as it comprises in everyday usage not only parishes, church districts and the regional and national levels of the church, but also independent diakonal institutions. How to relate the different levels and organizational forms of Protestant welfare activities to the term 'church' and to develop an appropriate ecclesiology are frequently-discussed questions in the German context.

for manoeuvre. From a financial perspective these organizations should, it seems, limit their activities rather than take on new ones.

The ambiguity can be seen very clearly in the responses of church representatives. Strong and positive expectations were noted with satisfaction in a situation which is perceived as increasingly secular. Yet it is the process of secularization itself which is causing the problem. Hence the dilemma. Of course the churches want to live up to at least some of these expectations, but they seem doomed to failure, as they have neither the financial nor the human resources to carry out their task. The following chapter both illustrates and explains this situation.

The Research Period

In many respects the research period can be considered 'special' – from a socio-political, religious and gender perspective. Almost all the interviews took place between November 2004 and September 2005 (i.e. before the 2005 election). During this time, the political situation became more and more complicated. The lower house of parliament (Bundestag) and the upper house of parliament (Bundesrat) consistently blocked each other – the coalition of Social Democrats and Greens had a small majority in the former, while the coalition of Conservatives and Liberals slightly dominated the latter. Although the need for fundamental economic and social reforms was on everyone's lips, very few changes could actually be accomplished. One which was, however, was the intensely-debated reform aimed at reducing both unemployment (Hartz IV) and unemployment benefits (ALG II). After January 2005, such benefits fell much more rapidly from an income-related level to one which provided minimal assistance only. It is no longer permissible to retain substantial savings whilst in receipt of unemployment benefits, or to receive high unemployment benefits for a prolonged period. These reforms affect the middle class very directly, in that it becomes increasingly difficult to maintain social status during extended periods of unemployment. This reform is seen as a major shift in the logic of the German welfare system.

Many of the interviews were conducted close to the death of John Paul II and the subsequent election of Benedict XVI. Since these two events dominated the media for weeks, the relevance of religion was more evident to many interviewees than it would have been otherwise. Two of the potential papal candidates came from Germany, one of them well-known for his rather conservative views on the position of women within the Catholic Church. This meant that a lively discussion regarding the roles of women was ongoing during this period. At the same time, family and education policy became a hot political issue, due in part to the rather mediocre German results in the second round of the OECD Programme for International Student Assessment (PISA).[3] As a result, the federal government

---

[3]   The OECD Programme for International Student Assessment (PISA) 'is an internationally standardised assessment that was jointly developed by participating

introduced a programme to develop both day-care in schools and preschool education. The final point concerns Angela Merkel's election in 2005. Although Merkel led the opinion polls during almost the entire campaign, many public commentators did not believe that she would become Chancellor, partly because of her gender but also because of her GDR origins.

Welfare and Church-Related Agents in Germany

The German Model of Delegating Welfare Provision

The German system is not the only one which gives churches and church-related organizations a significant role in welfare (see the other case studies in this book). It is, rather, the post-war preference for independent welfare providers over public ones which is unusual – a policy which has strengthened the position of independent welfare organizations in general and church-related ones in particular. These non-profit organizations include the Protestant Diakonie, the Catholic Caritas, the organization of the workers' movement (*Arbeiterwohlfahrt*), the German Red Cross, the Jewish Zentralwohlfahrtsstelle der Jüdischen Gemeinde and the umbrella organization for the remaining ideologically-based welfare agents (Deutscher Paritätischer Wohlfahrtsverband) (Boeßenecker 2005; Bundesarbeitsgemeinschaft der Freien Wohlfahrtspflege 2002; Falterbaum 2000). To avoid the situation that occurred under National Socialism,[4] the Federal Republic of Germany strongly affirms two things: multiple levels of political decision-making and the use of independent agents. In the field of welfare, the principle of subsidiarity – itself of Catholic origin – became a guiding principle.

Although Germany is known as the country of the Reformation, it has been shaped by biconfessionalism since the sixteenth century (Schilling 1998). It is clear, moroever, that Catholicism has had a stronger influence than Protestantism on social policy in the twentieth century (Kaiser 1998). But quite apart from this, biconfessionalism was one factor that led to a relatively early separation of church and state under the Weimar Republic (the first democratic state). Legally and formally, the Constitution of 1919 introduced state neutrality in the field of religion. This meant that both the Catholic dioceses and the regional Protestant

---

countries and administered to 15-year-olds in schools. The survey was implemented in 43 countries in the 1st assessment in 2000 and in 41 countries in the 2nd assessment in 2003'. See http://www.pisa.oecd.org/pages/0,3417,en_32252351_32235907_1_1_1_1_1,00.html or OECD (Organization for Economic Co-operation and Development), *Programme for International Student Assessment, Learning for Tomorrow's World. First Results from PISA 2003* (Paris 2004).

4   One of the strategies of the National Socialists was to force the independent organizations and associations working in all sectors of society to become uniform organizations led by the Nazis.

churches became independent of the state. That said, both the Catholic Church and the various Protestant churches remained corporations under *public* law, strongly involved in tasks such as education and welfare (see articles 135, 137, 140 and 141 of the Weimar Constitution). The Federal Republic of Germany maintained the Weimar legislation on religion. Indeed the prominent role of church-related organizations within the German welfare system is due at least in part to the legislation on religion, in so far as it entitles organizations as well as individuals to claim the right of freedom of religion. This right is applied, amongst other things, to the welfare work conducted by church-related organizations (Winter 2001).

Given this background, it is easier to see why the independent church-related organizations became major providers when the welfare system was expanded, specialized and professionalized during the 1960s and 1970s. The state, however, still has important obligations. At the national, federal and municipal levels, the state – together with the different schemes of independent and compulsory social insurance – must ensure both the finance and the delivery of social and health care, but need not provide these directly. Delegation, in other words, includes the reimbursing of costs for legally-guaranteed social services. Currently, between 30 and 60 per cent of all services are run by independent welfare organizations (depending on the field of social work). Among them, church-related agents are still the most important (Bundesarbeitsgemeinschaft der Freien Wohlfahrtspflege 2002).

As mentioned in the introduction, the German economy and welfare system are facing major challenges – a situation perceived as a crisis by both experts and citizens. Indeed, it seems to be more difficult for Germany than for other European countries to adapt to rapidly changing conditions – notably to an ageing population, to shifting values and to the forces of globalization. The national rate of unemployment, which has been between 8 and 10 per cent for almost 20 years (and in some regions up to 25–30 per cent), is regarded as a major social problem[5] – one which undermines the social insurance system, a situation made worse by the costs of reunification (Strohm 2000; 2002). At the same time, demographic shifts are challenging both pensions and health insurance (Landsberg 2003), and as the welfare system's sustainability is increasingly called into question, the motivation to contribute declines accordingly (Deufel and Wolf 2003; Keupp 2000). There is, finally, a heated public discussion about the high costs of labour in Germany. Radical cuts in the welfare system will – it is claimed – increase competitiveness (Sinn 2004).

In the same period, German society has become markedly more diverse – this is important from a welfare perspective. Since reunification, the population can be divided into three major groups: roughly 26 million Catholics, a similar number of Protestants, and about 23 million people who are officially registered as 'Others'

---

[5]   After 2005 (the time of the data collection) the German economy experienced an upswing which has helped to reduce unemployment. As a result, the welfare system was evaluated more positively. But as only a few fundamental reforms have been effected, it is very likely that similar problems will be perceived and discussed as the current recession makes itself felt.

– including 3.3 million Muslims, 1 million Orthodox Christians, 360,000 members of Free Churches, and more than 100,000 Jews, Hindus and Buddhists.[6] It follows that the Catholic and Protestant churches can no longer work on the assumption that they represent the overwhelming majority of the German population.

One further change directly influences both the churches and church-related organizations in the field of welfare. During the 1990s, a welfare market (in the form of controlled competition) began to emerge, including commercial providers. The aim was to limit – indeed to reduce – welfare costs (Schmidt 2005; Olk 2001). All of these factors can be seen in the Reutlingen case study which concentrates primarily on the services provided by Protestant agents. The emphasis lies on the questions raised both by and for church-related welfare in this rapidly changing context.

The Case of Reutlingen

As in many other countries, there are considerable regional variations regarding the welfare engagement of the churches and church-related organizations in Germany. This is due to different regional traditions, and to the different histories of East and West Germany. In selecting our case study, we chose a city which represents the traditional West German model, bearing in mind that it is this system, with its strong integration of church-related agents, which has become the dominant model in the country as a whole. Such integration is certainly true in Reutlingen (Schmidt 2005; Leis 2004a; Leis-Peters 2006).

The city has approximately 110,000 inhabitants, and is a part of the federal state of Baden-Württemberg. The town is situated between the Mittlerer Neckar and an upland agricultural region known as the Schwäbische Alb. Many large companies, such as Daimler, Porsche and Robert Bosch GmbH, are based in the industrial Mittlerer Neckar. It remains, even now, one of the motors of the German economy. Reutlingen is a popular place to live for many commuters who work in this industrial region and in Stuttgart, the capital of the federal state, roughly 50 km away.

The town dates back to the eleventh century. During the sixteenth century, it became a centre for the German Reformation. In 1524, the citizens of Reutlingen forced their government to introduce and to maintain the new teachings of the Reformation (Brecht 1995). In 1530, Reutlingen was one of the two German towns which signed the Augsburg Confession. Consequently, a strong identity as a Protestant city persists, though the figures tell a different story. After World War 2, the city became more and more mixed denominationally. Many of the refugees from former German areas in Eastern Europe who came in the 1940s and 1950s,

---

6   The numbers for the two folk churches are relatively exact due to the church tax system (which includes these two churches and is connected to the public tax system). When it comes to other religious organizations, the statistics rest on estimations and information provided by the organizations themselves (http://www.remid.de).

and many guest workers who moved to Reutlingen during the 1960s and 1970s, were Catholic. Today Protestants still form the largest religious group, but with only 42.8 per cent of citizens belonging to the Evangelical-Lutheran Church, there is no overwhelming majority. Catholics constitute 23.9 per cent of the population. Apart from these two groups, public statistics reveal only the so-called 'Others' (33.3 per cent). This group comprises other Christians (the Orthodox and members of the free churches), Muslims, Jews, Buddhists and Hindus, as well as people who do not belong to any religion. The latter is the largest group within the Others (Stadt Reutlingen 2005).

In 2004 and 2005 Reutlingen still had a comparatively low rate of unemployment (less than 6 per cent). This is below the average rate for Baden-Württemberg (about 6.5 per cent) (Stadt Reutlingen 2005) and far below the unemployment rate for Germany as a whole (about 11 per cent) (www.destatis.de). In the same period the percentage of Reutlingen's inhabitants without a German passport was about 15 per cent, Turkish and Greek citizens constituting the largest groups among them (Stadt Reutlingen 2005). Other groups of immigrants include German repatriates. Since the end of the Cold War, thousands of people with German origins who had been living in Eastern Europe, mainly in the former USSR, have come to Germany. They have German passports and are, therefore, not counted as citizens with a foreign passport. Nonetheless, many of them face similar problems to other immigrants concerning language and integration.

From the middle of the nineteenth century, Reutlingen underwent an early industrialization, mainly in the areas of engine construction and textile and paper production, and right at the end of the war, the city was destroyed by bombing. As a result, Reutlingen is no longer an historic city. The destruction caused by the war, together with an early economic upswing in the 1950s and 1960s which saw the replacement of many of the remaining old buildings, have marked the townscape. It is the structure of the city as a whole, with its pedestrian precinct and huge market place in the city centre, which is most indicative of the long history of the town. The modern city has expanded mostly by incorporating many of the neighbouring villages.

As in most of the federal states in the western part of the country, it is difficult for women in Reutlingen to combine work and family. The supply of day-care is insufficient. Roughly half of the children aged six and under living in Reutlingen are offered a place in a kindergarten.[7] These kindergartens are obliged to care for the children six hours a day, Monday to Friday. Care covering the whole day is rare; in 2004 such provision was available for only 580 children (out of about 6,300 aged up to six) (Stadt Reutlingen 2005).

One of the important service-sector employers is the Bruderhaus Diakonie (a church-related organization). This is one of the major diakonal institutions in

---

[7]   Usually children start kindergarten at the age of three. This means that most of the places are offered for children who are three years or older. Until very recently, mothers were expected to stay at home with younger children.

Germany, and has its headquarters in Reutlingen. In 2004 the Bruderhaus Diakonie had about 3,500 employees in 14 districts (*Landkreise*) in Baden-Württemberg, roughly 1,500 of these in the district of Reutlingen. The presence of the Bruderhaus Diakonie in Reutlingen, and the strong representation of church-related actors in the local welfare provision in general, are among the factors which make Reutlingen a highly pertinent case study.

Church-Related Welfare Provision in Reutlingen

As in Germany in general, a variety of church agents and church-related organizations are involved in welfare work in Reutlingen. The following figure shows the different types of church-related groups providing welfare within the framework of the regional church, the Evangelische Landeskirche in Württemberg, to which Reutlingen belongs (see Figure 6.1).[8]

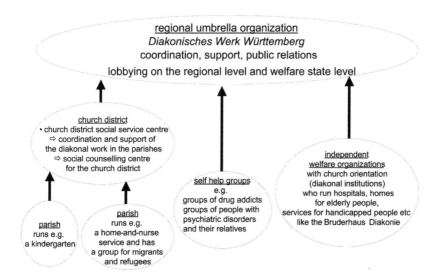

Figure 6.1   Structure and Levels of Diakonal Work in Württemberg

Altogether there are 16 Evangelical-Lutheran parishes in the city of Reutlingen, with a total of about 43,000 members. The parishes are governed by a male or female senior priest along with the church council. During the study period, 28 parish priests, two hospital chaplains, one youth chaplain, two student chaplains and a chaplain to refugees were working in Reutlingen. Fourteen priests and

---

8   There is no national Protestant church in Germany, but several regional Protestant churches with different church histories and different Protestant traditions. The Evangelical-Lutheran Church in Württemberg has about 2.3 million members.

teachers were teaching religion in the schools of Reutlingen, and about 100 church employees were working in the parishes, including eight deacons (mostly in the field of youth work), the staff of the 11 parish-run kindergartens, church musicians, administrators, property managers and sacristans. Many of them were only employed part-time – church employees are increasingly being replaced by volunteers.

Women dominate the Protestant church numerically. About 57 per cent of all church members are women. There are also many more women than men employed by the church. Nevertheless, more men hold top managerial positions or are priests. In the Evangelical-Lutheran Church in Württemberg, only about one-third of the priests are women. These proportions are reflected in Reutlingen, where 12 of the 28 senior priests in Reutlingen are women.

The *parishes* in Reutlingen are actors in the field of welfare. Indeed many of the activities defined as core parish tasks in parish documents and interviews can be regarded as welfare work or, at least, as having a 'welfare orientation'. This work is mainly financed by the churches themselves, which means mostly by church taxes.[9] It includes:

- worship services
- baptisms, weddings, funerals
- instructing confirmation candidates
- teaching religion in school[10]
- work with children and young people
- work with elderly people
- pastoral care.

It is clear, however, that some parishes in Reutlingen are more active in social projects and in collaboration with the municipality than others. This depends very largely on the theological style of the parish council (a lay body) and of the senior priest. Some parishes, which prioritize welfare, run both associations and/or groups of (diakonal) volunteers – for example, support groups for people caring for sick relatives, associations which collect money for needy people within the parish and widespread visiting services for lonely people. Kindergartens are also prioritized. Eleven of the sixteen parishes run a kindergarten. Unlike the activities listed above, more than 90 per cent of the cost of kindergartens is reimbursed by the municipality.

The so-called Vesperkirche is a prominent example of an independent welfare association which is not linked to a specific parish, but is closely connected to the

---

[9]   The church tax is linked to public income tax, and amounts to 8 or 9 per cent of total income tax. The decline in church membership leads very directly to reduced revenues. The parishes become increasingly dependent on collections and donations.

[10]   The workload of a full-time priest within the Evangelical-Lutheran Church in Württemberg includes teaching at least six lessons per week in a publicly-funded school.

church in Reutlingen. For five weeks in the winter, one of the old churches in the city centre becomes a meeting room for people from different social backgrounds, and a place of welcome for the homeless, the lonely and for people living in poor accommodation. The church is open from 9am to 6pm and offers coffee, sandwiches, cakes and lunch. Doctors and hairdressers offer their services free. Programmes for children and cultural events are organized. The primary aim of the project is not to provide indigent people with cheap food and services, but rather to encourage interaction between people living in different circumstances. This project is run exclusively by volunteers and is financed by donations.

The majority of the volunteers are women. This is true both of the Vesperkirche and of parish-related projects such as the visiting services. The Vesperkirche is a good example of how women and men undertake different tasks within voluntary projects. The women who are active in the Vesperkirche focus on meeting people from different social backgrounds, while the men undertake organizational or practical tasks (like fetching the food or preparing rotas).

A whole range of *self-help groups* are mostly independent, but closely connected to parishes. The majority of them are for alcoholics, drug addicts, relatives of addicts and people with mental illnesses.

The *church district* of Reutlingen offers the following welfare activities:

- a Christian home-nursing service responsible for an area of approximately 25,000 inhabitants
- a social service centre providing various forms of counselling: educational, family, psychological, for refugees, for women considering an abortion, for alcoholics and drug addicts, and for women who have violent partners. In addition, the centre organizes services for elderly people and the *Reutlinger Tafel* ('table of Reutlingen') project[11] run solely by volunteers
- a centre for youth work
- a family training centre offering courses on preparation for childbirth, cooking, and changing role-models.

The first two organizations listed are predominantly publicly funded.

Independent church-related welfare organizations are also engaged in welfare activities. The previously mentioned Bruderhaus Diakonie is an important provider in the Reutlingen municipality and district. The following list demonstrates the breadth and depth of services that it offers:

1. Help for elderly people, including
   - six homes, especially for people in need of nursing care (one of the homes specializes in geriatric mental illness)

---

[11]   In this project volunteers collect food which supermarkets can no longer sell and would otherwise be thrown away. This food is then distributed very cheaply to people on low incomes.

- two home care and home nursing services
- two food services
- an open meeting centre
- a counselling centre.

2. Help for people with disabilities, including
   - a home
   - several homes for collective assisted living
   - flats for individual assisted living
   - mobility services
   - several assisted places of work
   - several support services for children with disabilities
   - a counselling centre for independent living
   - a leisure association bringing together people with and without disabilities
   - a service assisting families with a disabled member
   - a retreat centre bringing together people with and without disabilities.

3. Help for young people, including
   - two training centres for young people with difficulties entering work
   - a social and training centre for young immigrants
   - help centres for young immigrants
   - a supervised centre for social and leisure activities
   - a bicycle centre run by young people
   - counselling for young people
   - a general school and a vocational school for pupils with special needs
   - a kindergarten for children with special needs.

4. Help for people with mental illness, including
   - two counselling services
   - a meeting centre
   - a supermarket run by people with mental illness
   - a factory offering jobs to people with mental illness
   - diverse assisted places of work
   - several homes for collective assisted living
   - flats for individual assisted living
   - a hospital specializing in psychiatry and psychotherapy.

The preceding lists show that the structure and the activities of both churches and church-related organizations in the field of welfare are complex and multifaceted, even at the local level. Consequently, it was difficult to choose a focus for our study. Considering the quantity and importance of their services, it would seem natural to focus on the Bruderhaus Diakonie. In the end, however, we decided to concentrate primarily on the parish and church district, whilst taking into account the independent providers, in order to make the results more comparable with the other case studies. Given the complexity of the situation, certain questions recur repeatedly: how are the responsibilities divided between the different levels?

And how does co-operation and communication between these levels work? These issues are clearly important but cannot – regrettably – be pursued in detail within the limits of this chapter.

Churches and Church-Related Agents of Welfare as Perceived by the Local Experts in Reutlingen

Churches and welfare work are strongly connected in Reutlingen. None of the interviewees[12] doubts that the churches have a role to play in this field. Indeed, many of the interviewees think that it is quite natural for churches to be involved in social activities. One of the representatives of the local population puts this as follows: 'The church needs to have social activities. Otherwise it is no longer the church' (m). Conversely, none of the interviewees could imagine an area of welfare in which church engagement would be questionable, and some maintain that it is precisely the welfare involvement of the churches that encourages people to remain within the church even if they do not participate in church activities themselves.

A few of the representatives of the public authorities point explicitly to the importance of the parish for networking at local level. The parish is perceived as an irreplaceable entity, because of the duty of care felt by church members for their neighbours. One of the representatives of the social services even thinks that parishes can function as bridges – in the sense that they can communicate the pressures and decisions of social services to the citizens. Being welfare providers themselves (e.g. in kindergartens), the parishes are aware of the limited room for manoeuvre in welfare provision. This distinguishes their views from those of ordinary welfare users or citizens.

Many of the church representatives think that the church could play a much more important social role if it had the resources to respond to even a few of the spiritual and social needs they are increasingly observing. Most interviewees refer to the church-related welfare services they know: the professional diakonal services of the Bruderhaus Diakonie, parish activities, or social projects like the Vesperkirche. However, hardly anyone can keep track of all such services. The representatives of the local population, in particular, have no idea about the organization and financing of church social work. They assume that all welfare services run by the churches or church-related welfare organizations are paid for by the same bodies (through church taxes and donations). They do not know that

---

[12] Thirty interviews took place in all, 15 with representatives of the churches and diakonal institutions and 15 with representatives of the public authorities, local politicians and an additional independent welfare organization. Four focus group interviews were also conducted: with a group of younger adults, a group of German immigrants from the former USSR, a group of students in the ninth year of elementary school and a group of students in the twelfth grade of grammar school.

most of these services are funded, like all welfare services, by public taxes and social insurance.

Change and Negotiation in the Funding of Welfare in Reutlingen

Even in a town like Reutlingen, where the churches and church-related organizations have dominated welfare provision for many years, co-operation between public authorities and church-related welfare providers has already changed. All welfare providers now have to compete for the contracts to run welfare services. One of the representatives of the social authorities puts it in these terms:

> Every welfare organization which wants public contributions for its projects has to lobby for it. There are no exceptions to this rule any longer. Even the churches and the church-related organizations, which used to have a privileged position, have to do this today. (m)

The church representatives describe the same development from their own perspective:

> We must beg for everything. Before the budget meetings in the town council, or in the district assembly, we go to the parliamentary groups to beg for funding … Some years ago we wrote an application letter and that was enough … Today you have to beg personally … Once we did not do that and as a consequence we got less money than all the others. (m)

In reply, the representatives of the public authority say that they treat the churches and the church-related welfare organizations like any other welfare provider. Yet some – quite clearly – have high expectations of them, particularly now that the public authorities are forced to reduce welfare expenses. For example, a new municipal strategy to meet growing needs and anticipated growing poverty in some districts of the town is much discussed in Reutlingen. The strategy involves both decentralization and differentiation, and the parishes have an opportunity to become important partners given that they have their own infrastructure in each of the districts:

> The parishes could be places of meeting. We do need these places right now. But as I experience it, the parishes have no tradition of sharing and no willingness to share … It is a pity, because we need meeting places in the districts and the parish buildings are already built. (f)

As is clear from the above quotation, however, some representatives of the municipality doubt whether the parishes are capable of realizing this partnership. They consider most of them to be quite middle class in focus, whereas the aim of the strategy is to create meeting places for socially deprived groups.

If it succeeded, such a development would offer a solution to the urgent problems facing the Evangelical-Lutheran parishes in Reutlingen. The financial difficulties of the Evangelical-Lutheran Church received a lot of coverage in the local media during the study period. Declining membership and revenues are obliging the church to think differently. Its present strategy is to sell buildings rather than reduce church activities. The parishes own about 60 churches, parish halls and other buildings, which cost a great deal to maintain. They plan, therefore, to sell or simply to close 11 churches and parish halls. In April 2005, the first of these church closures was announced. This provoked many emotions and a lively debate in the media. Some interviewees reacted strongly to this decision. The discussion made some of the church representatives realize that their buildings were of common interest.

> It was quite astonishing for me. Now, when it is about closing this building, a building where much is happening and where many people come, not only Protestants, ... it is becoming more and more a kind of town district centre. There has been an outcry ... People say we want to do something about that. (f)

The Tensions of Being Both a Welfare Provider and a Critical Voice

The church representatives worry not only about the financial situation of the church, but also about current social trends. They perceive growing poverty and social exclusion. One reports:

> I sometimes get scared when I think of the changes within the welfare systems ... We can notice the consequences of the changes today already. It is obvious that more people come to us to beg for money ... not homeless people, people who live here. (m)

Many of them feel theologically challenged to help:

> You can't only preach with words. To preach is also to do social work. These two ways of preaching belong together. If you stay at home all day to study the Bible and to prepare a sermon you have stopped being the church. Everything the church is talking about must be exemplified by its actions. (m)

In one sense, the needs of the public authorities and the churches seem to complement each other. However, both sides have the same aim: to reduce expenses. As a consequence, co-operation is dominated by financial negotiations. A church representative complains, 'The social laws no longer focus on the person in need. It's all about money. Money seems to be the most important thing' (f). Some public authority representatives fear that church-related providers exploit public funding for their own purposes. They propose that welfare activities which are delegated to the churches by the public authorities, and therefore mostly paid for by them, should be labelled more correctly as run by the church (or a church-related welfare organization), but paid for by public money. At the same time, the church representatives admit that they are less flexible than before, for financial reasons. A good example can be found in the day-care centres for children. In 2004, the municipality asked the Evangelical-Lutheran parishes in Reutlingen to take over two kindergartens. According to one church representative, the parish finally accepted the request, but only after the municipality agreed that it would pay almost 100 per cent of the costs (m).

The growing competition between welfare providers affects both church-related and public actors. The church-related actors point to the advantages they have compared with public providers: 'As independent welfare actors we have a community orientation like the municipality, but our routines are not as ponderous as theirs' (m). On the other hand, some representatives of the public authorities regard the abandonment of public welfare provision as a risky strategy:

> From my perspective it is not good that we hand over services and institutions run by the municipality to other providers. We lose our competence if we don't have the experience of working in the field any longer ... Soon, we will not run services and institutions for elderly people ourselves any longer. Then, our role will change. (f)

Both the public authorities and the church-related providers feel under pressure from the high expectations of the public (welfare is much appreciated in German society); to be the one who cannot provide what is necessary is not a position in which either the public authorities or church-related welfare actors want to find themselves. Indeed the welfare engagement of the churches and church-related organizations is taken for granted by the local population. This engagement often informs a positive attitude towards the church and is seen as enriching welfare provision: 'Now, when both the municipality and the state are running out of money it is good that the churches are active in the social field. They can offer services where the municipality is forced to close' (f). The church representatives are well aware of such expectations. One says:

> The church has to be close to the people. If we imagine that the church becomes alive in the Sunday services, it is only for a certain small part of our church ... We have to be present in a city in addition to these Sunday services. And we are only present if we do justice to our diakonal mission. If we are no longer active in this context, we will disappear. (m)

Quite apart from this, the involvement of the churches and the church-related organizations in the welfare provision of Reutlingen gives them a special position in public debate. They are expected to contribute to the discussion about welfare. The representatives of the public authorities, in particular, think that the churches represent one of the few institutions left which contribute significantly to public debate, at both the national and local level: 'When I say that there are poor children in a kindergarten and they need support no one listens. If the vicar talks about the same subject everyone listens. I am not insulted by this fact. I think we should co-operate in this matter' (f). However, the fact that it is the municipality which delegates social tasks to church-related welfare providers affects their ability to criticize. One of the church representatives admits:

> It is not easy to deviate from the social policy of the public authorities if you are closely connected to them financially. If I am dependent on public funding I am a partner and can criticize on a professional level. But to put my foot down by saying: 'Not with me!' That's difficult. (m)

Local population representatives want the churches to stand up for the poor, but not through statements, discussions or sermons. They expect the churches to contribute to public debate though deeds, not words. For them, projects like the Vesperkirche are more significant than any paper or speech.

In short, the majority of interviewees express an interest in the welfare involvement of the churches. There are some, however, who refuse to accept the status quo, and want to change society – in order to improve the conditions for the poor and excluded regardless of available resources. Their motivation could be described as 'visionary'. Some of the 'visionaries' among the public authority representatives think that they need to work with every possible partner in order to achieve their aims, and consider the churches in this light. Others are of the opinion that it becomes more difficult to achieve visionary aims if too many actors are interfering, particularly if the actors are as traditional, powerful, privileged and conservative as the churches.

A second group focus on the current conditions of the welfare system. They are aware of the present economic limitations and try to develop sustainable concepts of (church) welfare work within these limitations. Their motivation is to do as much as possible within the financial and social restrictions. They could, therefore, be labelled 'financial managers'. Once again, some 'financial managers' from the public authorities are interested in co-operation with every possible partner in order to help as many poor and needy people as they can. The churches and the diakonal institutions make good partners, because they work relatively professionally and can mobilize support and volunteers easily. Others, however, think that – as the municipality has to pay anyway – co-operating with too many partners means a loss of resources and energy, as every partnership requires (difficult) negotiations.

Among the church representatives, attitudes are also divided. Here, some 'financial managers' want to focus on fewer welfare activities and perform them in a professional and effective manner. Others would like to co-operate in as many welfare projects as possible, as this strengthens the presence of the church in society. To attract attention in the realm of welfare is very important for the church at a time when its membership and economic resources are shrinking.

Gender in Church-related Welfare Provision

An area in which the churches and the church-related organizations receive less approval is that of gender. In many of the interviews, the discussion of day-care for children raised this as a significant issue. Many interviewees agree that women get too little help to enable them to combine family and work, because traditional family and gender models still dominate. The churches are associated with these models, particularly by the representatives of the local authorities and the local population. Though only a few interviewees state it directly, the influence of the churches is held responsible for the persistence of traditional family and gender models in German society. One interviewee says: 'The churches have to understand that all-day day-care for children is not an idea of Satan. There are many examples from other European countries which have done this before. And they survived' (f).

The interviews show, however, that the self-perception of the church in relation to gender differs from the external perspective. On the one hand, the church representatives think that the Protestant churches have done a lot of work on questions of gender and equality. Some refer to the theological discussions about justice for women during the 1970s and 1980s which continue today. They mention institutions which were established as a result of these debates, such as offices for women's affairs. Others refer to specific events and to groups for women and men in the parishes. In addition, some interviewees point to the fact that the gender situation is less problematic within Protestant circles than it is within the Catholic Church. The representatives of the public authorities and the local population, however, perceive the gender situation within the church very differently. Several of them think that the church lags behind wider society on these issues. Others believe that the church generally has a very conservative view of women. Some interviewees do not differentiate between the Protestant and the Catholic traditions at all, and the majority of interviewees are quite pessimistic about questions of justice regarding gender. They think that traditional family and gender models will persist in Reutlingen and in German society more broadly. Interestingly, the market economy is considered to be the most probable source of change: if the traditional models no longer fit the needs of the market economy, they are likely to decline.

Challenges Regarding Motivation in the Realm of Welfare

The growing influence of the market economy more generally is an important issue in all the interviews. Most interviewees agree that welfare provision is becoming increasingly market-oriented. Even voluntary initiatives like the Vesperkirche must adjust to these conditions, if they want to continue in the long term. These adaptations do not only have practical consequences, they also influence the outlooks of welfare actors, and consequently, in the long run, the ideology of the welfare organizations themselves.

Interestingly, there seems to be little need for deep theological motivation for church involvement in the field of welfare. The few theological ideas that did arise are quite general. They involve notions of social engagement, what it means to be a member of the church or to be a Christian, Christian responsibility for the neighbour in need and Christian anthropology – in other words ideas which are comprehensible to most people. One explanation for the absence of extensive, in-depth theological justification could be that churches and welfare are so closely related in Reutlingen that this aspect of their work is considered self-evident. At least two facts support this explanation: the number and variety of the welfare activities carried out by the churches and church-related organizations, and the long tradition of involvement in this field.

Much more important to the interviewees was the tension between declining resources and strained finances on the one hand, and growing needs and expectations on the other. This is hardly surprising. As most of the interviewees deal with financial questions on a daily basis, it becomes more and more natural for them to think in terms of fiscal rather than theological arguments. And since practical social work is increasingly driven by financial questions, monetary concerns are likely to grow, to the point of dominating reflections in the field, irrespective of the training and background of the person involved. That said, the interviews do point to a need for a more distinct Christian profile for church social work. Indeed, many interviewees think that a clear Christian profile would strengthen their position in the welfare market. Ironically, an increase in theological reflection has been provoked by the market.

The representatives of the church, public authorities and local population all think that the church is needed as an open and welcoming meeting place in society. Some hope that church buildings can become places of encounter for people with different backgrounds. At the same time, some interviewees express the wish that the churches stick to their traditions and act as a critical voice in society, representing Christian values in an increasingly pluralistic and – as some put it – value-neutral society. However, to be simultaneously open-minded and welcoming, and traditional, clear and critical, is an almost impossible target. It reflects very directly the ambiguities highlighted in the introduction.

Concluding Reflections

The documents, interviews and other material gathered during the research period all show that the churches and church-related organizations have been, and still are, important welfare agents in Reutlingen. It is almost impossible for the representatives of the public authorities, the churches and the local population to imagine a welfare scenario without them. At the same time, the importance of the churches for society in general and for many individuals is decreasing (Schloz 2003). It is also clear that the fundamental changes taking place in German welfare as a whole directly affect the position of church-related providers – not always positively (Degen 2003; Grözinger and Haas 2004; Bruderhaus Diakonie 2005). Given the magnitude of all these changes, it is hardly surprising that the (economic) problems of German society, of the welfare system in general and of the place of churches in this are by far the most important subject for interviewees. All other questions are related to this issue.

Hence the complexity of the situation in which the churches face high, but diffuse expectations (Leis-Peters 2006). In general, all interviewees want the churches to be more active in the field of welfare: they should pioneer more welfare programmes, open their church buildings as meeting places and be a prophetic voice on behalf of the needy. The churches, however, have been forced to prioritize. From an insider's perspective it might be easier to close their welfare services, on the grounds that they are not part of their core activity. Such a decision, though, would be difficult for many church members (both committed and less committed) to understand. The public appreciation of their welfare work gives even insiders the feeling that the churches have too much to lose if they restrict their activities in this field.

From the point of view of the general public, the demands made on the churches and church-related organizations in terms of welfare reflect the hope that at least one institution will fill the gap as public welfare decreases. High and flattering expectations, however, are not always helpful. The more so as the process of secularization takes its toll, in that the churches have to handle these expectations against a background of shrinking resources. The problem is exacerbated by the fact that those who are not involved in the churches are simply not interested in how they resolve this problem – hence their dilemma.

Chapter 7

The 'In-Between' Church:
Church and Welfare in Darlington

Martha Middlemiss Lé Mon

By Way of Introduction

As the train pulls into Darlington station I look down on a town which, architecturally at least, clearly tells the story of its past. The town is still centred on the market square which was the focus for its formation in the Middle Ages as the area, on a trade route from London to the North, attracted merchants. The town grew gradually until a major expansion during the industrial revolution. Its location gave the area a natural role in the development of the railways and associated heavy industry. The railway and terraced housing built for workers are still in evidence today. However, the lack of billowing smoke and factory buildings betrays the fact that Darlington, like many other towns in England with similar histories, is no longer dependent on heavy industry for economic growth and employment. Rather, the majority of jobs available today are in the service sector, and the average wage is low as a result.

Once again, the architecture tells of a social mix in the town not immediately evident from the statistics. A walk through districts on the east side of the town soon betrays the low incomes of the inhabitants, a clear contrast with the relatively affluent districts concentrated in the west. This proximity of wealth and poverty explains the fact that, statistically, the town as a whole is not counted amongst those areas of Britain that are most deprived. The national index of multiple deprivation places Darlington as the ninetieth most deprived of 354 authorities nationally. However, 44 per cent of the residents of the town live in wards (administrative districts) that are in the 25 per cent most deprived in the country (Darlington Borough Council 2004).

A walk into town from the station reveals further information about the residents. During this short stroll I pass only white faces. Figures later confirm that I ought not to have been surprised. Like many towns in the UK outside of the major urban centres, Darlington has overwhelmingly small numbers of residents from ethnic minority communities. This absence is reflected in the cultural and religious profile of the area.

With this in mind it is unsurprising that, when I sit looking out over the town from the train window, the clear presence of Christianity in the shape of steeples and spires is not matched by the obvious presence of a mosque or gurdwara, although they do exist. Church buildings dominate the skyline, and the presence of one large church in the marketplace, next to the council building, is witness to the role that the church has played in Darlington's past. The suspicion that first impressions might not be all that they seem, however, is confirmed by the fact that one church building near the centre of town turns out, on closer inspection, to be a carpet warehouse. Even the physical structure of the town can provide an indication of the changes that have taken place in patterns of religious affiliation and influence. How and to what extent, however, this has affected the majority church in Darlington in the field of welfare is a more complex question and the reason for my visit.

As the only representative of both the liberal welfare regime and of the Anglican tradition in the WREP project, and indeed in Europe, the study for which I made my way to Darlington is important. The liberal welfare system bears resemblance at some levels to the social democratic model. However, in its mixed model of welfare it lies much closer to countries such as the United States and Canada. But unlike these two nations, and in line with much of the rest of Europe, England has an established church with a tradition of involvement in the welfare system, both through its parish model and its formal and informal influence. This has led to the majority church having a role within the mixed-model system alongside other voluntary bodies, as with many faith-based organizations in the United States. Simultaneously, however, it has an ambiguous yet nonetheless privileged position more familiar to a European setting. Finally, in relation to this last point, the demographics of the country must be taken into account. Britain has a long history of immigration from a wide variety of countries, often connected to its colonial past. This has led to an increasingly ethnically and religiously plural society, where, despite tensions in a number of areas, the presence of a number of different faith groups is taken for granted. Consequently, policy discourse is focused on faith communities rather than churches. This focus also appears in interviews at local level, and has fuelled assumptions that the role of the established church is one of spokesperson for all faith communities, and also that the church has a duty of care to all regardless of religious affiliation or the lack of it.

In addition to being the formally established church, the Church of England can claim to be the majority church by virtue of the fact that about 50 per cent of the population claim affiliation (Ipsos Mori 2006). No such survey has been carried out in Darlington specifically, but given that in the 2001 census 79.8 per cent of the population of the town identified themselves as Christian (above the national average of 72 per cent) there is little reason to suppose that figures for denominational affiliation should be significantly different from the rest of the country.

As the existence of the carpet warehouse implies, however, these figures are not representative of the numbers of regular churchgoers. In the diocese of which Darlington is a part, 1.57 per cent of the population attends a Church of England church on a weekly basis (Archbishops' Council 2003a). It is not that the Christians in the town are going elsewhere for worship – none of the free churches or other denominations in the town report significantly large congregations – but rather that most people do not go to church at all.

This said, the fact that the Church of England is the established church means that, at local level, each parish priest bears pastoral responsibility for all 'souls' resident within the parish boundaries. At national level, too, the church retains certain responsibilities and privileges. What this means in practice, however, can vary from place to place and – as will be made clear below – the church's role is perceived somewhat differently by representatives of the church, representatives of public authorities and by the general public.

The Wider Context

It is clear that the church's role in the nation has changed over past decades and that the challenges faced by the welfare system have both altered and deepened. Against this background, it is pertinent to ask of a local level study, what is the role of the church in welfare today as both actor and social voice? Is the understanding of what this role is – and what it should be – shared by those who represent the church and those who represent the official welfare system? It was to explore these issues that I ventured to Darlington. The material presented below is based on interviews with priests in the Church of England working in Darlington; representatives of the local public authorities, both councillors and employees in the welfare sector; and representatives of other churches and the voluntary sector in the town.[1] The aim was not just to gain information about the activities of the church in this sector, but also to learn more about the attitudes of those concerned in one way or another with church involvement.

In order to understand the role and perceptions of the local church in general and its role as a welfare agent in particular, it is necessary first to sketch the national context of which it is a part. This involves looking at the specificities of the English case in comparison with the rest of Europe, in terms of the position of the church, the welfare system which covers the country, the current challenges it faces and the role that gender plays in all of these. Following a presentation of this

---

[1]   Twelve parish priests (ten male and two female) were interviewed, as were nine representatives of the public authorities in the field of welfare (one male and eight female). Both elected representatives and employees were included in this category. The gender imbalance in both categories reflects the situation on the ground. In addition, interviews were held with a number of representatives of the voluntary and community sector (three) and of other denominations (four). The first two groups provided the material presented below, which formed the basis for analysis, while the latter categories have been used here as an additional source of information in sketching the background.

Also useful for this chapter is Davis et al. (2008). This report – published shortly before this book went to press – is described in more detail in endnote 3 to Chapter 1 of this volume.

background, the chapter sets out some of the key findings of the study, and suggests analytical categories which highlight differences and similarities in the church's role when viewed either as an arena or as a subject in the field of welfare.

The Welfare System in Britain

The British expression of the liberal welfare regime exists as a balance between family, market, voluntary sector and public provision. The state may still retain overall control over welfare, but the public sector acts increasingly as commissioner rather than provider of services. Over recent decades, both voluntary and private sectors have taken on larger roles in partnership with the state, providing services totally or partially funded by the state.

Underlying this structure is a philosophy of welfare where social assistance is considered to be a favour rather than an entitlement. The clearest example of this in Britain today is the government's 'Welfare to Work' policy. This is a policy of enabling and encouraging as many people of working age as possible, women in particular, to participate in the labour market. The aim is to improve the economy in general, increase the working population who fund welfare for the very young and the very old, and enable individuals to support themselves as pensioners to the fullest possible extent.

Recent Challenges to the Welfare State   The welfare system has been put under considerable strain in recent decades due to a number of demographic and social factors. The first of these is the fact that, as in much of Europe, the population is ageing. Since 1971, the proportion of people in Britain aged 75 and over has risen, while the proportion of those aged under 16 has declined (Office for National Statistics 2001: 5).

Family and household composition have also changed dramatically. Household size, for example, has shrunk, and the number of lone parents – and lone mothers in particular – has risen dramatically (Office for National Statistics 2001: 16 table 3.2, 19 table 3.6). These changes severely test a system based on male employment, and could have important consequences given the system's reliance on large amounts of informal care. This dependence on both voluntary organizations and the family has been particularly emphasized since the reforms of the 1980s and 1990s. The family, and women in particular, took on a great deal in terms of hidden welfare work, as much care that had taken place in institutions moved 'into the community'. Large amounts of care take place in the home in Britain today. It is particularly striking that nearly 60 per cent of those cared for at home receive no visits from health, social and voluntary services. Today women are still both more likely than men to be carers and to have the largest caring commitments (Mahler and Green 2002: xi, 2). Statistically, women are also disproportionately likely to be working in the public sector. The majority of women in work are employed in this sector and, within the sector, female employees significantly outnumber men (National Statistics Online 2008).

Women also spend more time than men caring for their children, a figure that holds even when comparing full-time workers. While the age of the youngest child clearly affects a mother's role in the labour market, the same is not true for her male counterpart (National Statistics Online 2004). That said, changes to parental leave rights in recent years as part of the 'Welfare to Work' programme mark a major policy shift. Yet despite this there is, Rake argues, an implicit gender bias built into the current framework, with its focus on paid employment as the basis for citizenship while the rights of women are often addressed within the sphere of the family (Rake 2001: 226). Maternity leave is significantly longer, for example, than the two weeks available to fathers. Recent reports that the majority of men do not make full use of this right serve only to highlight the gender dimension of issues such as the lack of accessible affordable childcare in the country, flexible working and parental leave (BBC News 2006). This is in contrast to countries within the social democratic welfare model where gender equality polices are paramount. In Britain, moreover, issues of gender equality – while generally addressed in terms of individual rights – are frequently part of a blanket approach to combat discrimination in society. The rhetoric is one of equality in general, not of gender equality specifically. Gender, race, ethnic and sexual discrimination are all included.

The major demographic shift outlined above does not represent the only challenge to the system. Differences in health and wealth in the population have also increased. Lone parents, for instance, constitute one group in society which is statistically likely to end up in poverty (Bradshaw et al. 2003: 18). A second example of such disparities can be seen in Darlington itself. The scores from the national index of multiple deprivation presented above represent significant differences in life expectancy, financial stability and quality of life for the inhabitants.

In addition to these large-scale changes, differences can also be seen in working patterns: unemployment amongst men is much higher than it was 50 years ago; women now make up nearly half of the workforce as opposed to 30 per cent at the time of the formation of the welfare state; and there is an increased 'flexibility' in the labour market, with many more people working part-time and in a self-employed capacity. The capacity of the labour market to support the welfare state has also shrunk. This, along with factors such as upwards trends in the use of health services (Office for National Statistics 2001: 7), and higher expectations of levels of care, has contributed to a situation where government funding of social services has increased. However, there has been no corresponding rise in equality of health and welfare amongst the population, or any sense that poverty has decreased.

The National Church and its Role in Welfare Provision

Historically the Church of England has had a considerable influence on the life of the nation and even on policy development. To this day, the Queen remains Supreme Governor of the church. This means that the Prime Minister can, on her behalf, influence the appointment of bishops and that Parliament retains some control over the church. The church, for its part, can influence the decisions of Parliament, given that the 26 most senior bishops hold seats in the present House of Lords. Here the bishops can contribute to the delay, amendment or even prevention of an Act of Parliament and, perhaps most importantly, have a platform from which to speak on national issues outside of their dioceses. The Archbishop of Canterbury, in particular, has a key role as the figurehead of the church. His speeches and sermons receive both media and political attention and he has access to the corridors of power, although less so than many of his predecessors who had regular meetings with the Prime Minister.

The Church of England frequently responds to consultation documents and reports or legislation from government. This is done via official responses or in comments in the press by individual bishops. In addition, the church publishes reports on issues of concern and individual bishops make statements in speeches and sermons. The broad nature of this approach means that it is impossible to discern any one 'church line'. The fact that the church is asked to, and actively responds to, government policy consultations is nonetheless interesting. In recent years, for example, the church has submitted official comments or commented publicly on issues such as civil partnership (Archbishops' Council 2003b), charities and charitable status (Archbishops' Council 2002), drugs policy (Church of England 2006b), employment regulations (Church of England 2006c), and asylum, immigration and citizenship (Church of England 2006a).

One report produced in the 1980s is also worth mentioning. 'Faith in the City' (1985) was explicitly subtitled 'A Call for Action by Church and Nation', demonstrating the church's own belief in its position to make recommendations for the nation as a whole (*Faith in the City* 1985). The twentieth anniversary of its publication also saw the formation of a Commission on Urban Life and Faith, instigated by the church but with a broad membership base. The report of this commission demonstrates, among other things, the church's view of itself as a key opinion-former on issues of social justice (Archbishops' Council Commission on Urban Life and Faith 2006). Interestingly, at the time of the publication of the report, the Archbishop of Canterbury was able to initiate a debate in the House of Lords on the contribution of churches to civic life.

Though this formal relationship remains unchanged, it is clear that the role which the church plays and the power which it wields within this framework do not. On the one hand, the Christian heritage of the nation, together with the ties of many non-churchgoers to the church, still exists. On the other, church leaders in England today would not use the language of their predecessors in calling Britain a 'Christian' nation. It is true that around 50 per cent of the population claims affiliation with the Church of England. However, as has already been demonstrated with reference to Darlington, only a minority of this percentage attends church regularly. What this means in terms of the personal spirituality of the citizens is a complex issue, but it is abundantly clear that the influence of the church on the lives of ordinary people is considerably smaller than it was a few generations ago.

In light of this change in society, the church increasingly emphasizes the need for good relations between the representatives of different faith groups in the country. It is hard to say to what extent the attitudes of the church and other faith groups are influenced by the current political climate on the issue or vice versa. It *is* clear, however, that in political circles the established church is increasingly seen as one of a number of faith communities in the country. A recent report produced by the Home Office recognizes the role of the churches:

> The Christian Churches have had an immense historic influence in shaping society, and make significant contributions in a wide range of areas such as community development, education, social inclusion and heritage. For these reasons the Churches have made and continue to make a particular and distinctive contribution to the development and implementation of Government policy in certain areas. (Home Office Faith Communities Unit, February 2004: 7)

The Church of England, moreover, has a particularly strong voice in this respect and is seen, at least to some extent, as the voice of faith in the public arena. That Anglican prison chaplains have responsibility for making sure prisoners of other faiths have access to their respective religious representatives is but one very practical example of this. That said, the report quoted above makes it quite clear in which direction government attitudes to the churches are moving. Specifically, it goes on to note the role that faith communities whose members are 'more recently settled in these islands' can play, and in an interesting indication of the declining official influence of the Church of England states that:

> [W]hile the Church of England is the Established Church in England, it should not be accorded privileged status in such consultations … if a decision is taken to canvas the views of the Church of England, for instance on matters with a doctrinal dimension, (e.g. civil partnerships), it would normally be appropriate to approach other prominent Christian traditions. (Home Office Faith Communities Unit, February 2004: 24 §2.2.38)

It seems, therefore, that in the eyes of the government the church retains an official position, but in practical terms it is increasingly seen as just one of a number of faith communities, and thereby of a number of organizations in civil society with which the public sector can co-operate. How, then, is this reflected at local level?

The Case of Darlington

Darlington has a population of around 98,000 and is a unitary authority, meaning that all decisions concerning both the town itself and the wider area are made by the same elected body. Its size means that Darlington is just big enough for such a solution to work, but at the same time this emphasizes something already felt by many in the town: that Darlington is a small town, somewhere where everyone knows each other. This may not be strictly true, but the interviews reveal that the same key individuals crop up time and time again in connection with a variety of issues in the town. Many witness to sitting on different committees and boards where the same faces circulate, a situation which has become all the more influential since the advent of the Darlington Partnership in 2002. This is one of a number of local area partnerships in the country between the local authority, local businesses and voluntary organizations in a given town. Working together for the development of the area and improved quality of life for residents, the aims of the partnership run parallel to those of the Council. The partnership is a formal expression of what was in the past a more *ad hoc* and less co-ordinated co-operation between authorities and other bodies.

It is clear that the interviewees see personal relations and the actions of key individuals as central to the success of initiatives in the area, and their responses to questions on church involvement in welfare are gauged accordingly. The fact that Darlington, with its marked divisions in wealth, misses out on extra funding reserved for priority areas suffering multiple deprivations, should also be seen as important background information. That the relative wealth of some areas of the town masks the deprivation in others is clearly a source of frustration to many involved in the welfare sector.

The Local Church as Welfare Agent

Unlike the German situation, church involvement in welfare provision in England is largely parish-based, and the actions of the church as welfare provider vary considerably from parish to parish. Also, unlike both Germany and Sweden, the parish priest is nearly always the only church employee. All other work in and by the churches is done by volunteers. Nonetheless, all parishes in Darlington organize activities for children and for elderly people which could fairly be described as welfare services. In this way, much church provision is focused on women, as they make up the majority of very elderly people in the town and are also frequently the primary carers for small children. For children, there are often parents' and toddlers' groups, and in the case of one parish a shoppers' crèche. For elderly people, both activities in the church building such as luncheon clubs, and home visits, are common. In addition, some churches run jumble sales, the primary purpose of which is to provide low-cost clothing. Similarly, in a couple of parishes a weekly coffee morning provides a meeting place for those who need it.

In all parishes, the clergy are actively involved in the local primary school and often sit as chair of the board of governors. In this capacity, clergy have an important role to play in the strategic planning and day-to-day running of local schools. They also carry out what they define as welfare work – that is, visiting parishioners in their homes or in hospital, either in person or by organizing rotas of volunteers in the parish. One priest also runs a 'surgery' at a local supermarket once a month, where he is available for anyone who wants to drop by and talk to him. Many priests, when interviewed, also note that much of the social work of the church is not organized directly by the church, but done by individuals in their capacity as individual Christians who are part of the church community. The churches also make their buildings available to a wide variety of community activities for which they are not responsible, but which could not take place without the availability of the building. In a number of cases, what was formerly the church hall has been converted into a community centre with a joint board of church and local community members.

Interestingly for the WREP project, with its focus on majority church activity, by far the most active in the social field in Darlington is the Baptist church in the town centre, which runs extensive programmes for homeless people and those with drug addictions in the local area. There are, however, other large-scale initiatives. First Stop, for example – a one-stop shop providing on-the-spot advice and assistance to homeless and unemployed people – was set up a few years ago at the initiative of the then town-centre vicar. His successor continues to sit on the committee. The Mothers' Union (a church-affiliated women's group) collects and sorts clothing and bedding for the shelter. There are two credit unions in the town which various churches helped to instigate in the early 1990s, and which make use of different churches as collection points.

Finally, it is important to mention that, over and above involvement in the town partnership, local community partnerships and schools, the church also formally interacts with the local authority in the welfare sector through its hospital, arts centre, college and police chaplains. The first of these is a full-time post within the health sector; responsibility for the other posts has been assumed by parish priests in the town.

Attitudes to Church Involvement in Welfare Provision

Representatives of both the churches and other organizations clearly understand the term 'welfare' to encompass more than the provision of practical services. Many do make a connection to the welfare system in the country, and through that to practical welfare provision, but the term is also seen to encompass a measure of general well-being over and above the material. In the vocabulary of the churchmen and women, this is something which is referred to in terms of spirituality and a relationship with God, while for others the vocabulary is more general. In common, however, is an understanding that people need support beyond the basic welfare services that the state or local authority can provide, not least in the current economic climate which has resulted in cutbacks in local services.

The View From Representatives of the Public Authorities   In light of the above it is perhaps unsurprising that representatives of the public authorities are eager for any partners who will enter the field of welfare provision and enable the local authority either to provide care more cheaply, or to provide services over and above those which they can offer themselves. What is perhaps more interesting is the clear assumption that the churches will – and are able to – provide such services with no strings attached, that is to say regardless of religious affiliation and without preaching. Such an attitude is often expressed in connection with comments concerning co-operation between public authorities and the church. It is accepted that churches may well provide extra services for their own members. Yet an understanding that the Church of England remains the established church, regardless of whether the commentator is in favour of this arrangement or not, leads – it seems – to an expectation that the church will contribute to the community in a neutral manner. This is not expected of other religious groups.

Conversely, in response to a direct question about whether the Church of England today retains specific responsibility in English society, many replies are negative. It is possible that this reflects a feeling that church influence has declined as society has become more plural. It might also reflect a more general trend in public discourse towards faith communities in general rather than one church in particular. Whatever the case, for most of those in the public authorities, the church commands little attention in the day-to-day planning of welfare provision. In the words of one public authority representative, 'I have to say that the church, and religion in general, is almost never mentioned' (f). Such a view – in contrast to the clear tendency in response to other questions to assume both a role for the church and the competence of the church – is of particular note. Perhaps one respondent articulated what many are thinking: that, as long as the Church of England is the established church with all the privileges entailed, it also retains a responsibility which other religious groups do not have (f). In many cases, however, it seems that responses are based not on reflection about the national situation, but on first-hand knowledge of the local.

Respondents know, for example, that the church is organized in parishes which cover all areas of the town, and therefore expect the church's work to include some measure of interaction with the local community, regardless of whether they (the interviewees) are aware of what is going on. They also accept that the churches have good local knowledge and expertise in fields such as the provision of spiritual support, the space for reflection, and the help and care of the vulnerable and deprived – something to be accepted gratefully, and indeed exploited. Here, however, there is a sense of frustration that respondents know so little about what the churches can offer, a situation for which they blame both themselves and the churches. When faced with an individual who needs extra social support not covered by the system, they feel that the church is an organization which could offer something at that level and probably does, but they feel unsure as to what this is and whom to contact in order to find out.

The View from Representatives of the Church If this feeling that the Church of England has a particular role and responsibility remains evident amongst representatives of other (secular) organizations, it is particularly strong amongst the representatives of the majority church itself. The church representatives interviewed were all ordained ministers and as such have a particular sense of responsibility for their parish and a strong identification with the institution. Many of them also mention that one thing which drew them to ministry in the Church of England specifically was the fact that it is the church for the whole nation with pastoral responsibility for all parishioners (not simply members of the congregation). It is not surprising, therefore, that they stress that the church is there for everyone. It both is, and ought to be, seen as providing neutral territory. In the words of one parish priest, 'That is the great advantage of the Church of England, that at its best it is seen as the best possibility of neutral holy ground. It belongs in that sense to everybody' (m). This must, however, also be seen in the light of comments made by representatives of other denominations in the town. From their point of view, the Church of England may be the obvious co-ordinator of ecumenical events, but this means that everything happens on its own terms (f). How neutral this 'neutral ground' is depends, in other words, on your perspective.

Despite noting the potential of the church to act within the welfare system, its representatives are quick to draw attention to its limitations. Many clergy feel, for instance, that they have a good awareness of the needs in their parish, and even of a number of individuals. They feel frustrated, however, by the lack of channels of communication into the official structures, which would enable them to act on behalf of parishioners, and by the lack of information about available services, which would enable them to point people in the right direction when the church itself cannot offer practical services. This latter point is closely connected to a second limitation – that of resources, both human and financial. The church, it is felt, should not overstretch itself in trying to provide services which it has not got the means to sustain; neither should it venture into areas where it does not have the expertise to provide an adequate and professional service. Drug rehabilitation programmes, for example, are seen as one area that should be left to trained professionals even if supported by the church. The contrast with Norway is striking in this respect.

The Church 'In-Between'

One point is clear: there is considerable ambiguity between the church's current role and what that role ought to be. This is true at several levels. Representatives of the local authorities have clear conceptions of what the church ought to do, yet they say in the same breath that they know nothing about the church and it is not their place to comment. They argue that in the field of welfare the church is a voluntary organization like any other, but then go on to ascribe to the church particular responsibility or expertise. Those who represent the church take it for granted that the church should be involved in welfare issues, and yet, faced with the realities of parish ministry and secular regulations, are equally quick to dismiss many courses of action as unfeasible. In other words, the church is given (more or less consciously) a distinctive role by the interviewees – a role that is seen as different from that of other voluntary groups or faith groups – yet it is in no way guaranteed.

The particular role ascribed to the majority church can be broken down into three different categories (see below). These have been distilled from the interview material because of their prevalence and because they are areas where representatives of both authorities and church paint a similar picture. This is not to say that there are no tensions between these groups; indeed they can be seen even within the 'common ground', revealing in what follows a complex and nuanced picture.

Before outlining these categories, however, one point needs firm underlining. As the discussion above shows, the general expectation that the church has a role to play in welfare should *not* be interpreted as an expectation that the church will provide practical welfare services on even a modest scale. Representatives of the local authority declare that the churches can do this if they want, but see other bodies as equally desirable partners. The church representatives, for their part, are willing to play this role where resources and competence allow. Yet they are equally quick to stress both that the church should not be seen as an alternative welfare agency and that resources, regulations and the need for professional competence are factors which limit such enterprises. Instead, the focus is placed on a much more diffuse role for the church – one, however, which is seen as specific to the Church of England. This is an 'in-between' role, expressed primarily in community-building and the provision of common space.

The Church as Neutral Ground

The fact that the Church of England has a presence in all areas of the town, and has resources, both human and financial, which most other churches do not, gives it a natural role in the local community. In many places, moreover, the parish priest is the only professional who not only serves but is resident in the neighbourhood. Similarly, the church building and connected church hall are often the only communal spaces in a residential area. This physical presence is familiar to local residents who use church premises not only for family events such as weddings, funerals and baptisms, but also for meetings and social clubs. They are used to the local vicar's involvement with the local school, visiting old people's homes and so on. In recent years in Darlington, this relationship has been formalized in many areas as local community partnerships. In most places the local vicar has been active in the process and either sits on or chairs the committee. In some areas co-operation has gone further and a deal has been struck whereby the church has given control of its hall to a joint church and residents' committee. This provides the opportunity to seek funding for refurbishment intended for community rather than religious groups.

As a result, a much wider variety of people now use the building and come into contact with the church. One vicar interviewed is convinced, for example, that efforts to be present when the building is being used for parent and toddler activities run by state-sponsored initiatives, has increased the number of baptisms in the church (f). Whether or not it is true that such initiatives have an effect on attitudes to the church and involvement in church life, it is clear that the churches do have a role to play in creating and preserving a sense of local community. The church representatives themselves see this as an important part of their ministry and of the church's contribution to welfare in the town. The church can, in other words, function as an arena for welfare, a space in which individuals can meet both with official welfare systems and with each other. Interestingly, despite its ideological and theological foundation, the church is seen in some senses as a form of neutral territory, on which all, regardless of religious affiliation or none, have a right to make a claim.

The Church as Mediator

The church is also, at least to some extent, a mediator. For example, many within the health and welfare sector in Darlington recognize that representatives of the church, and the parish priest in particular, have a good knowledge of the local community and expertise in areas connected to welfare. There is, however, a feeling both on the part of those representing the welfare system and of those within the churches that this competence could be used to greater advantage if the channels of communication were improved. Whatever the case, both where this communication functions well and where it is seen to be lacking, the church is often in a position to act as a mediator between individuals in need of support and the official welfare system. The church, in other words, is seen as a potential source of information and support in the relationships between individuals and the welfare system.

In addition, the church is seen as a place to turn when support from the official systems is inadequate, or when individuals lack trust in the authorities and therefore refrain from making contact via the official route. This occurs for various reasons: because of a mistrust of authority, a fear that support provided by authorities comes at a price (for example, for homeless under-18s the requirement to return home) or – particularly amongst elderly people – because of the stigma attached to means-tested benefits. This preference for non-official routes of support is not always something which is specific to the established church or even to churches in general; indeed, it seems rather to be a characteristic of the voluntary sector. Be that as it may, the clergy in Darlington report a strong expectation that the church has a duty to help people in need, including numerous examples of people knocking on the door of the vicarage wanting money or food. For respondents from both church and other organizations in this study, the fact that the church is one institution that people turn to when they do not trust the authorities is a further example of the position which the church holds between state and individual. It is not part of the official welfare system, and yet it is an assumed actor in the field.

The Church as Critical Voice

The third element of the church's role 'in-between' is its social voice: that is to say, its capacity to engage in public debate over welfare issues at all levels. Representatives of all churches who were interviewed argue that the church has a duty to speak out on moral issues, and for most this is a theological issue which reflects the very nature of Christianity and the role of the church in general. Interestingly, those interviewees who are connected to the public authorities often share this view, although not always the theological motivation behind it. Broadly speaking, however, churches are seen to have a particular duty to speak out about injustices given the moral stance which they claim.

The Church of England is seen as having both a duty and an opportunity over and above the norm: a duty to speak out because of the privileged position it has, and an opportunity to make use of its unique access to the corridors of power. Many refer, in particular, to the position of the bishops in the House of Lords, but also feel that even outside this forum their status gives to bishops a voice in the media and in political debate. At local level, similar responsibility is seen to rest with parish priests. In particular, those clergy who are school governors, or sit on other committees which oversee aspects of welfare provision in the town, see themselves and are seen by others as having a unique opportunity. They are knowledgeable about the local area and the workings of the system and yet, unlike those employed by the system, are able to speak out without fear of losing their job. As one representative of the local authority says:

> Every organization needs checks and balances … And I think that the church and faith groups have a role to play in providing some of those checks and balances against the state … We all need critical friends and I think the church can, that is one of the roles that faith groups can occupy. (f)

That the church should speak out alongside other pressure or faith groups seems to be taken for granted on all sides, and there is little evidence of the old maxim that church and politics do not mix. This is not to say that people do not have reservations about the church's role. Both church and public authority interviewees feel that the church should make sure that it is properly informed before it gets involved, and that it should be fully engaged with society and the local community if what it says is to be taken seriously.

It is significant that several interviewees from the local authority mention particular individuals in the church who have spoken out on social issues, and express admiration for them, but at the same time the interviewees are sceptical towards the church as an organization, partly because of the church's tendency to focus inwards on itself and on its obvious internal disagreements. One such is the long-running debate over the ordination of women to the priesthood. For many with little or no involvement in the church itself, this serves as proof that the church is out of touch with modern society. It may, however, be the relatively high expectations about what the church *should be* that lead to such harsh criticism. As one welfare sector employee says when reflecting on the church:

> You just look and think Gandhi was right – I like your Christ and I don't like your Christians ... I like the Church of England, but Anglicans irritate me ... Not all Anglicans, the idea of the church ... I think that there were always strong individual voices that strove to be heard, it's how do you reconcile the difference of opinion and then the difference of activity, but you know if we can't have high expectations of the church, what else can we have high expectations of? (f)

Conclusion

What, then, it may be asked, is the future for a church which is still the established church and physically present throughout the country, but at the same time has to face the reality that falling congregations mean fewer resources, human as well as financial, with which to sustain both the worshipping life of the church and its outreach to the wider community? What, more precisely, does this mean at local level, given the high expectations of the church which still prevail, not least on the part of the public authorities in Darlington – themselves conditioned by the role which the church has played in the past? It is this last factor, perhaps, which can provide a clue.

It has become clear, for example, that in Darlington, largely because of its size, particular individuals and their relationships with each other are the deciding factor in the conception and success of initiatives within the town. This, in the context of the English welfare system based on co-operation between actors from different sectors, means that there is potential for the church to capitalize on the fact that it is still perceived to have a role to play should it wish to be active either in the provision of, or the debate about, welfare. The corresponding downside, however, is that almost all initiatives are dependent on particular individuals and are therefore fragile – these people will not be there forever. A second point follows from this. If, for whatever reason, the church should decide *not* take up its potential role in welfare debate and provision, those working in the public authority are equally willing to turn to others. In the words of one such employee:

> If you had interviewed me ten years ago, five years ago the answers would have been very different ... The two main Christian churches have actually lost the buck seat. Now I don't know their business, it may well be that their number one priority is to try and save the core business and welfare is not their core business ... Why have the churches become disengaged? We didn't fall out, they just lost engagement which seems to me to be crazy. There is an open door and a seat at the table, but they don't seem to want to know. (m)

Maybe the church really does want to focus on its 'core business'. Clergy in Darlington were quick to point out that they are not employed as untrained social workers. However, their understandings of the role of the church, including a belief that this role necessarily includes engagement with the local community, coupled with a defence of the parochial system, indicate that they have no wish to become disengaged; indeed, they see the church as a key actor in the social field. Why such tensions appear between church and public authority when there is so much agreement on what the church is able to do, is no simple matter to determine. Yet the very fact these tensions exist means that the church can in no way take for granted that the role which it can assume today will be there for the taking in the future, if it is not actively preserved.

How this will turn out is something that the townscape cannot reveal to me now, although the fact that the conversion of church halls in recent years has been to church and community halls and not to carpet warehouses may, perhaps, say something.

Chapter 8

Church–State Relations in France in the Field of Welfare: A Hidden Complementarity

Corinne Valasik

Following the celebrations surrounding the centenary of the law of 5 December 1905, which established the separation of church and state in France, is it possible to speak of a formal or *de facto* collaboration between political and religious institutions in addressing social problems? Does the church, which has long assumed a charitable role, still have a part to play in the now highly-professionalized social sector? To attempt a reply to these questions, 29 interviews were held in Evreux with those holding responsibilities in this area: elected politicians, ordained and lay Roman Catholics, members of associations, journalists and volunteers, both believers and non-believers, together with several focus groups. These were complemented by on-the-spot observations in the places where welfare is provided.

Exploring Evreux

Evreux is a typical French provincial town. The centre is built around an eleventh-century cathedral dedicated to the Virgin Mary. Close by are the buildings of the town hall, more recent but no less imposing, located on a large square where a market is held twice a week. This layout, with two centrally-located bodies alongside – yet with no knowledge of – each other, provides a good illustration of the relationship between the Catholic Church and the political establishment in France. Equally historic are the canals which flow through the town centre alongside the River Iton. Formerly there were washing places here, and some local people would like to see these restored to preserve a local memory.

Indeed, Evreux feels its identity threatened by its proximity to Paris, situated as it is in Normandy, 100 km north-west of the capital, making it part of the Paris conurbation. More and more inhabitants of the town work in Paris, spending less and less of their time in Evreux. The effect of this exodus is apparent in the atmosphere of the town. The centre where the majority of businesses are located is quiet most of the time. It provides mostly local shops – clothes shops, hairdressers, a bookshop, food shops – but no large shopping centres and very few car parks, these being located outside the town. Between 12.30 and 2.30, and after 6.30 in the evening, Evreux shuts down, and it is hard to believe that it is a town of 54,076 inhabitants and the administrative centre of the *département* of Eure. In these quiet periods one can walk in the park which links the station to the town centre, or go out of the town to take a walk in the woods, to go horse-riding or to play golf. Indeed, the tourist office promotes the town's proximity to nature as an attraction to visitors.

One can also go out to two areas above the town centre which are also part of Evreux, which lies in a basin. To the north is the quiet residential area of Saint-Michel, which can be reached by car or bus or by a stiff climb. This is an area of detached houses standing in their own gardens, where birdsong and church bells are the only sounds to break the silence, and where it is not easy to find someone to ask the way if you get lost. For a more lively area one must go to the La Madeleine-Nétreville district, to the south of the town centre. This, too, is reached by car or bus; on foot you go under the railway and then through a long tunnel before another long climb. Nétreville is an area with both small houses and apartment blocks, most of them quite widely spread out with green spaces between them.

La Madeleine, however, presents a different appearance. Here, a large quantity of social housing was rapidly built in the 1960s to cater for the arrival of French and immigrant workers. Some 54 per cent of the dwellings in Evreux come into the category of social housing, and most of them are in this area; the quality of the buildings is not good, and they are showing their age. A general programme of renovation is under way, but money is short; of an estimated cost of €45 million, only €14 million had been released at the time of the fieldwork. Tower blocks face each other separated only by tiny areas of concrete, so that the occupants of one building can overlook those in another. The lower floors are dark, as are the walkways between buildings. The only colour is provided by the large number of cars in the car parks. There are few shops, only a greengrocer and a small supermarket.

It is not a district which is easy to reach without a car; there are buses to and from the centre but they are infrequent outside rush hour and there is no service after 8 pm. They are used only by the residents of La Madeleine; the other inhabitants of Evreux seldom go there, viewing the area with a mixture of alienation and fear. The local press regularly gives expression to the growing feeling of insecurity in the community. The responses of the local authority are pre-eminently repressive: installing CCTV cameras on the streets and buses; increasing the police presence from nine to 18 officers; repeated identity checks to crack down on illegal immigration; calling on the public to report any antisocial acts. This unease, and the division between areas which it brings about, was reinforced by the disturbances of November 2005, when the curfew imposed in La Madeleine was the strictest anywhere in France.[1] This was the scene of the most serious incidents reported in the *département* of Eure: around 30 cars were burnt by demonstrators, together with three shops, a police station and several phone boxes. The confrontations between law enforcement officers and around

---

[1]   The curfew used the 1955 law declaring a state of emergency which was applied during the Algerian War, and since then only in New Caledonia in 1984.

100 young people armed with baseball bats, *pétanque* balls, stones and metal bars caused damage to a school and the annexe to the town hall and injured a number of people.[2]

La Madeleine is thus a district with an accumulation of problems: badly built and badly located, it is where the majority of the victims of the economic crisis live – those who depend on welfare and have little prospect of a more secure future. It is these major social questions that the French state and the Catholic Church are trying to address.

Welfare in the French Context

In the typology established by Esping-Andersen (1990) and generally followed in later studies, France belongs to the corporatist (that is, the conservative) model of welfare. This means that social security benefits and labour law reinforce distinctions of status, with numerous social funds being restricted to specific groups of people. Wages, social security benefits, and so on, are negotiated between representatives of the state, the unions and management. The social security system which was established after World War 2 was conceived as a support for workers, but payments have increasingly been extended to those who are not in work and to immigrants. In the 30 years between 1945 and 1975 the welfare system, understood as 'the state as provider' in the pursuit of wellbeing and comfort, has brought about a profound change in French society, notably in the role and position of women. The welfare system has enabled women to acquire autonomy in relation to their partners, while also gaining protection against such risks as divorce, death of a partner, illness and so on. At a time of economic crisis, therefore, it is women who are most strongly affected by restrictions on the welfare budget, as they are more dependent on it than men. Women are not only beneficiaries of welfare but also constitute the majority of those who work in the system (in the tertiary sector, as medical and social workers and so on).

The financing of social security – that is to say pensions, unemployment benefit, and healthcare – has long been a concern of politicians, without any real solutions being found. With unemployment around 10 per cent, and nearly 15 per cent of people in short-term work, the demands on the social security budget have increased while available resources have diminished. Any redistribution of social expenditure is regularly resisted, and payments are thinly spread among the most deprived and much more generously among the better off. In 2000, of a population of 60 million, France had 4.5 million people living in poverty and 5 million just above the poverty line, at a time when social expenditure increased to 54 per cent of GDP (Observatoire national de la pauvreté et de l'exclusion sociale, 2002).

---

2   'La Madeleine sous le choc', *Paris-Normandie*, 7 November 2005.

Political Decentralization and Charitable Associations

From the 1980s onwards the French state has adopted a policy of decentralization of *compétences*[3] aimed at revitalizing local and national democracy. The term 'territorial unit of the Republic' has been redefined and, since 2003, has been applied to the 36,778 *communes*, 96 *départements* and 22 *régions* of metropolitan France, as well as to the overseas territories and those with special status. These are all governed by the same rules with a legislative assembly elected by universal suffrage (for example, the town council) and an executive power elected by the assembly (for example, the mayor). Social action is the area in which decentralization has been most developed. At regional level, the Regional Directorate for Health and Social Affairs (DRASS)[4] co-ordinates and oversees the action taken at the level of each *département*. At the level of the *département*, social action is directed by the Departmental Directorate for Health and Social Affairs (DDASS).[5] It is for the *département* to define policy for social action in line with the broad outlines laid down by the state. The *département* is responsible for welfare payments as a whole (the legal conditions for entitlement to benefits being fixed by the state) apart from family allowances which remain within the competence of the state. The *département*, therefore, administers five types of social benefits: welfare support for children; disability benefit; social and employment benefits, for example the *Revenu Minimum d'Insertion* (RMI);[6] benefits for elderly people; and medical benefits. Some 43 per cent of the Eure *département* budget is devoted to welfare payments, which is in line with the national average.

Since 1986 the *communes*, too, have had a direct involvement in the administration of welfare through the Communal Council for Social Action (CCAS). The Communal Council is legally independent of the municipality which finances it, and is directed by a board of management made up of elected members designated by the mayor and representatives of voluntary associations. The purpose of this body is to analyse the social problems of the community and to oversee the management of nursery schools, child care and old people's homes, and to propose solutions for the needs of social assistance in the community.

The process of decentralization which began in the 1980s has brought about a greater clarity in the areas of competence of each body and has resulted in greater autonomy for the *départements* and *communes*, especially in the area of welfare. However, there is still some confusion between the areas of competence of the state, the *département* and the *commune*; the *commune*, for instance, remains

---

[3]   '*Compétence*' is defined as an area of aptitude established by law and entailing specified rights which are delegated to the body which exercises them and puts them into effect.

[4]   There are 22 Regional Directorates (DRASS) in France.

[5]   There are 102 Departmental Directorates (DDASS) in France.

[6]   The *revenu minimum d'insertion* (RMI) provides each person aged over 25 with a minimum income.

responsible for managing shelters for homeless people, although these are also the responsibility of the state. Establishing partnerships between the various bodies is, therefore, a complicated matter.

The *communes* previously had a role in the management of social problems, but their scope for decision-making and experimentation was limited; initiatives came mainly from the voluntary sector, which is very active in France although, paradoxically, it is rarely studied. As France is a very centralized country there has traditionally been very little interest in 'intermediate structures', particularly as far as welfare is concerned. It is the welfare state – *l'Etat-providence* – that is perceived as being responsible for social matters.

Indeed, the republican ideal is very largely founded on a distrust of any intermediate structures which might come between the state and the citizen (see Ion 1997). Until the beginning of the twentieth century, for example, the state refused to legislate on the freedom of association, fearing that this would benefit the Catholic Church. The law of 1 July 1901 did establish the freedom to create a voluntary association in France, but one of its objectives was to reduce the influence of Catholic congregations in France. According to this law, no formalities are required to set up such a body, apart from making a declaration at the *Préfecture*; but the *Préfecture* has no right to give an opinion on the proposed objectives of the association (unless they appear to be illegal). It is the association's members who define its objectives, articles and the internal rules of the association. Only those associations recognized as providing a public good (which can be linked with a religious denomination) – and, therefore, recognized by the state – can receive state funding, in which case they are subject to a financial and legal audit by the state. Thus this law, which is generally perceived as being relatively liberal, requires associations to submit to state control when they need financial support (Laville and Sainsaulieu 1997).

In the first part of the twentieth century many powerful associations were set up, both confessional (see below) and non-confessional, the latter encouraged by the state. Alongside traditional activities such as charities, new areas of activity were developed, notably cultural and leisure activities. After World War 2 the state became a welfare state which aimed to combine economic development and social protection. Gradually some associations, recognized as providing a public good, became semi-public institutions, working in co-operation with those of the state. More flexible in their structure and way of working, these associations were asked by the state to carry out certain assignments: providing additional help to underprivileged people, helping them in their dealings with bureaucracy and so on. Progressively, whole areas of welfare management came under the direction of a voluntary sector overseen by the state. This collaboration was encouraged by a flourishing economy which enabled the state to provide regular funding to these organizations.

The 1982 laws on decentralization brought to an end the state support of these associations. Virtual monopolies of services offered by associations, such as home-help and child-minding, were now called into question. These services were now considered potential sources of employment, and the state authorized private companies to enter this sector. For example, it is still the case that parents can benefit from state aid, in the form of a reduction in income tax, if they employ a child-minder rather than a subsidized organization. Laville and Sainsaulieu comment, 'Associations and private companies are thus required to compete in the name of job creation' (Laville and Sainsaulieu 1997: 366).

At the same time, faced with high levels of unemployment and social exclusion, the state is turning to the associations for help in the area of social and employment benefit. Within the framework of national policy, employment contracts (*contrats emploi-solidarité*) allow people to work for an association provided this does not compete with existing jobs. These contracts are short-term and are appropriate primarily for those in difficult financial and social circumstances. In exchange, the associations benefit from tax relief and exemption from social charges. It should be noted that the state no longer has the same financial resources as in the past, and public subsidies now depend on the results produced by these associations. Therefore, subsidies are now granted on a less regular basis and are also regularly reassessed by the state. Confessional associations can benefit from state funding, if their objectives are recognized as providing a public good and on condition that they do not engage in proselytizing. Thus, associations working in the area of welfare can benefit from state recognition, but at the same time they are under tight control by the state if they rely on subsidies for their continuing existence.

The Role of the Catholic Church in Welfare

When asked about their religious affiliation, 62 per cent of people in France declare themselves Catholic, making Catholicism the majority religion. Church–state relations are defined within the framework of the law of 9 December 1905, which was passed at a time of conflict between the state and the Catholic Church, not as a contract between partners but as a unilateral act on the part of the state aimed at limiting the influence of religion in education. The law was applied in the face of opposition from the Vatican, expressed in the encyclical *Vehementer Nos* of 1906, and is the conclusion of the process of secularization (*laïcization*) which began with the French Revolution. It does not, however, define *laïcité* as such, but sets out the principles that 'the Republic does not recognize, fund or subsidize any religious body' (article 2) and that it has the obligation to protect the religious freedom of the individual. The churches no longer have any standing in public law, and therefore have no legal basis for intervening in the political arena. The principle of *laïcité* applies to all public institutions. The fifth Constitution, passed in 1946, referred back to the law of 1905 in defining France as a 'secular (*laïque*) Republic'.

The law is more flexible in its application than these general principles suggest. The communes and the state allow the churches to use church buildings built before 1906 without charge. The clergy are able to benefit from the social security system, and their national insurance and pensions are substantially supported by the contributions of all citizens. Private religious schools can, under certain conditions, be financed by the state. However, the definition of *laïcité* has been reaffirmed in the law of 15 March 2004 which, in response to the demand by Muslim girls to be allowed to wear the headscarf in secondary schools, forbids the wearing of religious dress or any 'ostentatious' religious symbol. This interpretation of *laïcité* is presented above all as promoting integration, allowing all to have equal status as citizens. It is in this context, too, that the French Council of Muslims (*Conseil français du culte musulman*) was set up in 2003, on the initiative of the Ministry of the Interior, to provide spokespersons for the Muslim community to engage in dialogue with the state.

Thus, religious bodies have no direct involvement in the public domain, which remains the responsibility of the state. They do, however, play an important part within the voluntary sector which, as we have seen, remains crucial in the management of welfare.

Welfare in Evreux: Town Hall, Church and Voluntary Associations

Several large international companies established themselves in Evreux in the 1960s, attracted by its proximity to Paris, its relatively low wages, the availability of public subsidies and its quality of life. This brought about a renewal of the local economy, especially the network of small and medium-sized businesses which sub-contracted to the large firms. In all there are 2,300 businesses in Evreux, providing approximately 32,500 jobs. Four major sectors predominate: pharmaceuticals, with GlaxoSmithKline the largest employer in the town with 1,850 employees; electronic and electrical equipment, with Deutsch and Schneider; printing, with Atlas Publications; and packaging, notably of cosmetics, with Mecanic Brochage. Increasingly, however, these large companies have relocated to Asia, especially China, in order to reduce their costs. There has been a steady loss of jobs for economic reasons, with the level of unemployment increasing year on year; from 8.3 per cent in June 2002, unemployment reached 9.5 per cent in 2003, with women and young people aged under 25 being the worst affected. Unemployment has become the major concern in the town; it is difficult for those who lose their jobs to find other employment in these areas of activity, with a consequent growth in demand for welfare services. This increasing insecurity of the workforce is a growing concern to locally-elected politicians who feel powerless in the face of this new situation.

Moreover, the town council's scope for action is limited by its own financial position. The town's debt rose in 2000 to €100.6 million, or €1,880 per inhabitant, compared with the average for towns of comparable size of €1,260 per inhabitant. By means of budget cuts, especially in the area of welfare where support for local associations has been reduced, the debt was brought down to €87.1 million in 2003. The challenges which the town now faces are broadly similar to those of other urban areas of the same size.

The Town Council and the Reorganization of Welfare

At the time of the fieldwork, the mayor of Evreux was Jean-Louis Debré, a member of the rightist UMP (*Union pour un Mouvement Populaire*), and also President of the French National Assembly.[7] He was close to the then President of the Republic, Jacques Chirac, and was Minister of the Interior between 1995 and 1997. He was unpopular for a time following his decision in August 1996 to order the police to remove a group of illegal immigrants from the church of St Bernard in Paris where they had taken refuge. After he took up the post of President of the National Assembly in 2002, however, his image changed. He undertook to modernize the working of the Assembly so that it more closely reflected the expectations of the people. His position enabled him to make personal pronouncements on the actions of the government of the day, with whose workings he was equally at home. Notably he opposed several of the laws on decentralization, and strongly upheld the 2004 law against the wearing of ostentatious religious symbols in schools.

Although Debré was a nationally-known politician, this was his first term as mayor of Evreux. He had been a member of the National Assembly for the Eure *département* since 1986, and won the municipal election against the communist Roland Plaisance, the incumbent mayor who had held the post since 1977. There was a comparable reversal of the political situation at the level of the region and in the *département* of Haute-Normandie, both of which moved in the opposition direction – that is, to a socialist administration.

In Evreux, Debré's administration sought to address the economic situation on two fronts: by making the town as attractive as possible to business by creating tax-free zones, adapting education to the needs of business and improving the road infrastructure; and by rethinking the local management of welfare, by reorganizing the CCAS (Communal Council for Social Action) to make it the facilitator for all social policy in the town. This policy rested on two principles: adapting the organization to the needs of those who use it, and improving the efficiency of its service to the public.

The Catholic Church Seeks a Voice

The focus of this study is primarily on the dominant religious tradition, which in France is the Catholic Church. As Evreux is the seat of a diocese, it is possible to compare social action at the level of the parishes with that at diocesan level. This study was conducted during the tenure of Bishop Jacques David,[8] who was

---

[7]   Debré's father, Michel Debré, was prime minister after World War 2 under the presidency of Charles de Gaulle, and took part in the drawing up of the fifth Constitution. His son is fond of referring to his family background, and places himself in the Gaullist tradition.

[8]   Jacques David was born in 1930, ordained priest in 1956 and bishop in 1981. Four years later he became bishop in the diocese of La Rochelle and Saintes, before being

replaced on 29 January 2006 by Father Christian Nourrichard, formerly Vicar-General of Rouen. Bishop David's first mission was to reunify the diocese after the removal of Mgr Gaillot as Bishop by the Pope in 1995. Bishop Gaillot's removal provoked vehement protests from Catholics and unbelievers alike; his last Mass, on 22 January 1995, was attended by 20,000 faithful in Evreux, with several thousand protesters in Nantes and hundreds in Nancy, Metz and Strasbourg. Mgr Gaillot is currently bishop of Partenia, a diocese which no longer exists.[9] Once things had calmed down, Bishop David sought to respond to the challenges currently facing the Diocese of Evreux: minimizing the effect of the shortage of priests, allowing the laity to play a fuller role in the life of the church through training and shared responsibility, and maintaining a balanced budget.

Bishop Jacques David put the question of welfare at the heart of his pastoral ministry. In his view, Catholics should be alert to all forms of exclusion and should try to respond to these. The church's ability to act is severely limited by its lack of financial resources. In 2004 giving from church congregations brought the diocese a total of €1,176,102, which was allocated as follows: 36 per cent for clergy stipends and expenses; 29 per cent for training of seminarians and pastoral work, essentially among the young; 16 per cent for Catholic groups and services; 12 per cent for general administration; and 7 per cent for the diocesan secretariat.

Welfare initiatives at the level of the parish offer meeting places, organized by lay people, for those with specific needs – such as alcoholics, single mothers and people with disabilities. These provide an opportunity for people to meet and talk, but seldom lead to any concrete action. The church therefore establishes numerous partnerships with Catholic movements such as Caritas (*Secours Catholique France*), the Catholic Committee against Hunger and for Development (*Catholique contre la Faim et pour le Développement*, CCFD), the Saint Vincent de Paul Conferences and so on. These are independent lay associations, movements or communities recognized by the church, at local, national or international level. They each have their own objectives and forms of teaching, and aim to develop a particular aspect of the church's mission; the church supports them by providing facilities – the loan of premises for meetings – and financially. There is little evidence in Evreux of the new communities claiming to embody charismatic renewal. There is some collaboration with non-Catholic associations when their mission is not seen as being incompatible with that of the church; this usually takes the form of exchanges of information, arranging meetings (such as those for illegal immigrants), sharing premises and so on.

The Catholic workers interviewed consider the church's role to be above all that of being available to listen to people and to accompany them in their daily

---

appointed to Evreux in 1996.

[9]   As he no longer has pastoral responsibilities Mgr Gaillot is not eligible to take part in the French Bishops' Conference, which has suggested various solutions to enable him to resolve this situation, all of which he has refused, causing some unease among his supporters.

lives, treating them not simply as workers, unemployed or excluded people, but holistically as individuals. They wish that the church's social teaching and action in this area – referring particularly to Caritas and the CCFD – were better known, while still respecting the spirit of the 1905 law. But they recognize that their attempts at communication usually fail, as one worker testifies:

> Not long ago a company laid off lots of workers. The bishop went to meet the unions and to talk to the workers. The press were informed but nobody bothered to come; they're not interested – and in any case, there's suspicion; because it's the church, people are distrustful. We don't seem able to escape from that. (f)

This distrust was also apparent in interviews with elected politicians, who initially refused even to discuss the church's welfare work at local level, on the principle of *laïcité*, before acknowledging that they had no idea of what this might involve. The person responsible for welfare admitted that he had never thought of asking the question: 'I've never asked myself what the Catholic Church did on the level of welfare. Perhaps I should have done, but no, I've never thought about it' (m). He continued, 'If the French bishops started intervening in political debate, in my opinion that would restart wars and tensions which we really don't need – we've got other things to do' (m). There is, then, no official collaboration between the church and political bodies in the field of welfare at local level.

The Voluntary Sector

The study revealed that a large proportion of welfare work is undertaken by the voluntary sector, in which confessional and non-confessional groups are working side by side. It has proved difficult to trace all the associations present in Evreux, as the municipal records are far from complete; moreover, the level of mutual recognition among the various associations is very low, which seems to point to a problem of organization in this sector.

One can, however, distinguish two broad types of organization in Evreux, depending on whether they see their mission as centred on the individual or as addressing a specific problem.

Long-Term Action   Some associations are aimed at meeting the needs of the individual within a given geographical location. Whatever difficulties a person may be facing, the association will try to respond to them by establishing partnerships with other bodies, while remaining the immediate point of reference for the individual. Such organizations may also offer group activities which promote training, such as the sewing and cooking classes for women of foreign origin living in La Madeleine. Such meetings enable the women bit by bit to broach the problems which they face and to seek advice from the volunteers – for help with literacy, support for children at school, alcoholism, financial problems and so forth.

Such associations seek above all to work through relationships between individuals and to recreate social networks among those who live in the same district. Their activities are essentially long-term and cannot be expected to deliver visible results within a prescribed timescale. In this respect there is little difference between confessional and non-confessional groups: Catholic associations are open to all and prayers or masses do not feature in their activities. Their Catholic allegiance is, so to speak, invisible, which enables them to collaborate more easily with others; this is, in any case, a condition of their partnership with other bodies. As the interviewee quoted above says, 'What counts is the quality of the work they do – that's all. If the Catholic aid agency stayed in its corner and wanted to pray to God at every board meeting, then it's clear there wouldn't be any understanding between us' (m).

Targeted Action   Other associations concentrate on specific types of problem, such as those concerned with housing. Some help clients to complete their applications for social security or to find housing, or they may agree to pay rent on behalf of the client for the time that they need to access more permanent forms of assistance. The most pressing problem at the moment concerns emergency shelters. Since places offering help and shelter for immigrants and asylum-seekers in Paris are already full to capacity, this need has shifted to other parts of the Paris conurbation, notably to Evreux which has few appropriate facilities available – all of them provided by the voluntary sector. Political asylum-seekers now use these facilities alongside the homeless people who are the facilities' regular clients, leading to frequent misunderstandings between the different groups which regularly break out into violence. Asylum-seekers have increasingly become the dominant group in these centres, displacing the homeless people who congregate elsewhere until other organizations arise to meet this new need (or existing associations extend their activities to deal with them). Officially, those who use these centres should not stay more than a few days or weeks, long enough to find a more permanent solution. In reality, the sector admits that they often allow people to extend their stay – thereby infringing the official guidelines – or else allow individuals to 'circulate' between centres so that they do not find themselves without shelter.

Such associations, therefore, aim to respond to a specific short-term problem. Unlike those described above, they do not deal with people who are already established in a locality, nor is it their goal to strengthen social networks at a local level. As the situations they encounter become more pressing, some find a way round the official guidelines and increasingly question the basis of their mission, as one worker for an organization explains:

The DRASS tell me I shouldn't keep people for more than three months, but what can you do in three months? The people who arrive here are physically and psychologically exhausted, they're at the end of their tether. That's the urgent need, to give them a place to breathe. It used not to be like that, but now that's what I see. I'm not an institution, I'm a human being faced with other human beings; I can't throw them out on the street just because that's what the rule says. No, I can't, that's not how I see my job. We've got to find other solutions. (m)

Thus the voluntary sector in Evreux fulfils certain functions of the state in the area of welfare. All those working in this field confirm that they are now facing new challenges. At a time of economic crisis, for example, they can no longer simply offer support which is aimed at enabling people to re-enter employment. Rather, each body adapts its provision according to an individual's chances of finding another job. Welfare workers struggle to redefine what is meant by reintegration and what to offer to those who have little or no prospect of finding a job at all. This explains why some clients of these groups consider them simply as providers of funds.

Welfare: What Does it Mean?

Each association thus has its own definition of welfare and the action needed to resolve the problems that it identifies. This diversity of approaches to welfare leads, moreover, to a proliferation of identical services provided for the same population in the same locality. Unsurprisingly, the lack of transparency encourages users to see themselves as consumers, choosing an association on the basis of what it offers rather than of its particular values. Those who work for such groups deplore this new type of behaviour, which they see as inconsistent and opportunistic, but which derives in part from the local situation. In the general lack of clarity surrounding the definition of welfare, individuals act according to their own interests without feeling committed to any particular organization, since all are seen as capable of providing the same kind of service; an association's confessional character does not seem to have any relevance in this context.

This lack of clarity in relation to welfare is reflected in the data emerging from the focus groups drawn from the wider community. One interviewee says, 'The welfare state, that's the social security, everything to do with aid .. Actually, I don't really know' (m). Another suggests, 'Welfare – it depends on the state, doesn't it? So whether it's local or not doesn't make much difference. Apart from that, there are some associations locally but I don't know anything about them. They help people' (f).

Indeed, those interviewed associate welfare with particular institutions such as ANPE (*Agence Nationale pour l'Emploi*) and the CAF (*Caisses d'Allocations Familiales*) – in other words, according to the needs they address, but without relating them to specific local bodies. They say that they are not very well informed by the media, and admit to not being very interested in what they call welfare matters, which they consider to be too complicated. Welfare is deemed a difficult subject, with its own technical language which is understood only by experts and makes it remote from reality. Paradoxically, the concept of welfare becomes clearer when it is linked to the role of voluntary organizations and the

Catholic Church; welfare then becomes charity, helping people in need. Welfare at a local level is identified, therefore, with visible individuals who are part of the community. Associations, including those with a confessional base, are recognized and legitimated. The confessional groups are seen as indispensible and complementary to other agencies, provided they 'neutralize' their Catholic affiliation. On the other hand, official representatives of the church should *not* intervene in public debate, even on welfare issues; religion should remain in the private domain. This suspicion extends to politicians, who are also seen as having lost their legitimacy. This view should be seen in the context of the wider crisis of public institutions in France, which are no longer seen as embodying shared or unifying values (Dubet 2002). Conversely, attachment to the idea of the 'social' – seen as the locus of resistance to the dominance of economics – seems to become stronger the greater the sense of dispossession.

The Concept of Subsidiarity between Church and State

Robert Castel (2003) has shown how the state has proved ill-equipped to deal with new social problems. Similarly, our findings suggest that public authorities are rarely in the forefront of finding innovative solutions to newly-emerged problems, but subsequently they can incorporate solutions proposed by the voluntary sector, whether confessional or not, into their own ways of working. The association L'Abri (Shelter) is a good illustration of this. Created in 1984 as an initiative of Caritas and supported by the local Catholic church, L'Abri provided shelter and support for those whose situation was extremely precarious and whom few other associations at that time were able to help. In 2001, the DDASS gave its approval to the Centre for Emergency Shelter (*Centre d'Hébergement d'Urgence*) which L'Abri had set up, with a guaranteed subsidy, professional social workers gradually replacing volunteers, and partnership with other agencies. In the years since then, L'Abri has completely changed its structure: having begun as a Catholic aid organization run by volunteers, it retains its voluntary status but is now managed and funded by public authorities.

Does Church-State Subsidiarity Operate in the Voluntary Sector with Regard to Welfare?

Identifying New Problems

The church, recognizing that local communities have been considerably weakened by the economic crisis, is seeking to recreate social links between individuals, by working through small-scale local groups which bring together the residents of a particular district or village. The pressing need is not so much to produce an agenda for social change as to enable individuals to rediscover what unites them over and above their differences. By encouraging and stimulating neighbourly relations, the church enables lay people to understand the difficulties that the population is facing. This information is then passed on to the different levels of the church hierarchy. The Catholic associations also have knowledge of the situation on the ground which is continually updated by their partnership – even if it is not officially recognized – with other associations working in the field. The analyses put forward by the Catholic associations, combined with the feedback they receive from the local communities and the experience of members of the clergy, gives the church as a whole a detailed view of the local situation. Finally, the press review organized by volunteers from one of the Catholic movements, Le Carrefour Rural, which is distributed throughout the diocese and also sent to all elected politicians, is a means of disseminating an overview of the information which has been gathered. The Catholic volunteers who were interviewed thus appeared better informed about current social problems in Evreux, especially in La Madeleine, than some of the elected politicians, who admit that they rarely visit the area except at the time of an election, which inevitably limits their ability to understand the local situation. They rely on the information provided by the associations with which they are in contact – that is, only a minority of them – and on the press. There is no meeting to discuss these matters between local politicians and church workers. As there is no co-operation between state and church on these matters, it is through the medium of the Catholic associations that some problems come to light and are brought into the political domain.

The church, then, gives material aid – loan of premises, setting up of networks, modest financial support – in the early stages of new groups or projects which arise to deal with recent problems such as illegal immigrants. This is direct aid which is not visible because it works at the level of the associations rather than of the church itself, as a lay worker pointed out:

> If all of a sudden there were no Catholic associations working in welfare, the state wouldn't be able to cope. But people find it hard to make the link between the church as an institution and the Catholic aid organizations which help thousands of people. (m)

The Local Authority Takes Over

The state, through its various institutions, is liable to take control of some activities carried out by the voluntary sector – the majority of which is Catholic in Evreux – but this involves a change of status and mission for the groups in question. The town council which took over in 2001 realized that the management of welfare was largely in the hands of the voluntary sector, and wanted to reassert its own central role through the CCAS. A new policy of 'contractualization' was put in place, whereby financial support was offered to those associations which could show tangible results in the short and medium term. This change in political direction brought about numerous conflicts in the voluntary sector, some members of which rejected any form of scrutiny by the state. Those who work in the sector raise questions about the criteria for entitlement to support. Some argue that, by giving more power to the communes, the laws on decentralization have indirectly created a new form of clientelism, whereby only associations which conform to the model put forward by the town council receive support, while those which depart from this norm are barely considered. The new conditions for entitlement to support are questioned:

> When there were people really doing a good job in the districts where there were problems, their subsidy was cut. So you have to wonder whether it was really because they considered they weren't doing a useful job, or whether it was just to make a point at the expense of the previous administration. (f)

Local politicians partly confirmed these suspicions, refusing to take the risk of supporting an activity whose results could not be measured in advance. The CCAS, too, was reorganized so as to reassert control over activities which had previously been carried out by associations – such as help with filling in forms for RMI (*Revenu Minimum d'Insertion*) – putting it in competition with the voluntary sector. At the same time, its links with institutions like the DRASS and DDASS have been strengthened, as an elected politician testifies:

> Some associations sometimes want to act as a filter between clients and politicians, and that's really a tendency we must resist … I think we must renew the link with democracy, and let the elected representatives take back power with citizens instead of working through this filter of the associations; that's the key issue at the local level. (m)

Thus the municipality can provide the financial support necessary for the association to function at a later stage, but only in the light of the results it produces: 'What we're trying to do at the town level is not to give handouts but to help them to relaunch … We have to give priority to helping those who want to be helped, those we can really count on' (m).

An example of this is the setting up of a social grocery store, which Caritas decided to establish in the face of the growing impoverishment of a section of the population. The municipality approved of the project and, at the time of the research, was trying to find some financial support to complement what has already been authorized by DRASS. The project is in line with the local authority's new priority for action, the issue of support for impoverished workers:

> The people that concern me today are precisely those who are on the brink of poverty: who still have an apartment but are struggling to keep up the payments, who have children but have difficulty in providing for them but who, despite everything, are still working. (m)

The social grocery, opened in September 2005, is now officially presented as an initiative taken by the local authority; the involvement of Caritas is hardly mentioned. Yet Caritas still manages the operation of the grocery, as is shown by the fact that an advertisement for 12 volunteers to work in the daily running of the shop was published on the Caritas website and not on that of the local authority; the advertisement specifies that applicants should be 'supportive of the aims of Catholic Aid [*Secours Catholique*]', which also offers training in welfare provision.

Elected politicians are thus anxious to reclaim their position at the centre of social action, as the instigators of new projects, as harmonizers of the various initiatives which already exist and as the primary, and obligatory, interlocutors for those with responsibility for welfare. This policy clearly shows that politicians have lost their grip on these matters in the past. The new policy was clearly helped by the personality of the then mayor of Evreux and the fact that he was also the President of the National Assembly.

Institutionalization of Voluntary Associations

At a third and final stage in the process, voluntary organizations can receive long-term financial support from state institutions such as DRASS. The association is then completely under the control of the state, which greatly reduces its capacity for experimentation. In return, the public authorities require the sector to become professionalized by employing professional social workers, which in any case meets the need of the associations themselves whose recurrent problem has been the lack of volunteers willing to commit themselves regularly in the long term, as most prefer only a short-term involvement. An additional difficulty arises from the increasing complexity of the law and the procedures governing welfare provision, especially since the introduction of decentralization. Finally, the voluntary associations receive less financial support than in the past. All these factors lead to a desire for greater professionalism in order to respond more effectively to social needs and to qualify for financial support. But it also brings about a more distant relationship with clients – one based on a professional ethic rather than purely human contact.

Some associations, therefore, have found themselves involuntarily under the control of public bodies. Moreover, projects which do not correspond to the model pre-established by the state, in particular those which seek to rebuild social links in the longer term, receive little support. The future of such associations therefore poses the question: are we facing an increasing homogenization in the management of welfare?

Conclusion: A Hidden Complementarity

In accordance with the principle of *laïcité*, there is no official collaboration between church and state in Evreux; nonetheless, co-operation does in fact take place between Catholic associations and the various levels of the state. Whereas public bodies seek to respond to social problems by analysing the specific needs of the different categories of individuals (such as unemployed or elderly people) at whom welfare programmes are targeted, local religious initiatives build on their traditional approach of 'knowing the territory' – that is, by identifying problems which they try to address through local action, by dealing with communities as a whole, and by seeking to promote interaction between the various elements which make them up.

There is a certain complementarity in these two approaches to 'the new social reality', raising the question of whether they provide a kind of division of labour in dealing with social problems. This does not run counter to the historical logic of secularization, but invites us instead to find new approaches to the place of religious institutions in late modern societies. Looking beyond this complementarity, however, another question emerges: that of the durability of these approaches which have grown up in Catholic soil – a question which applies in fact to the whole range of welfare initiatives. Since it appears that projects which do not correspond to the model predetermined by the state receive little financial support, are we not witnessing a homogenization of the management of welfare leading both to greater uniformity and a growing remoteness in human relationships?

Following the outbreak of urban violence in France in the first two weeks of November 2005, the then prime minister, Dominique de Villepin, acknowledged that the cuts in subsidies to voluntary associations had been a mistake and promised to reverse them.[10] The French Bishops' Conference, meeting in a plenary assembly at Lourdes in November 2005, doubted whether repression was an answer to the 'dramatic tensions of our time' and insisted on the importance of 'all the work done on a day-to-day basis by very many associations and institutions in order to create bonds of solidarity to enable us to live together in brotherhood' (Ricard 2005). On this point, at least, church and state agree.

---

[10] 'Dominique de Villepin choisit l'état d'urgence', *Le Monde*, 9 November 2005, p. 10.

Chapter 9

What Kind of Church? What Kind of Welfare? Conflicting Views in the Italian Case

Annalisa Frisina

The Catholic Church is currently an important but controversial ingredient in the Italian 'welfare mix' (that is, the particular blend of state, market and third-sector providers). By means of the Vicenza case study in the Veneto region, I would like to demonstrate just how contentious the presence of the church really is.[1]

Representatives of public authorities and the local church generally encourage the dominance of the Caritas-Diaconia association (discussed in detail below), and value the public visibility of the Catholic Church as a welfare actor. Conversely, citizens' groups and representatives of private social organizations would prefer an increased secularization in Italian society – that is, a socio-cultural transformation in which the institutional and political roles of the Catholic Church are reduced. Interviewees from citizens' groups and lay organizations systematically refer to the Italian Constitution rather than to any religious imperative when discussing motivations for welfare and social commitment.

This study shows a plurality of perspectives, conceptions and practices of welfare within the Italian Catholic world. Importantly, the word 'church' is shown to mean different things to different interviewees: representatives of public authorities and the local church imply an 'official' or institutional church, while citizens' groups and representatives of lay social organizations refer to a 'lay church', a community of believers sharing the aspirations of civil society as a whole. As the lay church struggles for the democratization of welfare, it also seeks the democratization of the official church.

---

[1] The Vicenza case study is based on 18 individual interviews and four focus groups. The individuals interviewed are divided among the following groups: six representatives of the state welfare sector (three women and three men); six representatives of the local church (three women and three men); six representatives of the main lay social organizations in Vicenza (two women and four men); three discussion groups with participants drawn from the local population (Focus Group 1: four women and four men; Focus Group 2: five women and five men; Focus Group 3: four women and four men); and one women's discussion group on gender issues, composed of 12 social workers and one nun, who acted as the discussion group leader.

Surpassing or Reframing 'Charity': The Limits of the Italian Welfare System

As the early chapters in this volume have shown, the Italian welfare system is a conservative/corporatist or a social-capitalist regime (Esping-Andersen 1990, 1999; Sainsbury 1999). It is characterized by a passive or reactive model of social policy, which de-emphasizes direct state intervention and stresses the need to moderate the harmful outcomes of market forces. Its focus has traditionally been on cash transfers to support families, rather than on direct provision of services (Sainsbury 1999: 17). The Italian welfare state has been strongly characterized by the principle of social insurance, based on labour-market participation (Ferrera 1998). At national level, interventions against poverty depend on the contributory capacity of the beneficiary, thereby excluding many subjects who are faced with a difficult situation precisely because they do not participate in the labour market. Expenditure streams are therefore beneficial only for a minority of the neediest subjects (Benassi and Mingione 2003: 92).

Another significant element of this regime has been the commitment to the the traditional family. The strength of familism in Italy (and in other southern European countries) has led some scholars to distinguish it from other conservative regimes in continental Europe (Ferrera 1996; Bernardi 1999; Boeri and Perotto 2002). In a conservative/corporativist or social-capitalist regime, female employment is regarded as a private rather than a public matter (Sundström 2003: 40). However, social policy choices still influence working women. In order to see how, we need only mention the lack of public provision for infants and elderly people, conflicting school and work schedules, the fiscal system of direct family transfers (tax systems penalize double-income couples), and the juridical regulation of female work.

Notwithstanding the remarkable increase in female education and the fact that female work has become qualitatively similar to that of men, the differences in the rates of activity between married men and women are still substantial. The growth of 'atypical' work has increased female participation in the working world, but it has been suggested that these new forms of work should be seen simply as the legalization of former and still active habits of 'underground' work (Trifiletti 2003). As opposed to what has happened in northern Europe through part-time work, purported 'flexibility' in Italy is often synonymous with precariousness; it helps neither to reconcile work and family, nor to guarantee a sufficient level of social rights. Studies on time-management prove unambiguously that female participation in the labour market does not bring about an equal distribution of family work (Balbo 1991; Santi 2003). The 'double-presence' model (where women labour full-time in both paid and family work) is still the most widespread. Faced with a sharp trade-off between motherhood and work outside the house, Italian women often renounce having children at all, the result of which is the so-called 'low-fertility balance'. If women are forced to dedicate many hours to housework due to lack of alternatives, they necessarily have less to invest in their careers.

Nowadays, though, more and more women aspire to economic independence and stable participation in the working world. The trade-off which formerly forced them to stay at home now spurs them to have fewer children and to employ immigrant women for assistance with domestic labour. In fact, immigrant women are now the main providers of care for elderly people in Italy (Castagnaro 2002).

Table 9.1   The Main Characteristics of the Italian Welfare Regime

Role of:	
Family	Central
Market	Marginal
State	Subsidiary
Social unity of solidarity	Relatives
	Corporations
	State
Dominant place of solidarity	Family
De-commodification rate*	High (for the working breadwinner)

* De-commodification is the right to an income independent from market participation (Esping-Andersen 1999: 43); it is a way to specify the idea of rights relating to social citizenship, as suggested by T. H. Marshall.
Source: derived from Esping-Andersen (1999: 85).

There are huge regional variations between local labour markets and local policies, and resources vary in important aspects. Municipalities influenced or historically dominated by centre-right parties (as in Veneto, where Vicenza is located) emphasize the differences between gender roles, and see care primarily as a private responsibility and (hence) a female task (Bimbi 1995). Since the end of the 1990s the Veneto region has been oriented toward 'a rather radical *liberist*[2] logic in which market regulation sharply prevails over public intervention, at the expense of the universality of the rights of social citizenship, but also of the multiplication of social capital as a latent factor of competitiveness' (Messina 2001: 179). Messina also notes the huge presence of Catholic non-profit organizations, to which much regional social service provision is devolved, discrete from private and state services. This delegation to Catholic associations entails a more

---

[2]   Note that the implication here is of economic rather than political liberalism. The term 'liberism' is used because it more closely reflects the Italian term *liberismo*, referring specifically to economic liberalism.

traditional range of social services compared with the more innovative Emilia Romagna region, historically ruled by centre-left parties.

Most social services are publicly funded but performed by non-statutory organizations, and the welfare mix varies greatly between local areas. It is not only a matter of the dosage of the ingredients in the blend; quite apart from this, the third sector is a very heterogeneous field when it comes to the types of organizations, experiences and social actors therein (De Leonardis 2002).[3] The supply of services depends therefore on the relations between local policies and organizations, and on the traditional aims and specializations of these groups (Sundström 2003).

There are few quality and purpose controls for third-sector services. As shown by the case of religious institutions operating in the field of personal assistance, there is little awareness of the importance of continuously training workers to meet the demands of a task of such significance (De Sandre 2003). Another problem is that of co-ordination deficit, which can lead to expensive 'mistakes'; some interventions are duplicated while others are completely lacking (Mingione and Andreotti 2001). Moreover, the tradition of 'charity' provided by religious institutions preserves deep-seated features scarcely compatible with universalistic philosophies of care (Mingione 2000). The data emerging from a recent national survey on social care services linked to the Catholic Church are not reassuring: almost two-thirds are not in the local administration lists regarding the programming of such services. It is interesting to note, however, that 57 per cent of church-related services benefit from permanent public financing (Sarpellon 2002: 222).

Christian associationism is more active than ever, covering all sectors of society and giving birth to the 'basic welfare' which plays such an important role in the Italian welfare mix (Diamanti and Pace 1987). Another national survey reveals that social assistance services connected to the Catholic Church have increased from 4,089 in 1988 to 10,938 in 1999, with a yearly growth rate of over 15 per cent (Sarpellon 2002: 18). In the earlier surveys the most common service was the provision of housing for seniors, young people and disabled citizens, as well as domiciliary assistance. Nowadays the most common services (more than one-fifth of church-related services) deal with 'emergency help': advice bureaux and the distribution of primary goods.

How can the growing presence of the church in welfare be explained? First we must consider the increasingly marginal role of the public actor (to judge from the shrinking funding available – see Pizzuti 2005). According to some interviewees, as we will see, this trend is dangerous: it may cause a return to a time dominated by traditional paternalistic paradigms, dictating that those who

---

[3]   'Third sector' means all organizations which are neither profit-oriented companies nor public bureaucracies, thus including heterogeneous phenomena such as non-profit, volunteer and non-governmental organizations, self-help groups and foundations (De Leonardis 2002; see also Barbetta et al. 2003; Dalla Mura 2003).

have resources must provide for those who do not, in the philosophy of 'assistance to the poor'. Workers – it must be remembered – had to fight long battles to reach a paradigm of citizenship based on social policies, universally guaranteeing the right to 'minimum standards of life' and promoting solidarity among individuals who perceive themselves as interdependent. A return to old-fashioned 'charity approaches' would, therefore, signal an interruption of the movement towards modernity and democracy.

So which church actors are operating nowadays within the Italian welfare system? What are their beliefs regarding welfare, and how do they act locally? It is important to remember that the Italian Catholic world is not homogeneous, and that Italian Catholicism may resemble a 'giant with clay feet' (Garelli et al. 2003: 307).[4] According to official statistics, 90 per cent of Italian citizens belong to the Catholic Church, but this does not imply high levels of orthodoxy. For example, 45 per cent of Italians think that 'clergy celibacy should be abolished' (Garelli et al. 2003: 299); and more than half of the population holds that there is 'some truth in all religions, and that Catholicism is not the only true religion' (Cesareo et al. 1995). Moreover, in a recent survey Italians were questioned about the introduction of the law recognizing civil unions, after the model of the French civil pact: 71 per cent declared themselves favourable,[5] in spite of the official position of the Italian Council of Bishops (CEI), which repeatedly declared the law to be morally unacceptable.

There exists, therefore, a multiplicity of ways in which to 'be' Catholic in this country, but Italy continues nevertheless to represent itself as a religiously homogeneous society, so much so that certain scholars maintain that, for Italians, Catholicism has become a means to believe in their collective identity (Pace 1998).[6]

Catholic associationism is both complex and plural, tendencies which increased after the second Vatican Council, an event which brought to many the hope of a different model: that is, a church no longer based on hierarchy and obedience. Consider Don Milani's famous phrase 'obedience is no longer a virtue' which became a slogan in those years (Pace 1998: 133). This hope seems as yet unfulfilled. The pyramidal, top-down organization of the church still remains. Catholic-inspired social assistance services are tied to the church in complex ways which Sarpellon has classified as 'active co-presence, influence, support, control'. A connection to the church grants advantages in terms of resources (access to

---

[4]   Unlike in other traditionally Catholic countries, the presence of the clergy in the Italian territory is still significant. However, the progressive ageing of the clergy is accelerating and new generations are lacking.

[5]   See the Italia 2006 report by the Eurispes institute: www.eurispes.it

[6]   This collective identity is once again experiencing crisis (Pace 1998), and the Lega Nord dimension of this crisis is – amongst other things – creating new 'internal enemies' such as immigrants and Muslims (Saint-Blancat and Schmidt Di Friedberg 2002).

premises and financial resources), and a stronger presence in the territory. The current tendency, however, is toward lay enterprise motivated by religious values, with the church present more as inspiration than as institution (Sarpellon 2002).

The limits of Italian welfare are many, and nowadays the thorniest issues relate to federalism and the new 'devolution' law, recently approved by the centre-right majority. The future seems to harbinger more regionalism and lower levels of economic redistribution, as well as greater socio-economic variation. State control versus local autonomy affects the outcome of local social policies and the maintenance or alteration of gender relations. According to Ferrera and Sundström, in under-institutionalized Italy, strong social and economic groups employ the rhetoric of subsidiarity in order to preserve social diversity and patriarchy (Ferrera 1998; Sundström 2003). What will be the church's future position? In the referendum on assisted procreation (12–13 June 2005), the church fought actively to prevent a quorum being reached (as indeed happened). However, the agenda of the church as a public voice is uncertain. In many respects, traditionalism has prevailed. Nonetheless, after many years of silence the Italian feminist movement has re-emerged to defend law 194 on abortion, against attacks from the centre-right government and church hierarchies.[7] Other actors, themselves church members, criticize the official church 'from within'.

Let us now consider how welfare works in a local context where the church has historically played a key role, asking who the key actors are in the present situation.

The Predominant Role of Caritas-Diaconia in Vicenza

Vicenza is a town of 112,717 inhabitants (52.3 per cent women),[8] located in the Veneto region in north-east Italy, at the centre of a very successful model of economic activity. Vicenza has a 2.5 per cent unemployment rate, lower than the national average. This rich industrial area is mainly composed of small and medium enterprises, spread throughout the province, which export up to 80 per cent of their produce. Handicrafts and other small enterprises are characterized by a heavy dependence on family work, extremely flexible working hours, and low overall expenditure. For this reason, enterprise in Veneto is said to be 'a model, a social identity and not only a means of production' (Del Re 1999: 104).

Vicenza has always been a traditional Christian-Democrat bastion and, during the time of the fieldwork, was governed by a centre-right majority (Forza Italia,

---

[7]   See www.usciamodalsilenzio.org A demonstration was held in Milan on 14 January 2006, involving circa 200,000 men and women of all ages.

[8]   This figure was current as at 31 December 2003: www.comunevicenza.it/ente/statistica/vedivicenza.pdf

Alleanza Nazionale and Lega Nord).[9] According to Messina, in Veneto relationships with politics have always been instrumental: people expect politicians to defend the 'traditional order' and safeguard the local community's interests (Messina 2004: 31). Lega Nord (the Northern League) finds fertile soil here, having become the main expression of this 'anti-political territory'. In fact, territory and local realities become touchstones of identity which in turn become ideologies employed against the state. For these reasons, Diamanti argues, the Veneto region can be considered 'an economic giant and a political dwarf, since the rapid expansion and success of the industrial districts have not been accompanied by an equally effective political development on either the cultural or the institutional level, or indeed of that of the local political class' (Diamanti 2003: 33). Frequently, local authorities delegate social policies in particular to third-sector associations.

The Veneto region is historically characterized by a 'white political subculture' (Trigilia 1986), organized around the church and its related associations: Azione Cattolica, Coldiretti and the various Acli (Catholic Associations for Italian Workers) (Della Porta 1999). The importance of Catholic associationism goes well beyond matters of faith and religion. It includes contributions to the organization and orientation of social life, support for local interests, and the provision of socialization, social assistance and training.

The church's presence in Vicenza's welfare system engages a broad variety of actors: the many parishes, with their various charitable practices (difficult even for the diocesan administration to keep track of); religious institutions, operating mainly in the field of education; and finally the heterogeneous world of Catholic associations, in particular Caritas-Diaconia, currently the main church-related actor in Vicenza's welfare system. Each of these is outlined below.

Parishes

Vicenza's urban area comprises 36 generally wealthy parishes. Every parish runs a small welfare centre, proud of its own welfare activities (which vary greatly between parishes). As with many congregations in the United States, church-run welfare centres are a source of emergency food, clothing and shelter; educational and leisure activities; space for community meetings and cultural events; and willing volunteers (Ammerman 2000). Some parishes move their charitable practices elsewhere, for example financing hospitals and schools run by missionaries in Africa. Despite various attempts by the Bishop of Vicenza to give a centralized and coherent appearance to the diocese's social work, each parish, supported by its parishioners, tends to act independently – both financially and in terms of areas of social intervention. An exaggerated local pride often clashes with the impossibility

---

9   In the elections of 25 May 2003, the centre-right obtained 53.8 per cent of the vote, while in the elections of 28 April 2008 the centre-left won with 50.5 per cent of the vote. This success was linked to the protest against the building of a new US military base in the town.

of managing numerous or complex cases. In this case, the parish helps spread awareness to other local welfare agents, predominantly the local Caritas-Diaconia association (see below).

Religious Organizations

The main religious institutions in Vicenza are the Ursuline Nuns of the Sacred Heart, with their mother-house in Vicenza; the Pious Society of St Gaetano (a male religious order); and the teaching Nuns of St Dorotea (a female religious order). These and many other organizations are involved primarily in education, operating mostly nursery schools. They are often very expensive and therefore considered schools for the wealthy. There are also organizations of nuns running retirement homes (namely the Nuns of Child Mary and the Nuns of Poor Women). Finally, it is important to mention the 'basic welfare' services provided by Franciscan friars and by the volunteers of St Vincent, who offer hot meals to those at the margins of society.

Caritas-Diaconia

Diaconia is an association under the same authority as Caritas, and the two are therefore effectively part of a single organization. According to the directives of the Italian Council of Bishops (CEI), Caritas should not be an agent that directly provides welfare services. As a result, Diaconia was created on the local level, allowing it to receive generous funding from both state and private sources.

Caritas-Diaconia defines itself as 'a pastoral organization of social activity at the service of Christian communities. The goal of its existence is to promote solidarity towards people who are suffering from poverty and marginalization.' Caritas exists principally because of the voluntary membership of people whose intention it is to carry out social work benefitting those who are 'less fortunate'. Caritas-Diaconia is the actor with the most visibility in the public domain, and legitimacy in the eyes of local authorities and powerful actors such as bank foundations. Caritas-Diaconia is the predominant player in debates and practices of social welfare in the Vicenza territory.

The ambits in which Caritas-Diaconia operates are heterogenous and complex. It runs the main sleeping shelter in town; manages a social and working rehabilitation project for (ex-) inmates; offers 'anti-usury' legal counselling; organizes self-help groups among people with psychological problems; provides training and volunteer work for young people, both on a local and international level; provides counselling for adolescents; provides information and guidance for foreign victims of prostitution, and for other women with serious problems, especially those caring for children; runs projects of social reinsertion for homeless people; collects funds for gypsy children to facilitate their schooling; helps families who require domestic assistance by putting them in contact with immigrant workers;

and accompanies foreign citizens with addictions or psychological problems as they are sent back to their home countries.

It is clear that Caritas-Diaconia often operates in areas where state intervention does not reach. Why does the state not reach these areas? The most common answer (given by Caritas and by public authorities) is that religious actors are 'on the frontline' and can discover new needs and report them to the state sector, which will then take care of them. Direct management of social services by religious actors is therefore temporary and ostensibly bound to emergency situations. In the case of a town shelter that stays open during the winter months, however, the 'emergency' aspect is questionable: this shelter has now been in existence for almost eight years, staffed by Caritas volunteers. The state actor, the Local Social and Health Unit (USSL 6) provides only the sheets and pillows! Clearly the state is asking religious actors, if only implicitly, to care for segments of society which, because of certain political choices, are not part of its political agenda, such as immigrants.

As we will see, there are many other Catholics engaged in social work within lay associations (like social co-operatives), who are very critical of the excessive presence of Caritas-Diaconia. There are, in fact, conflicting points of view regarding the kind of presence the church should or should not have in welfare.

Polarized Views: Public Authorities and Church Representatives versus Lay Organizations and Local Population Groups

Representatives of public authorities and local church representatives generally encourage the presence of the Caritas-Diaconia association, and value the public visibility of the Catholic Church as a welfare actor.

Individuals working in social care for the Social Services of the Vicenza Commune, the Institution for Public Assistance and Charity (IPAB),[10] and the Local Social and Health Unit 6, believe that the mix of public and private social services works properly in Vicenza. In their opinion, it is not necessary for the public authorities to direct and control the good functioning of welfare. The fundamental thing for them is mutual trust, and in the case of Caritas-Diaconia they feel certain that shared values exist as a foundation for social work. Public authorities and church representatives are often very closely connected: a former president of Caritas-Diaconia, for instance, is now in charge of a local health authority. These tight bonds facilitate a shared vision of welfare and favour trust-based relationships, which in some cases seem to lead to a 'blind faith' in Caritas-Diaconia: 'You can always trust Caritas, it is very easy to manage projects together' (m, public representative). According to the public authorities, social

---

[10]   IPAB is one of the largest public organizations active in providing assistance to elderly people, and is endowed with considerable assets – including funds, art and real estate – inherited from local benefactors.

work provided by the church is indispensable because of its social capital (above all, its many volunteers); its economic capital (for example, the facilities it owns, which can be employed for the good of the community); and its cultural capital (the values that can motivate social commitment and engagement).

Representatives of the Diocese, of Caritas-Diaconia and of local religious institutions, also value the presence of officially church-related actors in welfare and think that the 'public' nature of their work is unproblematic. Over the last decade the church has become increasingly involved in social service provision. This new predominance of the church is thought necessary by religious actors because of the current political and economic context, and is considered proof of the strength of the evangelical message:

> Due to the economic crisis of north-eastern Italy linked to the relocation of enterprises, and also due to the lack of new social policies, the poor are becoming poorer, the middle class is disappearing. The wealthy remain rich and if they feel like it they do some charity work … For us who believe in a Christian message it is important to share resources, to create synergies, to promote solidarity rather than charity. (f, church representative)

The growth of Caritas-Diaconia, and the fact that it operates in diverse fields, is seen positively: this association is considered able not only to act but also to 'bear witness', that is to carry out cultural and 'human' promotion along with its social work, 'relating more than … performing' (m, church representative).

Church representatives believe church-related social services have added value offered by their spirituality: in their opinion, practising Catholics who do social work are likely to make the services offered more humane than those provided by state actors:

> We have a vast demand for our services because here it is not like a public office, it is not cold … They ask us for something more humane, they come in need of a saviour and we help them. Compared to public service, here we have a different fund of human experiences and a different motivation. (f, church representative)

However, among church representatives there are also the critical voices of Ursuline Nuns who think church actors should call the state back to its duty to work for the common good:

> As religious congregations we were born between 1800 and 1900 in response to the primary needs of people, and hence with a series of primarily social activities … There is a demand to provide once again certain social services formerly offered by the church as charity. Thus they will no longer be granted as citizenship rights. This is a huge problem; it is like losing some hard-won conquests of civilization. Over the last ten years, the region, provinces, communes and bank

foundations have been willing to give more and more funding to religious organizations simply because it is convenient for them ... Most of those who work in this sector are not aware of certain ongoing dynamics and, above all, of their consequences in the long term. (f, church representative)

This point of view upsets most public authorities and church representatives interviewed, but it is welcomed among the other important actors in Vicenza's welfare system, such as the lay social organizations (social co-operatives, for instance).

The latter express strong criticism against local welfare, mostly regarding the weak role of the state sector, the patronage system and the private interests which waste resources and cause inequalities. The growing role of bank foundations is also seen as problematic, because bank foundations rarely distribute funding in a public and universal manner:

Some of the procedures to obtain funding are official, as happens when applying for funds from the Province or the Region. But on the private level, as with bank foundations, it is those who can speak louder who decide where the annual funding will go, those who manage to have a person in the council. And so it happens that public bodies or the diocese get most of the funds, and whatever is left goes to everybody else. (m, representative of a lay social organization)

Here is one reason that Caritas-Diaconia's social work is considered problematic by representatives of lay social organizations – it monopolizes the little funding available and does not work according to a 'public and democratic' logic:

At the present time in many local contexts Caritas is an organization like many other co-operatives and associations, but it is stronger and at times even competitive ... Then there is a risk that because of scarce funding these dynamics will take over everything and there will be no room for critical reflection. (m, representative of a lay social organization)

Behind this critical attitude rests the fact that the state seems more 'lenient' with church-related actors; democratic parameters (like transparency of balance sheets and controls on the level of professionalism of personnel) seem not to apply. A return to the past is feared, since it was only thanks to public intervention that, to give but one example, retirement homes run by religious entities were forced to meet minimum legal standards. Yet some church-related actors still find it difficult to adopt a truly democratic perspective – and instead invoke 'Christian love' to legitimate their social work. This position is strongly criticized by the representatives of lay social organizations:

Professionalism is needed, love is not enough. But love is for free, and so it is convenient for public authorities to exploit this situation using volunteers even if they end up doing damage ... Some Christian associations ... abuse the word 'love' in all possible ways. They tell the state sector that they need money, but then they refuse to discuss the way they manage it. We [social co-operatives], believe instead that the task of the state sector is always to plan, co-ordinate and control. Church-related organizations have to accept this too, if they intend to be a public service, that is to say 'for everybody'. For example, we do not choose who we want to help ... There are those who say that they do social work for the love of Jesus. No, I do it because the person in front of me has rights! ... For a serious evaluation of social interventions, matters of faith must not be considered, we must face our commitments to real actual people.' (m, representative of a lay social organization)

Many workers involved in the social co-operatives of Vicenza are Catholics, but choose a secular approach, as they base their work on constitutional principles, appealing for instance to Article 3 of the Constitution, which states that it is a duty of the Republic to remove economic and social obstacles which hinder the full development of the person.[11]

As opposed to representatives from public authorities and local church representatives, these workers clearly show a different perception and awareness regarding the visibility and commitment of Christians. No need is felt to publicize or 'wave the flag' of the Christian inspiration of their social work: 'The gospel tells me to blend with the people, to disappear like the leaven to bring growth to the common good, because I care about human beings, about persons' (m, representative of a lay social organization). These critical Catholics think the church should promote a new civic sense and develop new, broader forms of solidarity. In particular, they stigmatize the use of religious difference to create social exclusion, as in the case of Lega Nord, which appeals to the 'Christian roots of the people of Veneto' in order to deny immigrants access to citizenship rights.

In discussion groups with participants from the local population, we found views on welfare and church that were similar to those of the representatives of lay social organizations. Most participants believe that a more active state sector is necessary in order to guarantee transparency in the allocation of funds, to make interventions really effective, and to grant social rights to everybody. Despite stressing the importance of actively involving citizens in the process of defining and satisfying needs, they are critical regarding what local politicians say about civil society:

---

[11]	Article 3 states, 'All citizens have equal social dignity and are equal before the law, without distinction of sex, race, language, religion, political opinions, personal and social conditions. It is the duty of the Republic to remove those obstacles of an economic and social nature which, really limiting the freedom and equality of citizens, impede the full development of the human person and the effective participation of all workers in the political, economic and social organization of the country.'

> They count too much on voluntary work … I witnessed the opening of a centre
> for the disabled, created entirely thanks to the efforts of families and volunteers
> … And there was also the inevitable politician who had the nerve to declare: 'I
> am proud of our people who have the strength to manage on their own!' What
> a cheek … Of course, well done Veneto people, well done citizens of Vicenza!
> And so they [local authorities] don't spend a single euro. (Focus group 1)

That said, local population representatives think that the church can contribute to
the well-being of citizens but that it should not 'bully' other groups.

In particular, young people believe that in some areas the church is the only
available alternative to paid facilities, such as for sports: 'So you go to the parish
centre to play soccer … But if you want to organize a cultural event, to whom do
you turn? I have the impression that politicians in Vicenza, no matter who they
side with, are not interested in young people' (Focus group 3). Indeed the focus
group with young people proved particularly interesting as it allowed generational
specificities to come to the fore. For example, beliefs about cultural policies and
the importance of social aggregation (not only of the young); the conviction that
it is necessary to conceive welfare anew in light of cultural changes resulting
from immigration; and the hope that it will be 'progressive Catholics' and the 'lay
church' who will play the main role in the future of Italian welfare.

Young students repeatedly stressed that welfare does not only concern 'social
activities for the needy', but also 'cultural activities which can improve the quality
of life in the urban fabric'. Only young people clearly expressed the opinion
that welfare involves developing the territory culturally as well as economically.
For young people, welfare is also important for social cohesion and peaceful
co-existence.

Finally young people believe that Catholic-inspired organizations active in the
social sector must change radically if they intend to provide a public service in an
increasingly multicultural society:

> Catholic groups, especially if they are traditionalist, receive more funding … If
> only parishes organize recreational hours, what will children of different religions
> do? … There are groups, those we have defined as progressive Catholics, who
> do not parade religious symbols and so they do not offend believers of other
> faiths or atheists … Sometimes a good deed that is done in a certain manner can
> have the opposite effect, it can be offensive. (Focus group 3)

It follows that progressive Catholics who 'do not turn religion into a façade', who
live by their faith but 'do not parade it' (Focus group 3) must play a leading role
in Vicenza's welfare in the future. From this discussion group emerges also a need
for a democratization of Catholic-inspired organizations – which seems above all
to be a generational concern:

> In my opinion church-related social organizations are mostly conservative, because they plan interventions from the top, they do what *they* think is right, they do not listen to the real needs of those who receive their help ... But there are young people like me, and younger organizations, who pay attention to these aspects. (Focus group 3)

This democratic challenge does not only involve the internal functioning of church-related social organizations, but is addressed to the institution of the Catholic Church itself.

An interesting contrast is beginning to emerge. Clearly questions on church and welfare took on different meanings for the two groups of actors: public authorities and church representatives refer to an official or institutional church; lay organizations and local population groups refer instead to a lay church or community of believers. This study, then, shows a plurality of conceptions and practices of welfare within the Italian Catholic world. In the next section the main trends discerned from the data will be analysed in a sociological, theological and gender perspective.

What Kind of Church? What Kind of Welfare?

All four types of social actors (public authorities, church representatives, lay social organizations and the local population) agree that the church plays a significant role in Vicenza's welfare system. All, too, link the growing predominance of the church during the last decade to state withdrawal from the field. However, while the public authorities and the local church representatives interviewed generally view church-related practical social work positively, representatives of lay social organizations and citizens' groups are more critical. They believe Caritas-Diaconia should improve its transparency and professionalism, and become more 'democratic', shifting from a model where decisions are taken top-down to a participatory model, which can co-operate better with other social actors involved in Vicenza's welfare system. They state specifically that 'the church' is much more than Caritas-Diaconia, as it includes a diverse community of believers who commit themselves to social work without publicizing their actions under the banner of institutional Catholicism.[12] Lay social organizations and citizens' groups wish for

---

[12]   It could appear contradictory that these actors affirm transparency as necessary to democracy, yet ask for the invisibility of church actors engaged in social work. From their perspective, however, these are separate issues. Transparency, in their opinion, is related to the good functioning of organizations which must be accountable for their actions (their use of funding, for example), and one of its major aims is to fight corruption. Invisibility, on the contrary, concerns the personal motivations and level of professionalism of individuals, who may be involved in social work for religious or secular reasons. In both cases, the actors cited are worried about the universality of social rights, and reject the patronage system. This

official church-related actors to be less involved in social work, and would prefer that they promote more public debate on such crucial issues as respect for legality, or solidarity among 'strangers' (Habermas 1997) – that is, citizens belonging to different cultures and faiths. A desire is clearly emerging for Italian society to become more secular, and for welfare to be more widely managed by lay actors, such as social co-operatives.

The table below sets out a schematic summary of the main points of view of the various actors, taking into consideration the following parameters: the type of 'church' commitment to social work ('official' or institutional church versus a 'lay church' or community of believers); whether tasks are prioritized by the church according to importance or need (practical social work versus cultural involvement or public voice); and the degree of public visibility that should be granted to church-related social work (publicity versus invisibility). What emerges is a polarity between two positions: public authorities and local church representatives, on the one side, and citizens' groups and representatives of lay social organizations on the other.

Table 9.2   Schematic Summary of the Main Points of View of the Various Actors in Vicenza

	Types of actors			
	Public authorities	*Local church*	*Lay social organizations*	*Citizens' groups*
Church commitment	official/ institutional church	official/ institutional church	lay church/ community of believers	lay church/ community of believers
Primary task	practical social work	practical social work	cultural involvement/ public voice	cultural involvement/ public voice
Visibility	publicity	publicity	invisibility	invisibility

There are, of course, conflicting opinions within each type. For example, among religious actors some believe that at the present time, the primary task of the church should be more cultural in nature, as in the case of the Ursuline Nuns. Others think that cultural and social work should proceed side by side. Nevertheless, the diagram indicates the most commonly shared points of view within each group of interviewees.

does not necessarily imply that religion must be restricted to private space: the interviewees admit that many social workers in the Italian welfare system are inspired or motivated by religion. However, they believe that religious identification cannot legitimate privilege and should not excuse exclusion in a society with growing cultural and religious diversity.

Theories concerning secularization are a primary issue in the social scientific study of religion. Certain scholars suggest shifting from a macro approach, within which secularization is a long process involving the whole modern history of western society, to a micro perspective, in which 'secularization is a property of action' (Turina 2005: 2). From this point of view, it is possible to observe empirically whether a domain of activity is likely to be 'secularized' or not, depending on whether the actor in question is concerned with the notion of God's will. What emerges from this research, then, is that social work carried out by Italian Catholics may or may not be *deemed* 'secularized', depending on who is being asked.

As we have seen, lay social organizations and the local population often refer to articles of the Italian constitution, rather than to the Gospel, when discussing welfare and motivations for social commitment. According to these interviewees, being a good Christian means being a good citizen. For this reason they expect the church to nurture the civic conscience of Italians, particularly regarding legality, as a founding principle of public welfare. Some stress that socially-involved Catholics cannot limit themselves to managing services; they must also contribute – along with other third-sector actors – to a political project, aimed at transforming society in order to achieve equality. Respondents therefore believe that social work carried out by Catholics should not be publicized as such, but practised within a shared democratic perspective with other socially-committed citizens. Finally, citizens' groups and other social organizations expect the official church to provide more of a cultural contribution, to promote a new solidarity among Italians. The current point in history is deemed particularly difficult in light of the unlimited individualism and growing inequalities created by the 'neo-liberist' model of development.

This kind of criticism against the Catholic Church 'from within' brings to the surface certain ongoing social transformations and poses serious issues on both cultural and theological planes: above all, what is the relationship between church and democracy in Italy today?

On the basis of the research data, I offer the experience of a worker-priest in order to stimulate further reflection. Having borne witness to the word of God in factories, this individual feels currently the need to testify to the values of democracy within the church as an institution:

> We, as worker-priests in Veneto, have painfully understood that we have nothing to bring to the table in a world torn by social conflict where trade unions are far ahead of the church regarding people's rights. We returned to the church with the conviction that our frontier lies here: bringing into the womb of the church what we have learned from democracy, from the joys and sorrows in the everyday life of people ... We have rediscovered the whole of mystical literature, which finds no boundaries in institutional religions, and then we have learned how to work, and much more, for example how to manage conflict ... We worker-priests

> suggest a lighter kind of mediation, a democratization of the church … But the
> church as an institution is still enormously heavy. (m, lay social organization)

This priest believes that it is necessary to make the Catholic Church more democratic from within. At a certain point in his life, he says, he felt the need to live his faith in a different way, giving up 'talking about God' and instead working side by side with those who try daily to create a fairer world. He believes his relationship with God is now more direct; he experiences spirituality more freely and finds inspiration for his social work in the writings of Christian mystics related to Protestantism. He would like the official church to acknowledge this 'other way of being Catholic'.

His story is only one case, but it clearly shows the individualization of faith in contemporary Italy. Moreover, it would be interesting to examine to what degree this reflects the development of the Italian worker-priests movement more broadly: have they returned to working within the official church, or are they still committed and involved in social work? This issue remains an unexplored research field. Whatever the case, this religious diversity requires a different model of social work: it is no coincidence that the worker-priest chose to work in a social co-operative, where decisions are made in a more participatory manner. Conversely, social actors related to the church as an institution carry out social work within more traditional and hierarchical structures, as in the case of Caritas-Diaconia. In response to a question about how the organization worked internally (for example, the nature of the decision-making process), the head of the legal department of Caritas-Diaconia responded as follows: the charismatic leader or Director 'is more or less in charge of everything, because he has prophetic abilities' (f, church representative).

The demand for the democratization of the church is closely related to another important issue, that of the relationship between Catholicism and feminism in Italy today. Our study has indicated that in Vicenza some believers are reinterpreting the history of the church from women's perspectives.[13] A typical example is the case of an Ursuline Nun who created a centre for gender studies within her religious institution and published a series of books on 'a Christian feminist from Vicenza', in order to increase her visibility and to start a debate on the role of women within the church.[14] This very enterprising nun has also created a working group of women who operate within lay social organizations, and want to reflect from a feminist perspective. They organize cultural events open to all citizens.[15]

---

[13] For an overview on a national level, see www.teologhe.org

[14] See *Il femminismo cristiano di Elisa Salerno e le sue prospettive* (1989).

[15] I decided to utilize this pre-existing group as a fourth Focus Group, composed of 12 social workers (employed in third-sector associations and social co-operatives) and one nun who acted as the discussion group leader. In this context more than in any other, it was possible for me to reflect on the relationships existing between welfare, religion and gender.

This women's group has brought to the surface some critical reflections regarding the potentially negative consequences of practical social work carried out by the church. According to these women, official church-related organizations simply try to fill in the gaps in the Italian welfare system, thus perpetuating a structure which is unfair towards women. In their opinion, the traditional idea of family (a male bread-winner and a female wife-mother) has to be questioned: the pluralization of family forms in Italian society demands changes in the welfare system (Saraceno 2003). By continuing to take for granted the traditional family model, other family models are excluded, including, for example, single-parent families, so that some lone mothers are reduced to poverty.

The women's group is particularly critical of the treatment of foreign carers:

> We discuss together family models and the people who will provide social care. How much is shared between men and women? Why do women have to bear the entire burden alone? Is it right to dump it on another [foreign] woman? This other woman also has a family … It is a chain reaction … Our current model [of welfare] is contributing to the disruption of the family structures of other countries, eastern Europe, for example, where women leave their children and their elderly to take care of ours. (Ursuline Nun)

Adopting this 'global perspective' (Ehrenreich and Hochschild 2004), women from the discussion group wish once again to question traditional gender patterns. This reflection stimulates a sense of social responsibility and solidarity that stretches beyond national borders. According to participants in the group, the emancipation of Italian women must not be achieved at the expense of women from other countries: for this reason, too, it is necessary to change the way in which the Italian welfare system functions.

If welfare should redistribute not only goods, but also power (De Leonardis 2002), what changes are necessary in order for women to become effective citizens? The concept of subsidiarity is questioned, namely the idea that each and every individual should be in charge of his or her own social responsibilities and that the state should, therefore, intervene only when strictly necessary. This often means that families are encouraged to manage on their own, even when they are not in a position to do so. The representatives of the female lay associations involved in local welfare believe that in Italy attributing responsibility to families amounts to putting the burden of social care on women, saying '[L]et us not forget that within families there are women, and that these cuts in social funding bear primarily upon women. People are not sufficiently aware of this' (Focus group 4).

Funding is another crucial issue: Italian social funding is among the most limited in Europe, especially regarding family and small children, unemployment and housing (Pizzuti 2005; 2006; 2007). In Vicenza, as elsewhere in Italy, bank foundations are becoming more and more important for the funding of welfare. Some interviewees reveal a growing concern that these new actors may not share their vision of citizenship as a political process of individual and collective social transformation. Quite apart from this, the welfare-mix in the Vicenza territory is both complex and 'porous', in the sense that public and private are so tightly intertwined that the same persons can find themselves playing roles that would normally lead to a conflict of interest (this can be seen in a number of biographical profiles). This is not necessarily a problem specific to Vicenza.[16] It is however a sign that a common Catholic cultural background is still operative. It is one reason, moreover, why some church-related actors continue to employ a paternalistic approach in social work, based more on good intentions than on professionalism, reproducing thereby both private interests and patriarchal attitudes.

All respondents, including church-related actors, criticize 'charity-approaches' which in the end prove humiliating, and claim that the manner in which social services are provided is as important as the social help itself. What types of social assistance, then, are more 'respectful'? If the aim is to create a welfare system where there is room for dignity, where people can feel they are all equal and experience their dependence on social welfare as a temporary phase of their lives and not as their destiny, Sennett (2004) argues that new social practices are necessary. These practices must not deal with needs, deficiencies or inadequacies, but must make use instead of individual capabilities (Nussbaum 2003). Promoting the participation of all male and female citizens therefore remains one of the main challenges for the welfare system. In Vicenza, and throughout Italy, citizens' groups are requesting involvement at a local level in setting the expenses of the public administration. Some communes have gone as far as introducing participative mechanisms to discuss certain balance sheet items with its citizens.[17] However, recent government manoeuvres have brought severe cuts in social funding, so much so that there may be little money left to fight over.

This study has revealed elements of the church engaged in 'pioneering' work, who have a critical stance towards the neo-liberist model of development, seeing it as a structural cause of inequalities. For this reason, it is not sufficient that the church simply 'fills in the gaps' in the welfare system, but that it be involved in social criticism in order to promote change. This 'lay church' shares the aspirations of civil society (Kaldor 2004) and, as it struggles for the democratization of welfare, seeks at the same time the democratization of the official church. A good example is the case of nuns who have started a process of 'criticism from within'

---

[16] The culture of legality is still weak across Italian society (Sciolla 2004), and the current government does not appear to encourage it; one example is the repeated official pardons granted for violations of local building regulations.

[17] See the website of the New Municipality Network, www.nuovomunicipio.org Moreover, after recent and conspicuous cuts in social funding, several national social sector associations have organized a counter-information campaign to force the government to use state funding 'for safeguarding rights, for peace and for the environment' (www.sbilanciamoci.org). However, this initiative has received no visibility in the mainstream national newspapers or on television.

from the point of view of gender, asking whether the church really does wish to be 'prophetic', or whether it will choose to remain conservative.[18]

---

[18]   The polarization present in Italian society is not a unique case. For instance, Radford Ruether notes that American Catholicism, too, entered the 1990s 'divided between movements of searching self-criticism calling for change and a hierarchy unable to accept the possibility of significant error, particularly on matters related to women, sexuality and centralized power. The conflict between a creative Catholic feminism and deep hostility to women's independence is a central expression of its polarization' (Radford Ruether 1995: 31).

Chapter 10

The Disgraceful and the Divine in Greek Welfare: The Cases of Thiva and Livadeia

Effie Fokas and Lina Molokotos-Liederman

A consideration of church welfare provision in the two Greek towns of Thiva and Livadeia reveals a kaleidoscope of practices and perspectives ranging from the 'disgraceful' to the 'divine'. For some inhabitants of these towns, it truly is disgraceful how little the church offers in terms of welfare services, compared with its assumed vast means; for others, church welfare activity in these towns is considered a true reflection of God's divine providence for his people. Understanding this complex and divergent picture requires insight into several factors: the wider context in which church welfare activity takes place, including the relationship of the Greek Orthodox Church to the Greek state; Orthodox theology and historical tradition in welfare provision; the nature of the Greek welfare system in general and, more importantly, its significant gaps. In the following paragraphs, we will offer a schematic overview of these three areas before turning our attention to the details of church welfare provision in Thiva and Livadeia and to the results of the research conducted there.

The 'Big Picture'

The divergence in perspectives on church welfare provision in Thiva and Livadeia stems very largely from the place of the church in general in relation to the Greek state, which may in some ways be described as a 'love–hate' relationship of both mutual support and unconstructive competition. The Orthodox faith is, according to the Greek constitution, the 'prevailing' religion of Greece, as represented in the country by the Autocephalous Church of Greece. The Autocephalous Church was established soon after the founding of the modern Greek state following liberation from Ottoman rule. This rendered it a symbol of national identity and Greek independence – both from the Muslim Ottoman Empire and from the Ecumenical Patriarchate, which remained under Ottoman rule in Constantinople. The 'prevailing' clause in the Greek constitution is accompanied by a number of privileges for the Orthodox Church in Greece, including the fact that the church is a public legal entity, enjoying not only tax exemption but also the payment of salaries for all clergy. These benefits, together with the financial strength the church enjoys, not least through mass land ownership (carried over from Ottoman times, when vast amounts of land were donated to the church by Orthodox subjects in order to protect the land from Ottoman confiscation), give the impression of a very well-endowed church. Meanwhile, the close links between church and state – making the church seem, to many, to be a fundamental component of state apparatus – lead to the conception held by many that the church bears joint responsibility, with the state, for welfare provision.

A sense of church responsibility for welfare also stems – as in other European contexts – from the theological position of the church on welfare, and the church's historical role in welfare provision. Much of the Orthodox theological teaching related to welfare is drawn from the sermons and writings of the 'Three Hierarchs': Basil the Great (c.330–379), Gregory the Theologian (329–390), and John Chrysostom (352–407). These texts form the theological underpinnings of what is considered the most vibrant period in church welfare activity – the Byzantine Era. The stark contrast between a church extremely active in welfare provision during Byzantine times and a much less visible role of Orthodox churches today is often explained with reference to the 'captivity' of the church during the Ottoman period.[1] That said, the church's substantial, if less visible role in welfare provision continued with the establishment of the modern Greek state. The church found itself in a particularly strong position in terms of land ownership: church lands were used for orphanages, hospitals and schools.[2] During World War 2, church welfare took an institutional form in the establishment of the National Organization of Christian Aid (EOXA).

Currently, the church at the national level oversees a moderately decentralized structure of welfare provision. Most church welfare activity is administered in the individual dioceses (the church is divided into eighty dioceses, or 'metropolises'), which watch over the activities of the individual parishes and monasteries. A non-governmental organization, Solidarity, is based in the Archbishopric of Athens. At a national level, the Synodal Committee for Social and Welfare Benefits deals mainly with research on social problems. Practical welfare activities based at national church level are twofold: emergency aid offered after crises such as earthquakes, floods and other natural disasters; and a cash benefit offered to Christian families in Thrace if they have more than two children.[3] Given the paucity of national-level church welfare activity related to the local level, it is fitting for the Greek case that our examination of religion and welfare took place at the local level.

A final part of the 'big picture' that needs to be borne in mind is the state of welfare provision more generally in Greece. The Greek welfare system can

---

[1]   On the changes in Orthodox welfare between the Byzantine Era and the experience of Orthodoxy under the Ottoman Empire, see Constantelos (2003).

[2]   For a discussion of the impact of church land ownership on later welfare endeavours of the church in relation to the state, see Diellas (2003).

[3]   This is considered a highly controversial measure, because of its perceived aim to bolster the Greek Orthodox community over and against the Muslim community based in Thrace.

be described as something of a late developer. It was strongly influenced by the welfare conceptions that prevailed at the time of the establishment of the modern Greek state in the nineteenth century. These included conservative ideas of social control, whereby the church represented the model of philanthropy and, together with the family, formed the social network which tended to welfare needs (Arapoglou 2004). The formalization of state welfare provision began with the establishment of the Ministry of Care in 1918 and the first social security scheme in 1934. However, the heightened welfare needs created during World War 1, the Asia Minor catastrophe and population exchange (1920s), World War 2, and the Greek civil war (1946–49) far surpassed state welfare provision capabilities. During the 1967–74 military dictatorship, no major developments in state welfare services took place. Accordingly, when speaking of a fully-fledged welfare system, we are more or less focusing on the post-1974 period, when welfare responsibilities of the state were embedded in the 1975 Constitution. Even so, in the years following the 1974 restoration to democracy, state welfare concerns were overshadowed by the aim to accede to the European Community. Once this had been achieved in 1981, a socialist party, the Panhellenic Socialist Movement (PASOK) came to power and introduced a wide range of extensions and reforms to the welfare system. Since then, party politics and occasionally EU pressure have influenced what has been a very turbulent path in welfare policy reform.

Today, the Greek welfare system is characterized by fragmentation and clientelism in the funding and delivery of social protection, resulting in large-scale inequities. Cash benefits predominate over other kinds of service transfers, and pensions form the majority of cash transfers. In very general terms we can say that the Greek system is based on a public–private mix, but the relationship between the roles of the public sector, private companies, non-governmental organizations and the family varies significantly across the spectrum of welfare services. The public medical system yields increasingly to private care schemes, and generally the system continues to rely on the family in nearly all aspects of welfare provision.

One of the largest problems facing the welfare system today is inadequate pensions. In Greece, as in all of Europe, the pension problem is exacerbated by related factors: an ageing population; low birth rates and hence fewer contributions to pension funds by the working population; the increased activity of women in the work force; and a new gap in care for elderly people resulting from women's increasing employment. (It must be noted, however, that Greece still lags behind other European countries in terms of female employment: 46.1 per cent compared to an EU25 average of 56.3 per cent.) Social security as a whole is considered a central challenge facing Greek society. Difficulties in introducing and implementing pension reforms are indicative of the stalemate often reached in general welfare reform efforts. Overall, the welfare system is plagued by a number of inherent contradictions, so that reform in one particular direction is often unconstructive. The system therefore suffers from gridlock, as reforms are always heavily contested in public debate – due not least to the many incompatible claims of various groups. Given the urgency for reform in the system as a whole, policies calling for gender equality slip down the priority list (as do those demanding the integration of immigrants and refugees into the welfare system).

Narrowing the Scope: The Welfare Scene in Thiva and Livadeia

Thiva and Livadeia lie 85 km and 135 km respectively north-west of Athens, and are the two largest towns in the prefecture of Viotia.[4] Their primary sources of income are agriculture and industry. The towns' main social problems stem from unemployment (mainly following factory closures in the 1990s); financial concerns specific to the agricultural sector (including changes to subsidies and poor weather conditions); integration, employment, and the social inclusion of immigrants; family-related problems (especially care for children and elderly people); and drug abuse. As such, Thiva and Livadeia are broadly representative of the major social problems present elsewhere in Greece.

The local public welfare services are similar to those in place throughout Greece: limited. The bulk of welfare services are based in the Welfare Office of the Prefecture,[5] which deals mainly with the provision of benefits to people with disabilities and the uninsured, and one-off allowances for emergency situations such as natural disasters. The municipalities themselves do not have dedicated welfare offices; rather, welfare activity is carried out only on an *ad hoc* and short-term basis, mainly through the Municipal Enterprise within each municipality (many short-term EU social programmes, in particular, are based at Municipal Enterprises).[6]

Unlike the state welfare system, the church welfare structure is relatively decentralized. Much of the church's social work is based in its various dioceses, the bishops developing their own welfare structures. The diocese we have chosen to study – the headquarters of which are based in Livadeia – is among the more active when it comes to welfare provision. A general observer of the church's welfare activity in these towns will notice a range of activities. The church runs two homes for elderly people (made particularly conspicuous by the absence of state-run homes for the elderly in these towns), and a centre for the housing and care of people with special needs or chronic illnesses. It also runs a large soup kitchen (*sisitio*), and an international conference centre – which, in addition to hosting conferences, also provides housing for visiting scholars and students,

---

[4]   The population of Thiva is approximately 23,000 and that of Livadeia 20,000. Prefectures are regional divisions introduced by the Greek state: there are 51 prefectures in Greece.

[5]   The Viotia Prefecture Welfare Office is based in Livadeia.

[6]   The municipal enterprise in Thiva is entitled the Municipal Enterprise of Cultural and Urban Development of Thiva (DEPOATH), and that in Livadeia, the Municipal Enterprise of Culture and Development of Livadeia (DEPAL).

and camps for Orthodox young people. Another noticeable, though not strictly church-based project, is the Centre for Rehabilitation and De-institutionalization: this boarding house for the de-institutionalization of mentally ill patients is in fact a joint initiative of church and state (see Augoustidis 2002: 42–48 for more information on this institution).[7]

Beyond these initiatives, which are organized and administered at diocesan level, each parish has its own programme of activities. In some church buildings in Thiva and Livadeia, the church runs soup kitchens for the poor, mostly operated by women. In one parish in Thiva a spiritual and cultural centre ('parish refuge') has been established, prominent not least for its impressive building, which houses a museum of church artefacts, a computer room, and recreational space for youth clubs, icon-painting courses and so on. Each parish runs several financial accounts to which parishioners can donate money to help poor people. There are also establishments called Associations for Women's Love which operate in several parishes to help the poor. There is a centre for mission and communication run by a monastery in Livadeia and a blood depository run by a parish in Thiva. One parish also maintains a bank account for the assistance of 'resourceless' young women.

The local church in Thiva and Livadeia has an especially strong focus on issues concerning psychological health. This is somewhat exceptional for local churches and is attributed to the work of particular priests in the area who have training in psychology and psychotherapy. Accordingly, the church has hosted a large international conference on Psychotherapy and Orthodox Christian Theology. Furthermore, there is a great deal of activity in the domain of psychological health at the diocesan level. This includes priest-led help groups for young couples, men and women; seminars where clerics learn about psychological and psychoanalytic themes and their application to pastoral care; and a psychological-help clinic housed in the Thiva diocesan building.

These examples of church activities are the most obvious and observable. Less conspicuous is, for example, the aid provided to economic migrants: many such individuals (often lacking formal rights to employment) seek work in the church which, due to its tax-free status, is able to employ them more easily than other institutions or agencies, and does so mainly for handy-work around church properties. In many cases, people in need of financial assistance are sent to the church by both state and privately-run welfare programmes. Also unobtrusive is the role played by the church in encouraging the local population to welcome the establishment of the Centre for Rehabilitation and De-institutionalization.

---

[7]   Fr Adamantios Augoustidis is the cleric who initiated this project, following the exposure in the international press of scenes showing the terrible conditions in the asylum for mentally ill people on Leros (established in 1956). The Centre originally housed patients from the island of Leros; it now houses patients from Viotia, Athens and other parts of Greece.

It should be noted, however, that another similar initiative in a nearby town was curtailed due largely to public protests.

Thus far we have described welfare activities carried out by the diocese and by individual parish churches. Another significant category of 'religion-based' welfare activity in Thiva and Livadeia does not, however, take place under the formal auspices of the church: namely, that done through private but church-related organizations. This study takes into account four such organizations: an orphanage; two homes for elderly people; and a religious association involved in a plethora of welfare activities. These organizations are legally and administratively independent of the church. However, many of their representatives also insist that they *are* the church, in the sense of the church as a body of believers.

With all of these initiatives, it is important to note the significant role played by individual agency. This is quite clear in the case of the psychology-related programmes, which, as we have seen, are the result of the fact that several clerics ordained in the Diocese of Thiva and Livadeia happen to have special training in this field. In the other programmes as well, little to no formal structure existed beforehand to host them. This must be taken into account when we try to assess how representative Thiva and Livadeia are of church welfare activity elsewhere in Greece. It is the case in most of Greece that church (and church-related) welfare is very much the result of individual initiative.

A Kaleidoscope of Perspectives

Following this brief overview of church welfare activity in Thiva and Livadeia, we now turn to consider perspectives of local individuals on this, gleaned through a series of in-depth interviews conducted in the locality. As noted earlier in this volume, one shared feature in the fieldwork conducted in all case studies was the use of seven common interview questions. In order to properly grasp the diversity of perspectives arising in the Greek case, it is useful to focus on individuals' responses to four of these questions in particular: 'What is welfare?', 'How well does the welfare system operate locally?', 'Should the church carry out social work?', and 'Should the church play a role in public debate?'.

What (On Earth and in Heaven) is Welfare?

In terms of local perspectives on the welfare system in Thiva and Livadeia and on the church's role within it, a great deal hinges on people's conceptions of the term 'welfare'. For some interviewees, the state immediately comes to mind: welfare is what the state provides, or ought to provide, for the well-being of its citizens. Interestingly, in answering this question, more than half of the interviewees refer specifically to the etymology of the Greek word for welfare – *proneia* – translated as forethought, or providence. Most interviewees then note that the Greek welfare system is not, in fact, characterized by such forethought; rather, through its emphasis on benefits, the system administers reactive rather than preventative help. One priest defines welfare thus:

> [Welfare is] all those steps that should have been taken before a person reached the point of extending his hand to beg for help. It is primarily a state responsibility. As the system is now, all we can do is try to mend traumas, heal wounds. This is not welfare. Rather, welfare starts from birth [i.e., by supporting a person from birth in order to live well and not fall into such trauma]. (m)

Three respondents say quite simply that welfare 'doesn't exist' – that is, that there is no state provision of welfare. For them, 'welfare' as a term is tainted, because of how poorly the state system works: 'It has a stigma ... it brings to mind the person who was hungry, poor, etc.'(f) (and, hence, the person neglected by his or her family and by society in general). These people view welfare as almost a dirty word, indicating the disgraceful state of the Greek welfare system, as well as the state of disgrace it represents when a family reaches the point of relying on state-based welfare.

Others, in the meantime, view welfare as a divine concept, indicating primarily God's providence and humanity's call to emulate it. For example, one priest refers to history, and to Byzantium in particular, to suggest that welfare has always been an important role of the church. Only in modern times, with the establishment of the modern Greek state, has welfare provision become part of the state's domain (m). Another interviewee defines welfare with reference to love:

> Our religion is love. We must help our fellow human beings in whatever way we can. God is love. Love came to us from Him. And we must give it to our fellow human beings. Christ said love others. We are called to extend love to all, both those who have and those who don't, and people of all nations. (m)

For these individuals, welfare is a broader concept than state provision. Interestingly, however, we cannot draw a religious/secular divide in definitions of welfare: several self-proclaimed religious individuals, and individuals working in church or church-related welfare services, defined welfare first and foremost in terms of state activities.

How Well Does the Welfare System Work (if at all)?

Assessments of how well the welfare system operates locally were overwhelmingly negative, insofar as the welfare system is defined as 'state provision'. For one interviewee, it is quite clear that the local welfare service functions 'terribly':

> It is based on benefits which are not enough to help in any case. And the contact between the state institution and the person in need is limited to this exchange

of money. It is bureaucratic. For me, it's not welfare at all. No one [in public services] looks at the state of his [the welfare seeker's] life. (f)

Similarly, one monk declares that 'wherever there is civil servant mentality, nothing can work well' (m). A priest explains:

> People in the civil service have a strange mentality that comes with a 'job for life'. They don't care especially for what they do, or about what they do. We see this in the way they treat the people they are serving. It is not a good attitude, which would be different if they were not there for life: they would have to continue proving themselves at work. (m)

In other words, it is deemed that the local welfare system suffers from a general condition ailing the Greek civil service.

Interestingly, several interviewees could not respond to this question, stating that they are not familiar enough with the local welfare system. For example, one priest declares: 'I don't know [about the local welfare system]. I hear that it's very bureaucratic, and that it takes a long time for anything to happen. So people can get help from the church in more simple forms' (m). He goes on to explain how this relative lack of bureaucracy in the church is one reason why so many people seek help from the church: they simply do not have the time or energy to wait and keep knocking at the door of the state. In this sense, the church is presented as more efficient in meeting people's needs. Another interviewee working in a church welfare programme is also hesitant to comment on the local welfare system, saying, 'I don't know enough. But if the employee is a civil servant, and if we judge by how the public system runs in general, it is more impersonal, more cold, more distant and foreign … or that's how I imagine it' (f). This response indicates that the assumption – even without rudimentary knowledge of what the state provides in terms of local welfare services – is that these cannot be quality services, because they are part of the public system.

Church v. State: Thrown into the 'Quality Competition' Ring

As we have seen, most respondents enter naturally into a comparison between state and church welfare services, with many contending that state services are bureaucratic and therefore faceless, impersonal and inefficient. This perspective, of course, influences their conceptions of whether the church should carry out social work. Several respondents emphasize a certain attitude or approach that one must have towards people in need: one must see the person as a *person*, and not as a case. In the interview research, both church and state representatives tended to point out that people in the church have such an approach. For instance, one respondent indicates that welfare requires that we 'see a person as a person, and his needs … not as state looks at the person, as a responsibility and as a faceless individual. Not an individual, a person' (f).

Furthermore, perhaps as a logical result of the consensus that local welfare services do not operate well, the majority of the respondents in Thiva and Livadeia consider that the church has an important role to play in carrying out social work, and should indeed play this role.[8] Beyond this reasoning, though, arguments are made in support of the church's role on two main grounds: first, and most frequently expressed, the church is better at providing welfare; and second, welfare provision is a fundamental part of the church's identity.

Regarding the first argument, people most often note that the church is love, and that people who work in church-based welfare services offer of themselves in the name of love. Thus, the church is much better able to care for people than other institutions, because love is what people need most. As one interviewee explains:

> State institutions are not like this. The quality of service in church institutions is much higher. The church draws its strength from the faithful ... it comes in to supplement the state not only in terms of gaps left in the system, but in terms of weaknesses in the quality of service especially: the state can't offer what we offer. (f)

Or as one monk says: in church institutions

> [people are not] looking at their watches waiting to get paid and to leave. They are close to the person, looking at the person as person, not as a case. They don't see you in terms of what they will get from you, but in terms of what they can give. What's missing in public institutions is the heart. A warm heart. (m)

In a similar vein, another interviewee describes the church and its welfare institutions as places which are 'more sweet, more warm, more human', and which 'can play a very important role in terms of the relief of pain, of abandonment of such people' (f). In this comment she reveals what remains a prevalent conception in Greece: that the sending of a family's elderly members to a care home is a form of abandonment. Consequently, church-run homes for elderly people are considered a compromise: still imperfect, but closer to family care than a state-run home would be.

In fact, amongst most respondents there is a general sense that people who work in church or independent organizations, either as volunteers or as lower-waged workers, care more about the people they serve. Furthermore, as several interviewees (even from state institutions) note, people will tend to tell a priest

---

8   Only two respondents feel quite strongly that, ideally, the church should not be involved with many of the welfare activities in which it is currently concerned: such involvement encourages, they claim, a confusion of church with state and perpetuates an unhealthy view of the church as part of the state. Yet even these interviewees argue that the church should play a role both because it is able to, and because the needs of people must be met.

their problems first, and are often reluctant to go and see a psychologist or a social worker. Finally, one further argument made is that the church can act more directly: someone need not go through ten committees and similar levels of bureaucracy in order to be helped by the church.

Interestingly, another positive comparison drawn with state-run welfare services is that because church-run services are based on love, and love will never run out, church welfare provision is more reliable. This argument is made especially with reference to several EU-funded programmes, which come with an expiry date; municipalities are meant to continue the programmes with their own funding, but expectations that this will actually happen are low in the local community. Accordingly, church-related welfare is considered a safer bet by some, because it is driven by love rather than by funds or political decision-making.

That said, the opposite view is also well-represented amongst interviewees from public institutions and from the local population. For example, one argument is that the state can and will offer services in an organized way and without expecting something in return. Conversely, it is said, when the church offers something, it 'wants you on its side', trying to win over your soul. In other words, state institutions are deemed philosophically neutral spaces while churches are not. Some interviewees also argue that church volunteer work is not stable enough; that volunteers cannot be relied upon for matters of such importance as social care, and that regular payment for work (as is the norm in public institutions) leads to greater reliability. Furthermore, it is claimed, the alleged 'facelessness' in public welfare structures is necessary: proper therapy requires a professional patient–client relationship, and in small communities, people may be too ashamed to take their problems to church or church-related institutions. In parenthesis, it should be noted that several interviewees representing public welfare structures and members of the local public were clearly suppressing somewhat low opinions of the church, saying they did not want to be negative or critical. These respondents tended to be more open with their views of the church after the recording device was turned off but, in general, respondents with negative comments regarding the church preferred to remain relatively, and consciously, vague.

Quite apart from this, the church is criticized by most respondents for not doing more in the domain of welfare provision, especially considering its vast social and financial capital. No one fails to praise those efforts already made by the church in Thiva and Livadeia, but there are very few (across all categories) who do not also say that much more could be done. One priest addresses this criticism by stating that the church plays a very important role, but that this is not necessarily evident to everyone, because it does so 'humbly and quietly'. He goes on to say that, on the one hand, this is a pity, because more people might come to help others, or to receive help, if they knew about the services.[9] On the other hand, he declares, 'it is

---

[9]   On the question of whether the church's role should be publicized, there is a significant discrepancy in people's views, including those of clerics: most feel that 'advertisement' is unnecessary, and is contrary to Orthodox tradition and to Christian belief

good that the left hand should not know what the right does.' In terms of visibility, the same priest notes that the church plays other roles in welfare provision beyond those normally discussed. For instance, aesthetics and tradition also comprise a large part of welfare. The church pays attention to the need of people for places to 'soothe their souls', offering – amongst other things – beautiful places to worship (the aesthetic element). It also connects them with their tradition (*paradosi* – this word has the sense of the passing on of heritage from one generation to the next, not of looking back), linking them to this significant source of identification (m).

The second group of arguments in support of the church's welfare activities has to do with the notion that 'the church' and 'social service' are indivisible concepts: social service is a fundamental aspect of the church's identity. Here one priest notes that '"work of church" and "social work" are indivisible. In my mind, they are synonymous ... I have no sense that what we offer is just ecclesiastical. It is social' (m). Or, as one administrator of a church-run welfare institution states, 'Our church is based on offering [*prosfora*], sacrifice, self-denial – at least, this is what Christ taught us: love others as yourself. These are the prototypes of our church, [to do this] without expecting something in return' (f). For another interviewee, considering whether the church should be involved in welfare activities, '"should" is the wrong word: there is no should about it. Church and social service are one and the same. Indistinguishable' (m). Likewise, one priest says the church not only *should* but *must* be involved in welfare (m).

Yes, the Church Should Speak Out, But ...

So from several different perspectives, there is general consensus that the church should involve itself in welfare activities. When it comes to church involvement in public debate, however, the picture is more complicated. Here people express interestingly mixed feelings, mainly formulating their responses in terms of 'yes, but ...'. Only one interviewee voices an unreserved 'yes' (f). It is important to note that most of the negativity in relation to this question is either directly or indirectly linked to critique of the national church and, mainly, of Archbishop Christodoulos, for his particular role in public debate on a number of questions, including social issues.[10] For example, as the priest quoted above explains, the ecclesiastical and

---

(noting the injunction in Matthew 6:3, 'But when you give alms, do not let your left hand know what your right hand is doing').

[10] It should be noted that the bishop of Thiva and Livadeia, Ieronymos, was Christodoulos' main rival for the archbishopric in 1998; the two subsequently had relatively tense relations, of which interviewees in Thiva and Livadeia are all too aware. Accordingly, quite often respondents make direct comparisons between the local and national church, and consciously endeavour to distance themselves from the national church, as represented by the then Archbishop Christodoulos (who has since been replaced by Ieronymos in the archbishopric, following Christodoulos's death early in 2008).

social problems are 'one and the same'. Hence, the church should have a voice on social issues. However, he continues:

> Sometimes there is a misunderstanding. Sometimes we feel that the Archbishop, Christodoulos, speaks for the Church of Greece. This is wrong. He *expresses* the voice of the church, and this he should do when he is invested the authority by the Holy Synod. The church should always speak discreetly, so you never feel 'oh, now the church people are talking again?'. This 'oh' means the person has become tired of us. So we should speak only when it is needed, and where it is needed. (m)

Another priest thinks this is 'a double-edged sword':

> Because yes, the church should express a public voice, but it is easily misunderstood. And here I am referring to the administration … it should express a public voice, but *very* carefully, that that voice will not be politicized, that it will always express its opinion when it sees something wrong, regardless of political stances. (m)

This view expresses a clear dismay over the politicization of the church and, based on this interviewee's other statements, it seems quite clear that these views are directed mostly at the church at the national level, where the political involvement of the church is conspicuous. Perhaps it is such pitfalls which lead others, such as the following commentator, to conclude 'I would prefer if it [the church] would mainly be involved with actions, rather than with words' (m). This, in fact, is a comment made by several individuals: the church would do best to remain in the business of action rather than words.

One priest offers a somewhat more nuanced response:

> It's a difficult question. 'Social issue' means abortion, and it means immigration [i.e., the range of social issues is large]. We need to narrow the bounds. The relation of the church and ethnos in Greece is particular. But I think the church should have a voice only in its domain, its space. In other words, it shouldn't talk publicly about abortion. It should talk [on this issue] only to its people, within the church. (m)

Here the respondent does not mean the church as a physical space but as a community of believers. Significantly, he is not equating 'Greek' or 'citizen' with 'the church':

> Not all of Greece or Greeks are Christian and belong to the church. I don't think the church should have a public voice on every issue … this is not the nature of the church. It is not the job of the church to solve social problems. That's the job of the state. The church can offer a voice, a view, but the church person

expressing a voice should (a) be speaking for himself (just like any citizen), but not offer it as *the* church voice – in other words, representatives of the church should not speak with disproportionate influence; and (b) the church should speak publicly when it is asked to, by the state. (m)

Here the cleric's view diverges greatly from the practice seen at national church level, where at the time of interview the Archbishop frequently spoke on social and political issues and received criticism for doing so – in many cases, in opposition to the state rather than at the latter's request.

Reflections

The research in Thiva and Livadeia offers much food for thought in seeking to understand European trends in majority church-based welfare activity. Throughout the process of gathering material and meeting with the other WREP participants to discuss the results, Greece often seemed an 'exceptional' case. For example, it was the only Orthodox country included in the study, so we were unable to test Orthodox versus Greek specificities against another Orthodox case study. Also, it was particularly difficult in the Greek case to provide statistics anywhere near the depth and breadth of those available in most countries involved in the WREP study (especially the Scandinavian ones). Such factors made the research more challenging, perhaps, but certainly no less exciting. Indeed, the enquiry produced very interesting results which require us to reflect on the Orthodox as well as Greek and southern European specificities, all of which influence the Greek case. We close this chapter, then, by presenting these reflections, first from a theological perspective, then from a gender perspective and, finally, from a sociological perspective.

Thinking Theologically

In analysing results from a theological perspective, it is interesting to note the repetition of the same Bible verses by many interviewees, and the fact that this applies to people working in the public sector and in private institutions as well as those representing the church. In general, the references to the Bible, to Christ and Christ's example, and to God's love, are surprisingly frequent, perhaps suggesting something beyond a simple reflection of the extensive religious education within the state school system. Many references are also made to Byzantine history, and to the traditions of the Orthodox Church, in terms of welfare provision; by comparison, there is very little reference made to Orthodox theology as such (only one priest mentioned the work, example and writings of St John Chrysostom).

The general picture that one receives, in the case of those who *do* make such reference, is one of people who are religiously-motivated in their welfare activities. However, there is little to suggest that they are motivated by Orthodox theology in particular. Rather, it is expected that the picture of religiously-motivated welfare activity in Greece, in terms of people's reflection on their own work, will resemble that in other case studies, and that a generally Christian sub-text will emerge from the WREP project, rather than a strongly denominational one. The exception in this case is the frequent recalling of Byzantine history and tradition. This tendency may be explained also with reference to the Orthodox Church's more general role in Greek society – as a repository of both historical consciousness and national identity. In light of this, it is not surprising that history is frequently evoked, and a pride in church history in particular.

The Woman's Place of Caring: Inside and Outside the Home

One of the most interesting elements of the Greek case study, when examined from a gender perspective, is that changes to the family structure – a good example being the entry of women into the workforce – are frequently linked to many of the social problems in Thiva and Livadeia, yet the people who play the largest roles serving in welfare programmes are women. In the Greek case it seems clear that women's role of caring in the home is continuing, but through various institutions, with either younger, employed women, or older women who were never employed or who are retired, now working as social workers or volunteers.

Clearly, women predominate numerically within the social activities of the local church. There tend to be similarities in women's and men's roles only where both are retired or senior citizens (for example, a couple may be involved in the same welfare activity). Yet even in this case the roles that they play seem divided: men tend to help in completely different ways from women. Male activities include (but are not limited to): offering part of a crop to the soup kitchen (which entails physically carrying crops which they have tended); gardening at the newly-established home for elderly people; and helping with technological or electrical problems in a given institution. Meanwhile, women visit and help care for the residents in church care homes; volunteer to clean and decorate church institutions; and cook for the soup kitchen (amongst other activities).

Especially interesting in the Greek case is the lack of hesitation with which interviewees tend to make generalized statements about 'women's nature' as caring beings who are 'better suited' to welfare activity and, by the same token, generalizations about men being 'ill-suited' to welfare activity and simply less capable of handling such work. In people's descriptions of the roles men play when they *do* engage in welfare work, there is a clear gender bias: men are only useful for outdoor activities, heavy-duty or 'messy' work (such as gardening), activities requiring strength, and typically (Greek) male social activities (such as playing backgammon and sharing an afternoon coffee with company at a café).

One further significant dimension is the fact that the gap left in care for the young and the elderly at home is, in many cases, being filled by immigrant women. These women, in turn, are creating gaps in welfare provision in their own homes (most often, it seems, abroad, in their home countries); but the money that they earn working in Greece appears to make this practical and worthwhile for them. The same tendency can be observed in Italy as, perhaps, in other parts of Europe. It would be interesting to learn more about how these new gaps in the households of immigrant women are being filled, and the extent to which this is simply a problem moving eastwards and southwards.

Lessons Drawn From Greek Society

A sociological analysis requires awareness of the fact that – as noted at the outset of this chapter – the state welfare system in Greece is, in general, very underdeveloped. The highly centralized system is basically replicated in all prefectures. Thus, the welfare system in Thiva and Livadeia may be considered to be equally poor as in most Greek towns – evidence of which is the fact that there are no state-run homes for elderly people in the entire prefecture of Viotia, whilst there are waiting lists at the church-run homes in both Thiva and Livadeia. Thus, it would be difficult for the local population *not* to appreciate the activities of the church in the domain of welfare, in the face of such dire need. Likewise, it is not too difficult for the local church to shine in this context. However, when one considers the relative monetary wealth of the national church – as many interviewees do – it is then harder not to criticize the church, since its welfare activities, unlike its financial capabilities, are assumed to be somewhat limited.

Furthermore, because of the close relationship between church and state, and the tendency to see the church's role as one of filling some of the many gaps left by the state, it is to be expected that, in most people's assessments of the welfare system and of the role of the church in welfare provision, they tend to compare the state's role with that of the church. The result is an interesting debate, seen above, over whether the church, or the state, is 'better' at welfare provision.

Equally significant is the extensive overlap between perspectives of the 'secular' and the 'religious', and of those representing the church or the state. There are cases of nearly identical responses from, for instance, a priest and a very secular person (in the shared view that the opportunity provided to worship in a monastery ought also to be considered a welfare service as it tends to people's emotional and spiritual needs). This fact may reflect close church–state relations, in the sense that the compulsory religious (mainly Orthodox) education in Greek public schools tends to transmit the same messages about the Orthodox Church to all Greeks. It may also (or on the other hand) simply reflect a conservative perspective as might prevail in any medium-sized European town. Finally, it may also (or instead) reflect a respect for the role of the church in welfare provision which has developed in that particular locality over the years, and which would not necessarily extend to the Greek Orthodox Church as a whole.

Based on the research in its entirety, we would like to close by suggesting that the question of whether the church or the state is 'better' at welfare provision – expressed in its own particular terms in the Greek context – seems to be one of the most interesting questions arising today, as European welfare states continue to shrink and other institutions (including churches) increasingly fill gaps left by the state. What is clear in the Greek case, however, is that the family (and, mainly, its female contingent) still wins the overall competition for 'best' welfare provision. The home is where needs are best cared for, and church and state are second and third choices for welfare provision. In fact, as regards care for children and elderly people, increasingly there are trends in Greece whereby church and state are, in fact, considered third and fourth choices, coming after rather than before the possibility of hiring an immigrant woman to care for children and elders within the home. Tradition in this sense is modified rather than abandoned.

Chapter 11

A Preliminary Conclusion:
Gathering the Threads and Moving On

Anders Bäckström and Grace Davie

The purpose of this chapter is twofold: it seeks first to draw together the threads that have emerged in the preceding chapters – doing so by reviewing very briefly the eight case studies contained in WREP, and then by looking at the common questions or themes that emerge from then. This done, the chapter moves in a different direction: it begins – albeit tentatively – to place these findings in an innovative theoretical framework, one which finds its focus in the complex interrelationships between religion and welfare in the long term. Not only does this underline the influence of religion on the different welfare systems that have emerged in different parts of Europe – a point already covered in the introductory material in this book – but it also looks in some detail at how these relationships may continue in the twenty-first century. How, in other words, are the shifts from modern to late-modern societies influenced by the dominant religious traditions of each of the countries under review? In so doing, this chapter points to the future – in part to the second volume, but also beyond. Indeed, if the conclusions emerging from the WREP project are taken seriously, it implies a thorough rethinking of how we understand the place of religion in modern societies, including Europe. That in turn means looking again at the concepts and tools that are available to us when we undertake such analyses, whether of welfare or anything else.

What this chapter does not do is embark in detail on the comparative perspective that is clearly a central part of the project as a whole. Such comparisons – set out within a sociological, theological and gender perspective – form the core chapters of the partner volume (see Bäckström et al. 2010).

Drawing the Threads Together

Bearing in mind that WREP was largely an exploratory study, from which no easy generalizations emerge, some of our findings are nonetheless striking. One of these is that the expected variations – for example in welfare regimes and denominational differences – not only exist in terms of structure but have imprinted themselves on the lives of ordinary people all over Europe. Such people are unlikely to have much knowledge of Esping-Andersen's regime-types, or indeed of the finer points of Lutheran, Catholic or Orthodox social teaching. They operate, nonetheless, with certain assumptions about values and human dignity, about welfare and well-being, and about the rights of citizens to a decent quality of life and appropriate levels of service from specified organizations. Such assumptions form patterns; it is these patterns that lie at the heart of the WREP project.

The Nordic Countries

In the Nordic countries, for example, an efficient, comprehensive and universal model of welfare is endorsed by all three groups of respondents: the representatives of the local church, of the local authorities and of the population. There is, moreover, a strong expectation that this model will continue: it is a 'good' thing. Classic Lutheran theology supports this position. Indeed, in many ways, the majority churches – though relegated to the margins in terms of the delivery of welfare – are similarly regarded. They too should be open to all citizens, and needs (material or spiritual) should be met regardless of personal beliefs. Even in the Nordic countries, however, the proportion of services delivered by for-profit and non-profit organizations has grown enormously in recent decades – a trend that has accelerated since the turn of the century. The point should not be exaggerated: such organizations work within a system of delegation, in which the state remains firmly in control even if other actors are charged with delivery. Despite modifications in practice, the 'norm' remains unchanged.

Gaps, nonetheless, persist – indeed, some are getting larger rather than smaller, for all the reasons pointed out in the introductory chapters of this book. Such lacunae are increasingly filled by the family, and – up to a point – by the churches. The latter, moreover, have a particular responsibility for the weak, and are commended for putting into practice the values espoused in their teaching; conversely, the temptation to indulge in party politics must be firmly resisted.

The Nordic countries quite clearly form a regime-type; their stories, however, are not identical. Finland, for instance, has had to deal with a particularly severe recession in the early 1990s, exacerbated by the collapse in the Soviet market. The response of the Lutheran Church to this profound dislocation in Finnish society – especially its care for the long-term unemployed – was widely applauded by the population as a whole. The church became an accepted player on the welfare field, a role that has continued. In Sweden, a rather different shift requires attention: the constitutional changes of the year 2000, in which the state church became a free folk church – a significant moment in all kinds of ways.[1] So far, however, it is clear that for most people, the Church of Sweden continues to inhabit a 'self-evident' place in Swedish society – not least in relation to crises or catastrophes (occasions when the normally invisible or implicit makes itself felt). Such episodes arise regularly in the lives of individuals and communities; at times, however, they involve the society as a whole. A particularly tragic example occurred after the

---

[1]   More detail about the constitutional changes in Sweden is given in Appendix 3.

sinking of the *Estonia* in 1994; another, though less obvious, took place after the East Asian tsunami at the end of 2004 which claimed a significant number of Swedish lives. In meeting these needs, the church is not only respected for its work, but sits easily alongside the claims of a highly secular society.

In the Norwegian case study, there is a different emphasis: it concerns the role of the Church City Mission and its charismatic leader. Here, the energy and vision of one individual is obvious – leading inevitably to questions about the future. Can this role be sustained? In the meantime, the Mission not only meets a very evident need, it also raises questions about values and the requirement for someone or some organization to assume a moral authority in the local community. The suggestion that, until recently, the role of moral guardian might have been fulfilled by the labour movement is interesting. Is it the case that an increased emphasis on efficiency and the importance of economic performance has left a void in the public discourse? For the time being, the leader of the Church City Mission has filled this gap, not only in articulating a particular, theologically-driven discourse, but in assuming a role that no other organization seems competent to fill.

Southern Europe

A very different picture can be seen in the south of Europe where there is a weak and somewhat rudimentary welfare system. Indeed, it is hardly an exaggeration to say that the roles described in the previous paragraphs are turned on their head. If in the Nordic countries, the family and the churches fill the gaps left by state provision, in the Mediterranean countries, it is almost the case that the state fills the gaps after the family and churches have exhausted their capacities – a situation that becomes all the more complex as the family alters in nature and traditional forms of female care begin to disappear.

The latter point, for example, is strikingly clear in Italy where the burden of the 'double role' has had unintended consequences, at least as far as the Catholic Church is concerned. The difficulties of combining responsibilities for the family with those of the workplace have not led to women doing more of the former and to an increase in the birth rate (as Catholic teaching might suggest); they have led instead to a marked decrease in the number of children and – very often – to the employment of immigrant women as carers within the home, especially for elderly people. Thus the focus on the family continues but mutates to suit the conditions of the twenty-first century. Some gain and some lose from these arrangements. If, on the one hand, this eases the burden for Italian women who wish to go out to work, it is rather more difficult for the families of immigrant workers – bearing in mind, of course, that such women are, undoubtedly, glad of employment of whatever kind.

At the same time, the Catholic Church has a very visible, if somewhat confusing, presence in the local welfare system – through parish work, large organizations such as Caritas-Diaconia, dozens of smaller organizations with various links to religion, and the religious orders (notably those of women). Interestingly the last of these sustains, at least in Vicenza, a sharp – and at times very critical – voice. Personnel, moreover, overlap – not only between religious organizations as such but between the church and the local authority: key individuals move back and forth between the two. Indeed, one of the most important questions to emerge from the Italian case is a persistent ambiguity about what does and does not constitute 'the church' at local level. Is it the local hierarchy, or is it a much wider variety of lay voices, brought together in the many different voluntary associations concerned with welfare, some of which are closer to the 'official' church than others? Answers to this question vary – in terms of both content and value judgements. One point is clear, however: that is, the widespread criticism of the state welfare system overall.

This is also the case in Greece, where expectations of adequate support from the state (quite apart from the provision as such) are markedly low. And, just as in Italy, there remains a very strong expectation that the family will care for its own, especially elderly members – a failure to do so is regarded as neglect. Provision by the church partially fills this gap, but the system as a whole remains unsatisfactory – some think that the church should do more, given its considerable assets; other think that it should do less, and stick to its primary (that is, religious) purpose. Such ambivalence is closely related to the ambiguity regarding the role of the Orthodox Church in Greek society more generally, a situation which is partly accounted for by the controversial role of the late Archbishop of Athens – a prominent figure at the time of the fieldwork. Clearly Archbishop Christodoulos raised the profile of the Greek Orthodox Church, notably with respect to the identity card controversy[2] – but at a price. There were many who resented this interference in the workings of the state, interventions that were considered inappropriate in a modern democratic society. In Thiva and Livadeia, however, the picture was rather different: here, there was respect for the local bishop (who in 2008 became the archbishop) and for the multitude of initiatives that take place under the auspices of the church at local level. More, of course, could and should be done, but for the great majority of Greek respondents, provision by the church is most certainly better than no provision at all.

Two questions are beginning to emerge beneath these debates which are common to all our case studies. The first is easily stated: is it the case that provision by the churches lets the state off the hook – in the sense that the church is fulfilling (at times very effectively) what many Europeans think is the role of the government, scrutinized by democratically-elected politicians? The answer tends to be pragmatic: better the church or the voluntary sector than nothing, but better still that an effective publicly-funded system takes over (but when?). The second concerns quality: who is the 'better' provider? Here the data reveal different voices. On the one hand are those who advocate the neutral, well-trained state professional, employed and salaried by the state. On the other are the supporters of more informal systems of care (including that of the churches), claiming that their services are more personal, if at times haphazard, and are based not only on

---

[2]	A full account of this episode can be found in Molokotos-Liederman (2007).

a genuine love of neighbour but on a thorough knowledge of the territory. Each group has its corresponding critics. Those, for example, who are uneasy about public provision talk about the inefficiencies of the state in southern Europe, and its extreme bureaucratization. The detractors of the churches, on the other hand, are concerned about 'strings' being attached to welfare – in other words, concerned that the giving of service might become conditional on church attendance or certain behavioural codes.

The In-between Cases

The plot thickens when we introduce the in-between cases: the very different situations in both France and Germany. If the first of these exemplifies the modern, centralized secular state par excellence, the second emerges from a very different history which necessitated – amongst other things – the deliberate dispersion of power and responsibility. Despite their differences, both belong in Esping-Andersen's continental and conservative regime-type, underlining a point already made – that this constellation is, in many ways, the most difficult to deal with, given its inherent diversity.

In France, for example, the separation of church and state is at its most complete; it is expressed both philosophically and institutionally in the principle of *laïcité*, implying the absence of religion in the public sphere.[3] The law of 1905 which established this system guaranteed that the individual would be free from the encroachments of religion. The church no longer had any standing in public law, with the implication that religion as such was relegated to the private sphere. An alternative, entirely secular system of government emerged to replace this, finding its political expression in France as 'an indivisible, secular, democratic and social Republic' (Article 1 of the 1958 Constitution). The French case study reveals, however, that both a range of voluntary organizations and the religious orders still play a part in welfare provision.[4] Indirectly, moreover, some of these initiatives are funded by the state. There is, in fact, a *hidden complementarity* between state and church as small, religiously-motivated and frequently precarious groups operate round the edges, providing innovative and barely visible forms of care – frequently relying on local knowledge that more formal organizations, even politicians, do not have. Their work with homeless people or asylum seekers offers an excellent example. Those in the know acknowledge the significance of this work, of which many – including the great majority of politicians – are unaware.

---

[3]   The notion of *laïcité* has already been explained in Chapter 8. It is important to grasp the tension between the understanding of absence as neutrality and the understanding of absence as hostility.

[4]   More detail about the place of the religious orders in the French case can be found in Mabille and Valasik (2004).

The situation in Germany could hardly be more different. Here, the principle of subsidiarity works in favour of the dominant churches, which remain corporations under public law, strongly involved both in education and in welfare provision. More precisely, both the memory of World War 2 and the policies of the Christian Democrats have favoured the delegation of large sections of welfare to the diaconal institutions, both Catholic (*Caritas*) and Lutheran (*Diakonische Werk*): in all, about 50 per cent of social care is supplied in this way. These institutions are largely financed through a variety of insurance systems, and together employ about one million people. But here, just as everywhere else in Europe, it has been difficult to keep up with demand. The problem is exacerbated, moreover, by the fact that the demands are growing at exactly the same moment as the resources of both churches and church-related organizations are diminishing – more rapidly than ever before. Despite the fact that a strong motivation to continue in membership – and thus to pay church tax – derives from the role that the churches play in welfare, there is a growing mismatch between the rising expectations of the population and the resources available to meet these. An already serious problem is compounded by the arrival of new for-profit actors in the welfare field, many of which are able to undercut the services offered by the voluntary sector. This is particularly true in the care of elderly people.

The Liberal Example

The liberal welfare-regime is different again. In England – as indeed in Britain as a whole – the market has dominated for some time: welfare provision is increasingly outsourced. Individuals, moreover, are expected to take responsibility for themselves. That said, the churches remain active at local level – offering informal care in diverse and imaginative ways, especially for very young and elderly people. Particularly important in Darlington, for example, was the provision of a 'neutral' space, within which a host of community activities can take root. Just how much is achieved in this way has only recently been acknowledged (see pp. 123–7). The parish system is clearly an important factor in this respect, providing as it does an almost unparalleled network of activities across the country. Resources, however, are limited, preventing the provision of social care on anything but a piecemeal basis. Despite the lack of money, one final point is important: the churches (not least the Church of England) have a potentially powerful voice at national level, which from time to time plays a significant role in British society. This was certainly the case under the Thatcher government of the 1980s: the moment, paradoxically, when the market system was most fully endorsed. There is an interesting parallel here with the Norwegian case: this essentially prophetic voice was heard most clearly when the Labour Party was in disarray. The void which opened up in political debate was filled momentarily by the churches.

Common Questions, Common Themes

Some common questions have already been mentioned: those that relate to the underlying responsibility of the state to provide for its citizens (should this or should this not be 'usurped' by the church?), together with the vexed question of quality (who, or which institution, is best suited to the role of welfare provider in late-modern society?). Both rest on the fact that there is a strong sense, right across Europe, that the state *should* take responsibility for the welfare of its citizens, but does not – and indeed cannot – fulfil all of its obligations to perfection. The problem, moreover, is likely to get worse rather than better, for all the reasons set out in the introductory sections of this book. Expectations are rising all the time; resources, however, are under constant strain – the more so since the 'credit crunch'.

The angle of questioning, however, differs and depends on your point of departure. In the north of Europe, for example, there is gratitude for a comprehensive system, alongside dismay that this will not, in all probability, be sustained in its present form. Elements of the market have already been introduced, albeit gradually, in the form of non-profit and for-profit actors. Interestingly, the Nordic churches find themselves on both sides of this debate: they are part of the voluntary non-profit sector and in this sense are invited to play a larger role in welfare provision, but at the same time their Lutheran understanding of the 'two kingdoms' leads them to be strongly supportive of a state system. In the south of Europe, an inclusive system of public welfare has never been fully established; it remains, none the less, an aspiration. In the meantime, what is to be done? Clearly, the situation would be even worse without the contributions of the churches – it is important, therefore, that these are maintained, as long as this does not detract too much from the underlying duties of the state.

In between these two extremes – in France, Germany and England – the stresses reflect the specificities of each case. In France, there is an interesting subtext: the state assumes not only the responsibility to provide for its citizens, but claims for itself a certain moral quality. In so doing it is taking on, quite deliberately, a role traditionally ascribed to the Catholic Church. Can such a role be sustained, however, in an increasingly plural society? The answer is by no means clear. In Germany, there is a systematic delegation of power, entirely understandable in historical terms, but problematic in recent decades. German unification, for example, has placed a particular strain on the system, the more so given the very secular nature of the former east. Equally difficult in a dispersed system is the lack of concentrated authority, which is required to make the radical decisions that are necessary, if Germany is to face the economic challenges of the twenty-first century. The opposite is the case in Britain, where a radical overhaul took place in the 1980s, leading to the systematic outsourcing of welfare provision. Such a process, of course, brings problems of its own – a fact that the churches have taken upon themselves to point out.

The situation is therefore complex, but a common – if unexpected – feature emerges from top to bottom in Europe: that is, the increasing rather than decreasing role of the majority churches in the voluntary sector, both as providers of welfare and as a 'critical voice' able to point out the less as well as more obvious deficiencies of the system. This is a situation in which local knowledge counts for a great deal. Particularly important, for example, is the work of the churches amongst groups of individuals – particularly homeless people or asylum-seekers – who do not fit easily into the system. Not only are the churches aware of their existence, they also have sufficient flexibility to circumvent the red tape that inevitably surrounds these necessarily marginal cases. A piecemeal system that offers emergency help in the short term cannot, however, be sustained for very long – an issue that most European countries have yet to address.

Bearing the above in mind, is it possible to suggest that a process of homogenization is taking place across Europe? And, always assuming that we can answer this question one way or the other, is this a good thing? There are clearly some signs of what has been termed 'convergence'. It *is* true, for instance, that the Nordic countries are adopting some aspects of both the continental and the market models – moving away from an all-encompassing state provision to a more diverse model. It is also clear that some elements of the Nordic model – notably those that concern gender and the care of children (the notion of paternity leave, for example) – are becoming more widespread across Europe. That said, there is clearly a very strong attachment to familiar ways of working: citizens in the north of Europe are not universally pleased about the changes taking place, and those further south do not always want Nordic 'norms' imposed on them. Indeed, the relative stability of the various regime-types is as noticeable as the changes that are taking place.

Interestingly, as far as the WREP project is concerned, distinctive 'theologies' are very much part of this endorsement – in other words, they both support and are supported by the regime-types in question. Luther's 'two kingdoms' have already been mentioned: here is a strong justification for inclusive state provision. Respondents from the churches in the Nordic countries were as proud of their national welfare systems as anyone else: the state is a central element in God's plan for salvation. Elsewhere – especially where the Catholic Church maintains a relatively strong presence – there is a rather different interpretation of 'salvation'. In Catholic social teaching, the state is quite definitely subordinate to the church. It follows that there are certain areas of society, not least the family, to which care is quite explicitly delegated (hence the importance of traditional female roles), but into which the state should not penetrate. Every infringement of this 'rule' is hotly contested.

In England, finally, political liberalism is endorsed to a certain extent by Reformed theology: it is considered a good thing to support oneself and one's family, as opposed to receiving care, though not to the extent that this tendency is found in the United States. One reason for restraint in this respect lies in the balancing force of a different theological current, deriving this time from Christian socialism. Equally significant is the presence of an established church. Indeed, the existence of a parochially-organized, majority church in each of the case studies under review is one of the unifying factors in WREP. It is also one of the most obvious contrasts with the United States, alongside the welfare state itself (see Berger et al. 2008).

An important question follows from this: are these two observations related, and – if so – in what way? One way of addressing these issues is to consider where the idea of solidarity, meaning a sense of belonging and an awareness of mutual citizenship, comes from. This notion is deeply rooted in the concept of social care, an idea that was traditionally kept by the churches, even if they failed at times to practise what they preached. Bit by bit during Europe's twentieth century, this responsibility for mutuality and social care was transferred to the state, where – very largely – it remains. This is not, however, a zero sum game. Rather, in the course of WREP (and indeed of WREP's successors), it is possible to detect a degree of rebalancing in these relationships, a point to be explored at length in the following section.

Before doing so, it is worth asking whether the notion of 'vicarious religion' might be helpful in this discussion. By 'vicarious', Davie means the notion of religion performed by an active minority but on behalf of a much larger number, who (implicitly at least) not only understand, but approve of what the minority is doing (Davie 2000, 2007b). Precisely this sentiment, for example, is one way of explaining the high levels of membership in the Nordic churches where levels of practice (and indeed of specifically Christian beliefs) are notoriously low. Practice and belief apart, it is beneficial for society that the churches are there, just as the welfare state is deemed an asset. In terms of the church, rather similar sentiments can be transposed to the Catholic or Orthodox parts of Europe, as indeed to Britain, despite the evident variations in the concept of membership and the absence of a church tax as a tangible means of measuring this. In short – as Davie has made clear – vicarious religion is pervasive across Europe, though expressed in different ways in different parts of the continent.

It is not possible, however, for 'vicarious religion' to cross the Atlantic. Up to a point, something similar can be captured in Robert Bellah's notion of 'civil religion' (Bellah 1970), in the sense of an underlying if not always articulate attachment to America; but the assumptions are rather different. For example, there is no sense here of a state or majority church operating on behalf of all citizens, whether they are believers or not. There is, instead, a myriad of competing denominations – in other words, a *market* in religion rather than a monopoly (historically speaking). Nor, in America, is there a welfare state in the European sense of the term. Indeed, in some sections of American society, there is a profound mistrust of such a thing – a view that sees the welfare state as the source of Europe's economic ills rather than the basis of mutual solidarity. It is something to be avoided at all costs (Muller 1997). The majority of Europeans, of course, have a different view (as do many Americans); they are not only supportive but proud of their welfare systems, as they are of the political values that these represent. These are deep-seated in

European societies, as the WREP data attests; they are unlikely to change in the foreseeable future.

There is, perhaps, a linking point: that is, the understanding of the state itself – something that is markedly differently on each side of the Atlantic. In the United States, there is no state in the sense that this is understood in Europe; it simply does not exist. Indeed, Americans are wont to use a different word: they talk about government rather than the state. In Europe, by contrast, there is quite clearly an entity called the state, together with its two off-shoots – one religious and one secular. The state, however, is subject to variation, just like the state churches and the organization of welfare. In the north of Europe, it takes a social democratic form, firmly supported by the churches. In France, it is not only strong but heavily ideological – this time challenging the dominant church. In Germany, the power of the state has been deliberately curbed; and in the Mediterranean societies represented in WREP, it exists but remains relatively underdeveloped. Only in Britain are there echoes of the American case, in the sense of a mistrust of the state per se – echoes which are themselves counteracted by an established church on the one hand and a tax-funded National Health Service on the other. If the former no longer attracts the active allegiance of the majority of the population, the latter most certainly does.

One final point concludes this section – one, moreover, that will be developed at length in the second volume. It concerns a further parallel between the majority churches of Europe and the different manifestations of the welfare state across the continent. In both cases, it is men who predominate in leadership and management and women who deliver care, a 'fact' that Europeans accept with equanimity – this is how it is. A telling example of such assumptions can be found in the opening quote in the chapter on gender in the second volume; it comes from the Italian case study: 'Speaking for myself, I would not leave my grandmother in the hands of a man … I find the idea of a male caregiver a bit funny!' The taken-for-grantedness of it all is the most striking feature. That disproportionate numbers of women are also found in the churches may or may not be a coincidence – it needs, and will be given, very careful thought.

Quite apart from anything else, the policy implications are crucial, in so far as they engage what has become known as a 'caring deficit' within western society. If women become overburdened by the expectations placed upon them, they may simply withdraw from their obligations, with serious consequences for care. A rather similar question is now being asked of the churches. If too many women no longer attend church and withdraw their support for its many voluntary activities, something of a crisis may ensue. It is this that returns us to the theoretical issues underpinning WREP, one of which is the nature of secularization, its impact on European societies and its possible futures. The fact that this process is itself gendered is in itself an important part of the puzzle (Aune 2008; Woodhead 2008a, 2008b).

Theoretical Implications

There are other links to be made with the idea of secularization – connections which constitute the theme of these final paragraphs. At one level, there has been a widely recognized decline in some indicators of religious vitality right across Europe – most obviously in church attendance and in the 'harder' indicators of religious belief. Nobody disputes that this is so. It is equally clear, however, that religion remains a significant element of modern European societies; indeed, its presence is growing rather than diminishing in public debate. A parallel development can be found in the delivery of welfare: our data reveal indisputably that – for different reasons in different parts of Europe – there are new 'spaces' opening up in the welfare systems of Europe, which religious people and religious organizations have been called upon to fill. Contrary to the expectations of many commentators, therefore, the growth of the welfare state should not be seen as synonymous with what has become known as the secularization process. The story is considerably more nuanced than that.

Understanding how these two dimensions interact, however, means taking a whole variety of factors into account. Among these are the constitutional arrangements of the country in question, its political evolution, the dominant theological tradition present in that part of Europe, the nature of the voluntary sector and the current economic situation. All of these will surface at some point in the following discussion, which brings together the work of two very distinguished scholars: one an analyst of welfare and the other a scholar of religion. What emerges, in fact, is a single story told from two very different perspectives.

Repeatedly in the preceding chapters, reference has been made to Gøsta Esping-Andersen's pioneering work on the welfare regimes of Europe. There is no need to repeat this over again, except to underline that – despite the caveats and criticisms outlined in Chapter 2 – his insights remain pivotal for all those who wish to understand the welfare state in Europe. For scholars of religion, however, an additional point is striking: the patterns or regime-types that emerge in the world of welfare relate very closely to the 'pathways' observed by David Martin in his equally seminal work on secularization (Martin 1978). Martin's central thesis is easily summarized: the process of secularization – strongly associated in the European case with the onset of industrialization and urbanization – is common to the continent as a whole, but unfolds differently within particular cultural contexts (Martin 1978: 4–5).

These contexts are determined by identifiable factors, for example the precise timing and the nature of what Martin terms 'crucial events' – namely the English Civil War and the American, French and Russian Revolutions, and the place of religion in these. Did these cataclysmic struggles occur over religion, against religion or through religion? The *absence* of such an event in the Lutheran countries is just as significant. The details are complex, but the underlying idea is simple enough. Emerging, in the fullness of time, from these various upheavals, are specific – and up to a point predictable – variations in the secularization process.

These include the American, the British, the French (Latin), the South American (extended Latin), the Russian, the Calvinist and the Lutheran cases, in which the decline – or more accurately transformation – of religion takes place in different ways. Martin's *General Theory of Secularization* (1978), supplemented by his later work on Latin America,[5] contains an account of each of these variations.

Not all of Martin's case studies are relevant to the WREP material or indeed to the welfare states of Europe. That said, the British, the French (Latin) and the Lutheran patterns most certainly are, and mirror very closely the regime-types explained in detail in previous chapters. Had there been a Calvinist example in WREP, something rather similar would have happened. Such connections are not difficult to explain: both theories (that of welfare regimes and that of secularization) draw on the underlying alignments and cleavages in European society identified by political sociologists in their work on the nineteenth century (especially the work of Lipset and Rokkan). Such cleavages are, in turn, determined by the 'crucial events' already outlined. It is simply that the story is told from different points of view: one scholar observes the emergence of the secular institutions required by a modern industrial society, the other documents both the influence and the adjustments of a territorially-based church to the upheavals and dislocations of the industrialization process.

One element in this transformation is the process of institutional separation or differentiation, in which tasks or areas of activity traditionally undertaken by the churches move bit by bit into the secular sphere. Such areas of activity include education, healthcare and – of course – welfare. In each situation, a particular variant of the welfare state emerges, as a similar goal (the separating out of welfare from the influence of the churches and the creation of an autonomous sphere with its own institutional norms) is achieved, or semi-achieved, in somewhat different ways. As we have seen, the role of both theology and ecclesiology in determining these pathways is increasingly recognized in the literature.

In parenthesis, it is worth noting once again the very different state of affairs that emerged in the United States. Here an entirely different mode of religious activity – what Martin calls 'an almost unqualified pluralism' – with no embedding in territory, and no long-term existence prior to industrialization, moved easily into the nascent cities of modern America. No great dislocation of pre-urban and pre-industrial patterns here – they simply did not exist. At the same time, a markedly different political system, deriving this time from a revolution built through religion rather than against it, resisted rather than encouraged the development of a welfare state in the sense that this is understood in Europe (Berger et al. 2008). Clearly, there is a relationship between the two developments, which needs careful examination. For a start, the myriad congregations that form the substance of American religious life are themselves a major component of the welfare system, both formal and less so. It is these organizations that offer lifelines to fragile and newly-arrived communities on the margins of American society.

---

[5] See, for example, Martin (1990; 2002).

A book on Europe is not the place to examine in detail the faith-based initiatives of the United States and the controversies that surround them.[6] It is, however, important to recognize that the very evident connections between the place of the churches in modern or modernizing Europe and the secular institutions that (on some readings at least) have come to replace them, do not simply stop once the welfare state as we know it is established. It is true that European populations have come to regard the state as the principal provider of welfare – that is quite clear from the data gathered in the WREP case studies. But they are equally aware that, in many parts of Europe, what is provided by the state is far from comprehensive, and likely to become less so given the pressures, both internal and external, to which it is exposed. These pressures were described in some detail in the opening sections of this book, and were given flesh and blood in the chapters that followed.

The crucial point to be made at this stage is that the pathways established by Martin in the secularization process, together with the particular regime-type with which they are associated, are as pertinent now as the welfare state begins to erode as they were when it was established. Almost all European societies are facing the same question: if the state is no longer able, or even willing, to provide a comprehensive system of welfare for its citizens, who is to be responsible for this task? It is equally clear that the churches, amongst others, have a role to play in these changes. Increasingly they are filling the gaps left by the state as the latter comes under strain. Careful scrutiny of the WREP data, however, encourages the following conclusion: that the factors which were present when the initial redistribution of responsibilities took place are still operative as the new situation begins to emerge. Or, to put the same point in a different way, the process of de-differentiation – the *renewed* co-operation between the churches and the secular sphere – is as culturally specific as its predecessor. It follows that there will be a relatively easy resumption of the welfare role on the part of the churches in some areas of Europe, and a much more difficult one in others – an idea to be pursued in our partner volume.

At this stage, three examples from the WREP project are enough to illustrate the point. In Italy or Greece, a very incomplete institutional separation in the first place has meant that the line between state and church remains essentially fluid. It can move back and forth as the situation demands. Greece evokes the specificities of the Orthodox world with its own understanding of institutional separation (a point recognized by Martin). Italy, in contrast, falls into the rather more antagonistic 'Latin' pattern, as does France. But as Martin makes clear from the outset, the details of the Italian case are very different from those of the French (Martin 1978: 124–126). In the former, the Catholic Church has retained a far greater influence at both national and local level – this was certainly the case in the welfare mix discovered in Vicenza. The contrast with Evreux is striking – so

---

[6] A good introduction to faith-based initiatives in the United States is provided by Cnaan (2002) and Cnaan et al. (2006).

much so that in Evreux the likelihood of any formal collaboration between church and state is, and is likely to remain, almost impossible. Co-operation exists in this locality, but informally, on the margins and out of sight, reflecting a national situation in which the church has been comprehensively displaced by the secular state. As we have seen already, the researcher engaged on the French case had difficulty persuading the public authorities to co-operate at all in a project that paid attention to religion. In Finland, finally, the very particular conditions of the recession in the early 1990s have led not only to a noticeable rise in the welfare roles undertaken by the churches, but to a gain in popularity as a result. The move away from the state and back to the voluntary sector (including the churches) as the provider of some elements of welfare may not be universally welcomed; nor is it necessarily ideal in terms of Luther's two kingdoms. It can, however, be achieved without major recriminations on either side.

Similar stories could be told of the remaining cases, balancing commonality against difference. No European society can escape the strains and stresses associated with providing welfare for an ageing population in an increasingly volatile economic climate. Each society, however, will deal with this within the specificities of its own history, aware of the limitations imposed by the past as well as of the opportunities offered by the present. Exactly the same parameters, moreover, will come into play when religious minorities are introduced into the discussion, both in general and in terms of welfare provision. This last is the subject of WREP's successor – the project known as WaVE (Welfare and Values in Europe). In this case – as was made clear in Chapter 1 – welfare has become not so much the focus of the study as such, as the 'prism' through which core values are perceived, with a particular emphasis on inclusion and exclusion. Precisely this issue, however, resonates differently in countries accustomed to a religious monopoly (historically speaking), as opposed to those in which there has been a degree of pluralism for some time.

Beneath these issues, a more profound question is beginning to emerge: it concerns the place of religion in the public discourse of European societies. In much of Europe, the following – necessarily unstable – situation pertains: a largely secularized population is increasingly obliged to address complex religious questions on a regular basis. The situation is made all the more difficult in so far as the process of secularization has deprived many of those engaged in these conversations of the knowledge, and therefore the vocabulary, necessary for the successful resolution of such questions. One of these concerns the place of religion and religious organizations in the delivery of services, including but not only welfare. The changing nature of education, it is clear, raises equally thorny issues. Another involves the very difficult questions of pluralism and tolerance which have arisen all over Europe, including, for example, the tensions between freedom of speech and the protection of religious sensitivities; pushed to the extreme, these inevitably collide. Whatever the case, it is necessary to take account of the minority religions in Europe, many of which have difficulty coming to terms with the public/private distinction which has become the crux of post-Enlightenment understandings of religious life in Europe.

Such discussions go beyond the parameters of this book. They will be raised again in the companion volume, which will probe in greater depth the 'logic' of a study that examines – through a comparative analysis of welfare provision – the growing significance of religion in the *public* life of Europe. How can the religious voice or voices be heard? And what tools and concepts are required of social science in order that we understand them better? How, finally, can the increasing presence of religion be seen as an opportunity rather than a threat – as a means of resolving a problem rather than exacerbating it? Finding constructive answers to these questions constitutes a demanding, but crucially important agenda – a fact that is increasingly recognized in both Europe and its member states. WREP, we trust, has contributed positively to this discussion.

Appendix 1
The WREP Team

In total, WREP has included 24 researchers from eight countries. The members of the co-ordination group are listed first, noting those who also undertook the Swedish case study. In addition to the Swedish material, Ninna Edgardh was responsible for the work on gender within WREP and much day-to-day management, Per Pettersson for the sociological analysis and overall scheduling, and Thomas Ekstrand for the theological dimension. In the remaining case studies, the senior scholar is named first, followed by the 'junior' researcher.

The Co-ordination Group

Anders Bäckström, Project Director, University of Uppsala: Sociology of religion
Grace Davie, Assistant Director, University of Exeter: Sociology

Members of the Swedish team

Ninna Edgardh, University of Uppsala: Ecclesiology; Gender studies
Thomas Ekstrand, University of Uppsala: Theology
Per Pettersson, University of Karlstad: Sociology of religion

Specialist advisors

Eva Jeppsson Grassman, University of Stockholm: Social work
  (now at the University of Linköping)
Bo Edvardsson, University of Karlstad: Business studies

Case Study Teams

Norway

Trygve Wyller, University of Oslo: Ethics
Olav Helge Angell, Diakonhjemmet, University College, Oslo:
  Sociology of religion

Finland

Eila Helander, University of Helsinki: Church and social studies
Anne Birgitta Pessi, University of Helsinki: Sociology of religion

Germany

Heinz Schmidt, University of Heidelberg: Practical theology
   and Hans-Georg Ziebertz, University of Würzburg: Practical theology
Annette Leis-Peters, University of Uppsala: Sociology of religion

England

Douglas Davies, University of Durham: Theology
Martha Middlemiss Lé Mon, University of Uppsala: Sociology of religion

France

Danièle Hervieu-Léger, EHESS, Paris: Sociology
Corinne Valasik, EHESS, Paris: Sociology of religion
   and François Mabille, Institut Catholique, Paris: Sociology of religion

Italy

Chantal Saint-Blancat, University of Padua: Sociology
Annalisa Frisina, University of Padua: Sociology

Greece

Nikos Kokosalakis, Panteion University, Athens: Sociology
Lina Molokotos-Liederman, University of Exeter: Sociology
   and Effie Fokas, University of Exeter/London School of Economics: Political
      science

The Benefits and Problems of Linguistic Diversity in a Comparative European Project

Martha Middlemiss Lé Mon

This short note on translation was prepared at an early stage in the life of WREP. Its contents, however, have resonated in every phase of our work. Hence the decision to reproduce it in full as an Appendix to this book.

An American company setting up a European arm would not always recognize the number and variety of languages that have to be grappled with in this part of the world, and the implications that these questions have for the success of the business in question. English, it is assumed, is sufficient as a means of communication. Similarly, in the international research community, the assumption that English is the common language is frequently made. Everyone, however, can relate frustrated accounts from conferences where a language barrier meant either that they were not understood or could not understand.

We were aware of all of this at the outset of the Welfare and Religion in a European Perspective project, but paid little attention to it given the good levels of English in the group and the fact that several of the researchers shared other languages in common. Gradually, however, as the project progressed, we realized that the language question struck at the heart of the very issues that the project was attempting to research. This was not simply a translation issue; it was more radical than that. Quite simply, key words did not exist in one or more languages in the countries under review. A key question became, 'Why not?' Paradoxically, however, the 'problem' offered new opportunities, as the researchers involved began to articulate values and concepts which were taken for granted in their native countries but not elsewhere. Queries about how to translate a particular word for use in an interview guide led to in-depth and very fruitful discussions regarding deep-seated cultural values central to the understanding of religion or welfare in a particular country, which otherwise might not have come to light.

Some Examples

A good example can be found in the concept of welfare itself. It was decided very early on in the project – in line with the general explorative methodology of the empirical research – to start with a very broad definition of welfare, giving interviewees the opportunity to define the implications of the term for themselves before proceeding with the rest of the interview. This produced interesting results, with a split appearing between those who saw welfare as something provided by the state (the 'welfare system'), and those who interpreted the word as having a broader meaning, encompassing personal health and well-being, spiritual as well as physical. Such responses were of considerable interest to the project, but even before that, it was important to check the word that was used to translate welfare in each national context. In French, for instance, no word exists that is a direct translation of the English word 'welfare'. The French welfare state is referred to as '*l'état providence*', a phraseology which, in referring *necessarily* to the state, cannot be used to ask questions of individuals regarding the assumed connections between the state and the welfare system. The same is true of the situation in Italy, where the researcher chose to use the English word 'welfare' in place of the Italian term, for this very reason (see Frisina 2006: 184).

Such problems were restricted neither to the concept of welfare, nor to words that exist in the English language but have no counterpart in others. We have struggled, for example, to find a suitable translation for the German word *Ökonomisierung*. One author, writing in Swedish, has translated the term as *ekonomisering*, which he defines as an 'ongoing process effecting societal functions whereby increasing numbers of social and cultural phenomena are turned into markets and defined in economic terms' (Mårtenson 2004: 1) (my translation). While the phenomenon is recognizable in an English context, the actual word does not seem to exist in the language. Terms such as 'marketization' are close, but do not have the same emphasis, while 'neo-liberalism' is too politically-loaded a term and 'economization' is just plain wrong!

Having native speakers involved in a project can, at times, be almost more of a hindrance than a help. The well-known quip that the United States and the United Kingdom are two nations divided by a common language indicates the problems that can arise if it is assumed that the English language transcends cultural context. The point can be illustrated with reference to religious professionals. For an English speaker familiar with the English context, the natural word to use for a priest with particular responsibility for a geographical parish would be 'vicar' or 'incumbent'. These words, however, carry meaning regarding the legal status of the said clergyperson. Using this term of a Swedish parish priest with management responsibility (*kyrkoherde*), for example, could be misleading for an informed English reader. The question then arises of what term should be used instead. 'Priest in charge' might seem a logical choice, if it were not for the fact that in the English Anglican context, a 'priest in charge' is a priest with specific responsibility for a particular church or church plant, but under the authority of the parish priest – precisely the opposite, in fact, of what is intended.

The above is an example from the church environment. Others can be found in issues that are key not just to this project, but to the developing structures of the European Union more generally. In trying to compare towns and their administrative structures of governance across Europe, for instance, we sought comparable terms to describe the different levels of responsibility. Again, we met with the problem that the obvious English term for one level – 'local authority' – has a very specific connotation in its native context, which may not be appropriate for what others are trying to describe. Similarly, the word 'region' is used in many different countries, but describes areas of quite different geographical sizes. Looking for guidance, we turned to the website of the European Union Committee of the Regions, hoping that for internal purposes at least some common terminology would have been created. Here it was possible to see which bodies from each of the countries in the project (except Norway) are represented in the Committee and therefore counted as regions, but there is no common terminology. The list of national delegations and their co-ordinating institutions, for example, lists the Swedish delegation as co-ordinated by the common office for the Federation of County Councils and the Association of Local Authorities, while the United Kingdom equivalent is the Local Government International Bureau, and in Finland the Association of Local and Regional Authorities (see European Union Committee of the Regions 2005).

Nor are such issues of context, themselves tied up with terminology, restricted to the domain of bureaucratic terms, whether ecclesiastical or secular. Issues of gender provoked similar discussions, both in terms of genuinely comparable material and of the relevant terms to use. Here it is important to remember that WREP has its origins in the Swedish context, where the issue of gender equality is well-anchored in both political and public debate. The language has a word for this phenomenon: *jämställdhet*. The fact that such a specific term exists is revealing of political and cultural thinking. More precisely, the issue is seen as specific and separate from discussion of other forms of inequality – in contrast to the United Kingdom, where there is no specific term and gender equality is seen as one form of equality among many (to be sought along with racial, ethnic and religious equality, to name but the most obvious). The contrast can be seen very clearly in a comparison of the case studies from Darlington and Gävle. Without thinking, interviewees in Darlington answered questions referring to gender inequalities with reference to inequality in general. In the French case, a further complexity is revealed. As Corinne Valasik notes in her report on the national situation in France, the issue of gender equality was largely absent from public debate until the late 1990s. The reason for this lies in the dominance of republican universalism, which has been seen to exclude the possibility of focusing on the rights of different sections of the population (Mabille and Valasik 2004: 255). It is hardly surprising, therefore, that no accepted terminology has emerged in this field.

Developing an Unexpected Methodology

What, then, is the significance of these considerations – both for the project as a whole and beyond its boundaries? One point is clear: the process of uncovering and fighting with the linguistic challenges in this project has revealed issues which have profound consequences for comparative projects in the humanities and social sciences and the development of suitable methodologies to support them. To shed some light on these bold claims, two issues, already hinted at in examples from the project, require further discussion at a more theoretical level: first, contextualization and the dangers of domestication (both linguistic and conceptual); and second, universalization and the problems raised by a search for universal models.

Contextualization

Each individual researcher was based in, and culturally conditioned by, the national situation in which he or she was working. This grounding in a particular situation – including a whole range of assumptions which inform our particular 'domestic representations' (to borrow a term from Lawrence Venuti) – has its benefits in enabling us to see what is different from our own case, but also what is similar. At the same time, however, as Theo Hermans has noted, these 'domestic representations' create their own forms of dyslexia, enlarging some similarities while generating blind spots in other areas (Hermans 2003: 382). Translation, in other words, wields considerable power in constructing representations of foreign cultures – both in relation to the foreign culture itself, and to the influence it can have on the domestic scene. In Venuti's words, '[T]ranslation projects construct uniquely domestic representations of foreign cultures, but since these projects address specific cultural constituencies, they are simultaneously engaged in the formation of domestic identities' (Venuti 1998:75).

For Venuti there is an ethical element evident here which suggests that a distinction should be made between bad and good translation. Building on the work of Antoine Berman, Venuti argues that bad translation is necessarily ethnocentric and 'forms' the foreign culture – carrying out a 'systematic negation of the strangeness of the foreign work' under the guise of making the text accessible (Berman 1992: 5). Good translation, in contrast, opens up a dialogue and allows for cross-breeding which can enrich the translating language (Venuti 1998: 81). The relevant question for a translator, or scholar writing in a foreign language, is therefore not simply what is the 'best' rendering of a term, but rather what is necessary to give an outsider access to the text (Hermans 2003: 382). Venuti concludes that any evaluation of a translation project 'must include a consideration of discursive strategies, their institutional settings and their social functions and effects' (Venuti 1998: 82). Any comparative project that makes use of different languages and draws from different disciplines should include such considerations.

A good example of such an approach – and one very relevant to WREP – can be found in the 'Teaching Travelling Concepts' project, which aims to track 'key feminist concepts across the geographical, political and cultural complexity that is contemporary Europe' (Babovec and Hemmings 2004: 333). For these authors, considering how the terms 'sex' and 'gender' travel is not simply an issue of creating terminology where it does not exist in the native language. Rather, the translation of such terms involves critique and/or acceptance of their use as a 'dominant feminist heuristic' (Babovec and Hemmings 2004: 335). Of the work within their own project they say:

> These 'translations' must therefore be understood not only as pragmatic ones, but also as theoretical and historically engaged approaches, that draw on, interpret and intervene within the fields that they seek to describe or transform. (Babovec and Hemmings 2004: 335)

The authors note in particular the English-language dominance of the field, and the consequences that insufficient attention to detail in the translation and adaptation of European concepts have on the breadth of feminist thought. Interestingly, they comment on a phenomenon also brought to light in the WREP project – namely, that:

> [T]he absence of such work perpetuates the lack of acknowledgement of either the different histories of feminist concepts (in the case of French and Italian traditions), or the fundamental epistemological challenges to an English language feminism that European translation evidences. (Babovec and Hemmings 2004: 335–6)

There is, in other words, much to be gained from a more reflexive approach to translation, not just for individual academic projects, but also for the development of and between academic disciplines. Concepts from feminist thought, for example (as, indeed, notions of welfare and welfare systems), are not only influenced by their national context, but also by their disciplinary affiliation. Quite clearly, some of these concepts have been incorporated to greater or lesser extent into more than one discipline. Bal, writing on this issue, maintains that concepts which travel between disciplines can offer increased precision and reach exactly because of this movement (Bal 2002: 37). This is only the case, however, so long as the movement entails a degree of reassessment and change – something rather different from the imposition of a concept from one discipline onto another (Bal 2002: 39). Concepts are interesting and valuable, in other words, not because they mean the same for everyone, but precisely because they do not.

Universalization

The discussion so far highlights the pitfalls that exist in attempting to work across geographical and disciplinary boundaries. At the same time, it automatically raises the question of the value and validity of universal models. Clifford Geertz articulates precisely this tension in his development of the concept of 'thick' description. Geertz argues that cultural analysis is, or ought to be, '[G]uessing at meanings, assessing the guesses, and drawing explanatory conclusions from the better guesses, not discovering the Continent of Meaning and mapping out its bodiless landscape' (Geertz 1973: 20).

For him, the problems with overarching models are clear, in that they tend to obscure the particular and interesting in the cultural context studied. The tension, however, between the need to 'penetrate an unfamiliar universe of symbolic action' and the need to advance theory, between the need to understand and the need to be able to analyse, is both large and 'essentially irremovable' (Geertz 1973: 24). Geertz writes as an ethnographer and anthropologist, but his observations are relevant to any scholar studying cultural phenomena and grappling with the need to describe and understand the specific, while also attempting to make the material accessible for comparison at an analytic level. Geertz concludes that the role of theory in ethnography is to 'provide a vocabulary in which what symbolic action has to say about itself – that is about the role of culture in human life – can be expressed' (Geertz 1973: 27). Two questions follow from this: can the reflexive approach be of use to other disciplines when approaching comparative studies; and can the idea of a linguistic 'toolbox' be of help to the issues which surface in translation within such enterprises?

In terms of the linguistic challenge – the focus of this briefing paper – one scholar who has already made the connection is Theo Hermans. He has made use of the concept of thick description, as articulated by Geertz, to develop the concept of 'thick translation'. In his discussion of cross-cultural translation, Hermans comes to the conclusion that Rodney Needham was correct in arguing that there is 'no metalanguage to hold the invariant of transcultural comparison' (Hermans 2003: 384). There is no way, therefore, to establish fixed points around which to carry out objective comparison, and all that can be done is to constantly revaluate and question the 'language that serves as our probing tool' (Hermans 2003: 384). Cross-cultural mapping, translation and comparison, then, are, of necessity, self-reflexive. We need, Hermans argues, to abandon ideas of achieving full and accurate reproductions, and rather see language as a tool which can assist in the cross-cultural mapping at which we are really aiming.

Thick translation, like thick description, is such an approach, which allows for a 'self-conscious moment' and which keeps the 'universalizing urge of theory in check' (Hermans 2003: 386). It makes conscious efforts to avoid imposing categories derived from one tradition on another, and – in making the translator or author's subject position visible – removes the illusion of neutrality which is otherwise a danger.

Concluding Remarks

Given the experiences of this project, we wish to support Hermans and Bal in their calls for a reflexive approach to language and the use of concepts which are negotiable. Both language in general, and concepts in particular, are not only tools of analysis, but 'embodiments of the cultural practice' – to borrow from

Bal – which we aim to understand better through using them (Bal 2002: 21). Bal uses the metaphor of travel to illustrate this circular process – a choice which is singularly appropriate.

Both travel between languages and travel between disciplines can enrich a project if the researchers are prepared to keep an open mind and adopt a reflexive approach. A project which risks questioning assumptions, and is prepared to go off the beaten track, may not be taking the easiest path; nonetheless, it has much to gain from and much to contribute to the development of appropriate methodologies for use in comparative research. Such has been the case in WREP, which has not only drawn from eight very different case studies, but has brought together fields of study that are seldom connected in the literature.

Appendix 3
The Principal Publications of the *From State Church to Free Folk Church* Project

The following reports from the Church-State Project have all been published by Verbum, Stockholm. They are listed here in chronological order.

1999

Bäckström, Anders (ed.). *Från statskyrka till fri folkkyrka. En religionssociologisk, tjänsteteoretisk och teologisk analys inför förändrade relationer mellan Svenska kyrkan och staten år 2000. Presentation av forskningsprojektet/ From State Church to Free Folk Church. A Sociology of Religion, Service Theoretical and Theological Analysis in the face of Disestablishment between the Church of Sweden and the State in the Year 2000. Project Description.* (This short book is effectively the project outline. It sets out the purposes of the project, which were: to study the disestablishment process as the church ceased to be a state church and became an independent folk church; to study, both theoretically and empirically, the relationship of the Swedish people to the church; and to analyse the self-understanding of the Church of Sweden from the following perspectives: service-theory, theology and gender.)

Bäckström, Anders. *När tros – och värderingsbilder förändras. En analys av nattvards – och husförhörssedens utveckling i Sundsvallsregionen 1805–1890.* (A decrease in participation in both Holy Communion and parish catechetic meetings are related to the comprehensive cultural changes that took place during the nineteenth century.)

2000

Gustafsson, Göran and Pettersson, Thorleif (eds). *Folkkyrkor och religiös pluralism – den nordiska religiösa modellen.* (Nordic 'civic' religion is characterized by a combination of passive church membership and comparatively strong participation in the rites/occasional offices of the church.)

Pettersson, Per. *Kvalitet i livslånga tjänsterelationer. Svenska kyrkan ur tjänsteteoretiskt och religionssociologiskt perspektiv.* (Nearly all Swedes have a relationship with the Church of Sweden, but rarely make use of its services. This ambiguous position is approached from a service-theoretical perspective combined with insights from the sociology of religion.)

Thidevall, Sven. *Kampen om folkkyrkan. Ett folkkyrkligt reformprograms öden 1928-1932.* (When Swedish society both industrialized and democratized, a reform programme for a modern folk church was introduced. Parliament, however, forced through a further re-organization, which led the church to a more defensive position.)

2001

Bäckström, Anders. *Svenska kyrkan som välfärdsaktör i en global kultur. En studie av religion och omsorg.* (What role does a national folk church play in the transfer from industrial society to a late modern service society? Can an institutional church find a place between an increasingly globalized culture and an increasingly privatized local identity?)

Edgardh Beckman, Ninna. *Feminism och liturgi – en ecklesiologisk studie.* (This study discusses church services celebrated in Sweden and the difficulty of combining feminist demands with traditional forms of Christian liturgy.)

Hansson, Per. *Svenska kyrkans organisationskultur.* (The cultural life of the local church is split: outwardly warm and generous, but inwardly less so. The changing relationship between state and church places heavy demands on the flexibility of the church.)

Jeppsson Grassman, Eva. *Socialt arbete i församlingens hägn.* (This book presents a picture of the social work undertaken by the Church of Sweden and other congregations in a Swedish municipality. Questions for the future include the following: will the parish be a provider of welfare services or will it become an independent voice in society?)

Sjödin, Ulf. *Mer mellan himmel och jord. En studie av den beprövade erfarenhetens ställning bland svenska ungdomar.* (In a postmodern and increasingly non-traditional society, trust in authority has decreased, especially among young people in their view of religion. The religiosity of young people can be characterized as seeking without really finding.)

2002

Bromander, Jonas. *Rum för röster. Sociologiska analyser av musiklivet inom Svenska kyrkan som det uppfattas av kyrkobesökare, kyrkomusiker samt kyrkokorister.* (While traditional worship services may be sidelined when society changes, participation in church choirs and church music remains considerable. Does a decreasing knowledge of the Christian faith affect the musical life of the church?)

Ekstrand, Thomas. *Folkkyrkans gränser. En teologisk analys av övergången från statskyrka till fri folkkyrka.* (This study discusses theological texts which attempt both to defend and to criticize folk church ecclesiology; it also looks at official reports produced by government committees from the 1950s onwards in order to prepare for the disestablishment of the Church of Sweden.)

Stålhammar, Bert. *Kyrkoherdens ledningsvillkor.* (The church's complicated organizational structure contains inherent uncertainties and contradictions which strongly affect the priest's capacity to exert effective leadership. Since the Church Order of 2000, the church has increasing opportunities to conduct its own business, which demands distinct leadership at all levels.)

2003

DeMarinis, Valerie. *Pastoral Care, Existential Health, and Existential Epidemiology: A Swedish Postmodern Case Study.* (This study examines the theological, ecclesiological and pastoral challenges facing the church in the first decade of the twenty-first century, in a postmodern context where there are no absolutes.)

2004

Bäckström, Anders, Edgardh Beckman, Ninna, and Pettersson, Per. *Religious Change in Northern Europe: The Case of Sweden.* (The relationship between church and state has been successively weakened, culminating in the separation of 2000. Religion, however, has not relinquished its role in late modern Sweden but faith and values have, to an increasing extent, been privatized.)

Bibliography

Aaraas, E. (2002). 'Skøytebane på Bragernes torg'. *Drammens Tidende.* 30 July.

Alber, J. and U. Köhler (2004). *Health and Care in an Enlarged Europe.* (Dublin: European Foundation for the Improvement of Living and Working Conditions).

Allardt, E. (1975). *Att ha, att älska, att vara: om välfärd i Norden.* (Lund: Argos).

— (1976). *Hyvinvoinnin ulottuvuuksia.* (Porvoo: WSOY).

— (1989). *An Updated Indicator System: Having, Loving, Being.* (Helsinki: Department of Sociology, University of Helsinki).

Almqvist, R. M. (2004). *Icons of New Public Management: Four Studies on Competition, Contracts and Control.* (Stockholm: School of Business, Stockholm University).

Ammerman, N. T. (2000). 'Congregation'. In W. C. Roof (ed.) *Contemporary American Religion.* (New York: Macmillan). 148–150.

Amnå, E. (ed.) (1995). *Medmänsklighet att hyra? Åtta forskare om ideell verksamhet.* (Stockholm: Libris).

— (ed.) (2005). *Civilsamhället. Några forskningsfrågor.* (Södertälje: Riksbankens jubileumsfond i samarbete med Gidlunds förlag).

Angell, O. H. (2004). 'Welfare, church and gender in Norway'. In N. Edgardh Beckman (ed.) *Welfare, Church and Gender in Eight European Countries.* (Uppsala: Uppsala Institute for Diaconal and Social Studies). 63–102.

— (2008). 'Religion and the media: The cultural role of a church-based welfare agent in a Norwegian local community'. *Journal of Contemporary Religion* 23 (2): 133–145.

Angell, O. H. and T. Wyller (2006). 'The Church of Norway as an agent of welfare – the case of Drammen'. In A. B. Yeung, N. Edgardh Beckman and P. Pettersson (eds) *Churches in Europe as Agents of Welfare: Sweden, Norway and Finland.* (Uppsala: Institute for Diaconal and Social Studies). 86–141.

Anheier, H. K. and L. M. Salamon (1994). *The Emerging Sector. An Overview.* (Baltimore: The Johns Hopkins University Institute for Policy Studies).

Anttonen, A., J. Baldock and J. Sipilä (2003). *The Young, the Old and the State: Social Care Systems in Five Industrial Nations.* (Cheltenham: Elgar).

Anttonen, A. and J. Sipilä (1996). 'European social care services: Is it possible to identify models?' *Journal of European Social Policy* 6 (2): 87–100.

Arapoglou, V. (2004). 'The governance of homelessness in Greece: Discourse and power in the study of philanthropic networks'. *Critical Social Policy* 24 (1): 102–126.

Arbetarbladet. (2004). Gävles fattiga ber kyrkan om pengar. *Arbetarbladet.* 4 December

Archambault, E. (1997). *The Nonprofit Sector in France.* (Manchester: Manchester University Press).

Archbishops' Council (2002). *Response of the Archbishops' Council of the Church of England to the Report of the Strategy Unit 'Private Action, Public Benefit.*

— (2003a). *A Year in Review 2002–2003.*

— (2003b). *Civil Partnership: Church of England Response to DTI Consultation Document.* (London: Church House Publishing).

Archbishops' Council Commission on Urban Life and Faith (2006). *Faithful Cities: A Call for Celebration, Vision and Justice.* (London: Church House Publishing and Methodist Publishing House).

Arts, W. and J. Gelissen (2002). 'Three worlds of welfare capitalism or more? A state-of-the-art report'. *Journal of European Social Policy* 12 (2): 137–158.

Ascoli, U. et al. (eds) (1997). *Comparing Social Welfare Systems in Southern Europe.* (Paris: MIRE).

Augoustidis, A. (2002). 'Cooperation of psychiatry and the church in a deinstitutionalization project'. *International Journal of Medical Health* 30 (4): 42–48.

Aune, K. (ed.) (2008). *Women and Religion in the West: Challenging Secularization.* (Aldershot: Ashgate).

Babovec, E. D. and C. Hemmings (2004). 'Teaching travelling concepts in Europe'. *Feminist Theory* 5 (3): 333–342.

Bäckström, A. (ed.) (1999a). *From State Church to Free Folk Church. A Sociology of Religion, Service Theoretical and Theological Analysis in the face of Disestablishment between the Church of Sweden and the State in the Year 2000. Project Description.* (Stockholm: Verbum).

— (1999b). *När tros – och värderingsbilder förändras. En analys av nattvards – och husförhörssedens utveckling i Sundsvallsregionen 1805–1890.* (Stockholm: Verbum).

— (2000). 'De kyrkliga handlingarna som ram, relation och välbefinnande'. In G. Gustafsson and T. Pettersson (ed.) *Folkkyrkor och religiös pluralism – den nordiska religiösa modellen.* (Stockholm: Verbum). 134–171.

— (2001). *Svenska kyrkan som välfärdsaktör i en global kultur: en studie av religion och omsorg.* (Stockholm: Verbum).

— (2002). 'Att definiera religion i en senmodern kultur'. In C. Dahlgren, E. Hamberg and T. Pettersson (eds) *Religion och sociologi: ett fruktbart möte. Festskrift till Göran Gustafsson.* (Lund: Teologiska institutionen). 79–95.

— (2003a). 'Svenska kyrkan som social aktör i en senmodern tid'. In *Årsbok för kristen humanism och samhällssyn 2003: Tillräckligt mänsklig.* (Uppsala: Förbundet för kristen humanism och samhällssyn). 32–44.

— (ed.) (2003b). *Välfärd och religion i europeiskt perspektiv: en jämförande studie av kyrkors roll som välfärdsaktörer inom den sociala ekonomin: projektbeskrivning.* (Uppsala: Institute for Diaconal and Social Studies).

— (2004). 'The church in a new century'. In O. G. Winsnes (ed.) *Contemporary Religion and Church: A Nordic Perspective.* (Trondheim: Tapir). 81–99.

— (ed.) (2005). *Welfare and Religion: A Publication to Mark the Fifth Anniversary of the Uppsala Institute for Diaconal and Social Studies*. (Uppsala: Institute for Diaconal and Social Studies).

Bäckström, A. and J. Bromander (1994). *För att tjäna: en studie av diakoniuppfattningar hos kyrkliga befattningshavare*. Svenska kyrkans utredningar. (Uppsala: Diakonistiftelsen Samariterhemmet).

— (1995). *Kyrkobyggnaden och det offentliga rummet: en undersökning av kyrkobyggnadens roll i det svenska samhället*. (Uppsala: Svenska kyrkans centralstyrelse).

Bäckström, A., G. Davie, N. Edgardh and P. Pettersson (eds) (2010). *Welfare and Religion in 21st century Europe. Volume 2: Gendered, Religious and Social Change*. (Farnham: Ashgate).

Bäckström, A., G. Davie and R. Kingsbury (1996). *Building a Future. The eleventh Anglo-Scandinavian Pastoral Conference, 1996 Tallinn*. (Uppsala: Uppsala University Faculty of Theology).

Bäckström, A., N. Edgardh Beckman and P. Pettersson (2004). *Religious Change in Northern Europe: The Case of Sweden*. (Stockholm: Verbum).

Bahle, T. (2003). 'The changing institutionalization of social services in England and Wales, France and Germany: Is the welfare state on the retreat?' *Journal of European Social Policy* 13 (1): 5–20.

Bal, M. (2002). *Travelling Concepts in the Humanities: A Rough Guide*. (Toronto: University of Toronto Press).

Balbo, L. (1991). *Tempi di vita. Studi e proposte per cambiarli*. (Milan: Feltrinelli).

Baldock, J. (1999). *Social Policy*. (Oxford: Oxford University Press).

Baldwin, P. (1996). 'Can we define a European welfare state model?'. In B. Greve (ed.) *Comparative Welfare Systems: The Scandinavian Model in a Period of Change*. (London: Macmillan). 29–44.

Barbetta, G. P., S. Cima and N. Zamaro (2003). *Le istituzioni nonprofit in Italia: Dimensioni organizzative, economiche e sociali*. (Bologna: Il Mulino).

Barbetta, G. P. and F. Maggio (2002). *Nonprofit*. (Bologna: Il Mulino).

Barzelay, M. (2001). *The New Public Management: Improving Research and Policy Dialogue*. (Berkeley: University of California Press).

Bauman, Z. (1998). *Work, Consumerism and the New Poor*. (Buckingham: Open University Press).

— (2002). *Society under Siege*. (Cambridge: Polity Press).

— (2006). *Liquid Fear*. (Cambridge: Polity Press).

BBC News. (2006). 'Men not using full baby leave'. http://news.bbc.co.uk/2/hi/uk_news/5232040.stm 01-08-2006

Beck, U. and T. Hviid Nielsen (1997). *Risiko og Frihet*. (Bergen-Sandviken: Fagbokforlaget).

Beck, U. and M. Ritter (1992). *Risk Society: Towards a New Modernity*. (London: Sage).

Beckford, J. A. (1989). *Religion and Advanced Industrial Society.* (London: Unwin Hyman).

Bell, D. (1973). *The Coming of Post-industrial Society: A Venture in Social Forecasting.* (New York: Basic Books).

Bellah, R. N. (1970). *Beyond Belief.* (London: Harper and Row).

— (1985). *Habits of the Heart: Individualism and Commitment in American Life.* (Berkeley: University of California Press).

Benassi, D. and E. Mingione (2003). 'La sfida del reddito minimo di inserimento nel welfare italiano'. In P. Calza Bini, O. Nicolaus and S. Turcio (eds) *Reddito minimo di inserimento. Che fare?* (Rome: Donzelli editore). 85–100.

Berger, P. L. (1969). *The Sacred Canopy: Elements of a Sociological Theory of Religion.* (Garden City, NY: Doubleday).

— (ed.) (1999). *The Desecularization of the World: Resurgent Religion and World Politics.* (Grand Rapids MI: Eerdmans).

Berger, P. L., G. Davie and E. Fokas (2008). *Religious America, Secular Europe? A Theme and Variations.* (Aldershot: Ashgate).

Berger, P. L. and T. Luckmann (1979). *The Social Construction of Reality: A Treatise in the Sociology of Knowledge.* (Harmondsworth: Penguin).

Berman, A. (1992). *The Experience of the Foreign: Culture and Translation in Romantic Germany.* (Albany, NY: State University of New York Press).

Bernardi, F. (1999). *Donne fra famiglia e carriera. Strategie di coppia e vincoli sociali.* (Milan: Franco Angeli).

Beveridge, W. H. (1944). *Full Employment in a Free Society.* (London: George Allen and Unwin).

Bexell, O. (2003). *Folkväckelsens och kyrkoförnyelsens tid.* (Stockholm: Verbum).

Beyer, P. (1994). *Religion and Globalization.* (London: Sage).

Billis, D. (2001). 'Tackling social exclusion: The contribution of voluntary organisations'. In J. Harris and C. Rochester (eds) *Voluntary Organisations and Social Policy in Britain.* (Palgrave: Basingstoke). 37–48.

Billis, D. and M. Harris (1992). 'Taking the strain of change: UK local voluntary agencies enter the post-Thatcher period'. *Non-profit and Voluntary Sector Quarterly* (21): 211–225.

Bimbi, F. (1995). 'Rappresentazioni e politiche familiari in Italia. Cure dei bambini, lavoro professionale delle donne e crisi politico-istituzionale (1980–1990)'. In *Politiche per le Famiglie, Quaderni di formazione e animazione.* (Turin: Edizioni Gruppo Abele). 58–71.

Blomqvist, P. (ed.) (2003a). *Den gränslösa välfärdsstaten. Svensk socialpolitik i det nya Europa.* (Avesta: Agora).

— (2003b). 'EU och välfärdens gränser'. In P. Blomqvist (ed.) *Den gränslösa välfärdsstaten. Svensk socialpolitik i det nya Europa.* (Avesta: Agora). 6–33.

Boeri, T. and R. Perotto (2002). *Meno pensioni, più welfare.* (Bologna: Il Mulino).

Boeßenecker, K.-H. (2005). *Spitzenverbände der Freien Wohlfahrtspflege. Eine Einführung in Organisationsstrukturen und Handlungsfelder der deutschen Wohlfahrtsverbände.* (Weinheim/München: Juventa).

Boll, F. (2008). *Der Sozialstaat in der Krise. Deutschland im internationalen Vergleich.* (Bonn: Dietz).

Bouget, D. and B. Palier (eds) (1999). *Comparing Social Welfare Systems in Nordic Europe and France.* (Paris: MIRE).

Bradshaw, J., N. Finch, P. Kemp, E. Mayhew and J. Williams (2003). *Gender and Poverty in Britain.* (York: University of York, Social Policy Research Unit).

Brecht, M. (1995). 'Matthäus Albers Theologie'. In M. Brecht (ed.) *Ausgewählte Aufsätze IV: Reformation.* (Stuttgart: Calwer Verlag). 237–268.

Bromander, J. (2002). *Rum för röster. Sociologiska analyser av musiklivet inom Svenska kyrkan som det uppfattas av kyrkobesökare, kyrkomusiker samt kyrkokorister.* (Stockholm: Verbum).

Bruce, S. (1996). *Religion in the Modern World: From Cathedrals to Cults.* (Oxford: Oxford University Press).

Bruderhaus Diakonie. (2005). *Gesellschaft vor sozialer Veränderung. Auswirkungen der Verwaltungsstruktur-Reform für die soziale Arbeit in Baden-Württemberg.* (Reutlingen). See http://www.bruderhausdiakonie.de for more information.

Bryson, L., M. Bittman and D. Sue (1994). 'Men´s welfare state, women´s welfare state: Tendencies to convergence in practice and theory?' In D. Sainsbury (ed.) *Gendering Welfare States.* (London: Sage). 118–131.

Bundesarbeitsgemeinschaft der Freien Wohlfahrtspflege (2002). *Die Freie Wohlfahrtspflege. Profil und Leistungen.* (Freiburg im Breisgau: Lambertus).

Butterwegge, C. (2005). *Krise und Zukunft des Sozialstaats.* (Wiesbaden: VS-Verlag).

Byrådet i Oslo (2002). *Frivillighet i endring.* (Oslo).

Carroll, J. W. (1991). *As One with Authority: Reflective Leadership in Ministry.* (Louisville, KY: Westminster John Knox Press).

Casanova, J. (1994). *Public Religions in the Modern World.* (Chicago: University of Chicago Press).

— (2001). 'Religion, the new millennium, and globalization'. *Sociology of Religion* 62: 455–473.

— (2006). 'Rethinking secularization: A global comparative perspective'. *The Hedgehog Review. Critical Reflections on Contemporary Culture* 8: 7–22.

Castagnaro, A. (2002). 'La rivoluzione occulta nell'assistenza degli anziani. Le aiutanti domiciliari'. *Studi Zancan: Politiche e servizi alle persone* 2: 11–34.

Castel, R. (2003). *L'insécurité sociale.* (Paris: Seuil).

Castells, M. (1996). *The Information Age: Economy, Society and Culture. Vol. 1, The Rise of the Network Society.* (Oxford: Blackwell).

— (1998). *End of Millennium.* (Oxford: Blackwell).

— (2000). 'The rise of the fourth world'. In D. Held and A. McGrew (eds) *The Transformations Reader. An Introduction to the Globalization Debate.* (Cambridge: Polity Press). 348–354.

Castles, F. G. (2004). *The Future of the Welfare State: Crisis Myths and Crisis Realities.* (Oxford: Oxford University Press).

Cesareo, V., R. Cipriani, F. Garelli, C. Lanzetti and G. Rovati (1995). *Forme del pluralismo religioso.* Turin: Il Segnalibro.

Chaves, M. and W. Tsitsos (2001). 'Congregations and social services: What they do, how they do it, and with whom'. *Nonprofit and Voluntary Sector Quarterly* 30/4: 660–683.

Church of England (2006a). *Asylum, Immigration and Citizenship Press Release.* http://www.england.anglican.org/cgi-bin/news/item.pl?id=170

— (2006b). *Drugs Policy Press Release.* http://www.england.anglican.org/cgi-bin/news/item.pl?id=247

— (2006c). *Employment Regulations Press Release.* http://www.england.anglican.org/cgi-bin/news/item.pl?id=196

Church Research Institute (2004). *Church in Change.* (Tampere: KTK).

Cnaan, R. (2002). *The Invisible Caring Hand. American Congregations and the Provision of Welfare.* (New York: New York University Press).

Cnaan, R., S. Boddie, C. McGrew and K. Kang (2006). *The Other Philadelphia Story: How Local Congregations Support Quality of Life in Urban America.* (Philadelphia: University of Philadelphia Press).

Comparing Social Welfare Systems in Southern Europe. (1997). (Paris: MIRE).

Comprehensive Diaconal Programme for the Church of Norway (1997). *National Council for the Church of Norway.* http://www.kirken.no/english/doc/Diakoniengelsk.doc

Constantelos, D. (2003). 'Some aspects of stewardship of the Church of Constantinople under Ottoman Turkish rule (1453–1800)'. In A. Scott (ed.) *Good and Faithful Servant: Stewardship in the Orthodox Church.* (New York: St Vladimir's Press). 105–118.

Curtis, J. E., D. E. Baer and E. G. Grabb (2001). 'Nations of joiners: Explaining voluntary association membership in democratic societies'. *American Sociological Review* 66 (6): 783–805.

Dahlberg, L. (2005). 'Interaction between voluntary and statutory social service provision in Sweden: A matter of welfare pluralism, substitution or complementarity?' *Social Policy and Administration* 39 (7): 740–763.

Dalla Mura, F. (2003). *Pubblica amministrazione e nonprofit: guida ai rapporti innovativi nel quadro della legge 328/2000.* (Rome: Carocci).

Daly, M. and J. Lewis (2000). 'The concept of social care and the analysis of contemporary welfare states'. *The British Journal of Sociology* 51 (2): 281–298.

Daly, M. and K. Rake (2003). *Gender and the Welfare State: Care, Work and Welfare in Europe and the USA.* (Cambridge: Polity Press).

Darlington Borough Council (2004). *Darlington Facts and Figures 2004.* (Darlington).

Davie, G. (1994). *Religion in Britain since 1945: Believing without Belonging.* (Oxford: Blackwell).

— (2000). *Religion in Modern Europe: A Memory Mutates.* (Oxford: Oxford University Press).

— (2002). *Europe: The Exceptional Case. Parameters of Faith in the Modern World.* (London: Darton, Longman and Todd).

— (2007a). *The Sociology of Religion.* (London: Sage).

— (2007b). 'Vicarious religion: A methodological challenge'. In N. T. Ammerman (ed.) *Everyday Religion: Observing Modern Religious Lives.* (New York: Oxford University Press). 21–36.

Davie, G. and M. Cook. (1999). *Modern France: Society in Transition.* (London: Routledge).

Davie, G., P. Heelas and L. Woodhead (eds) (2003). *Predicting Religion: Christian, Secular, and Alternative Futures.* (Aldershot: Ashgate).

Davis, F., E. Paulhus and A. Bradstock (2008). *Moral, But No Compass: Government, Church and the Future of Welfare.* (Chelmsford: Matthew James Publishing).

De Leonardis, O. (2002). *In un diverso welfare. Sogni e incubi.* (Milan: Feltrinelli).

De Sandre, I. (2003). *Istituti religiosi e strategie di servizio alle persone: una ricognizione sistematica.* (Padua: Fondazione Zancan).

Degen, J. (2003). *Freiheit und Profil. Wandlungen der Hilfekultur: Plädoyer für eine zukunftsfähige Diakonie.* (Gütersloh: Kaiser).

Del Re, A. (1999). *Donne in politica. Un'indagine sulle candidature femminili nel Veneto.* (Milan: Franco Angeli).

Della Porta, D. (1999). *La politica locale.* (Bologna: Il Mulino).

DeMarinis, V. (2003). *Pastoral Care, Existential Health, and Existential Epidemiology: A Swedish Postmodern Case Study.* (Stockholm: Verbum).

Deufel, K. and M. Wolf (2003). *Ende der Solidarität? Die Zukunft des Sozialstaats.* (Freiburg im Breisgau/ Basel/Vienna: Herder).

Diakonisches Werk Württemberg (2005). http://www.diakonie-wuerttemberg.de

Diamanti, I. (2003). *Bianco, rosso, verde ... e azzurro. Mappe e colori dell'Italia politica.* (Bologna: Il Mulino).

Diamanti, I. and E. Pace (1987). *Tra religione e organizzazione: il caso delle ACLI.* (Padua: Liviana).

Diellas, Y. (2003). I Symvoli tis Ekklesias tis Ellados stin Diamorfosi tou Kratous Pronoias kai i Symmetochi tis sto Systima Koinonikis Frontidas. http://www.ecclesia.gr/greek/holysynod/commitees/welfare/Welfare-0004a.htm

Diocese d'Evreux (2004). Le diocese en chiffres. http://www.evreux.catholique.fr

Dobbelaere, K. (1981). 'Secularization: A multi-dimensional concept'. *Current Sociology* 29 (2): 3–153.

— (2002). *Secularization: An Analysis at Three Levels.* (Brussells: Peter Lang).

Donegani, J.-M. (1993). *La liberté de choisir. Pluralisme religieux et pluralisme politique dans le catholisme français contemporain.* (Paris: Presses de la FNSP).

Dubet, F. (2002). *Le déclin de l'institution.* (Paris: Seuil).

Durkheim, E. (1979). *Suicide: A Study in Sociology.* (London: Routledge).

Edgardh Beckman, N. (2001). *Feminism och liturgi – en ecklesiologisk studie.* (Stockholm: Verbum).

— (ed.) (2004). *Welfare, Church and Gender in Eight European Countries: Working Paper 1 from the Project Welfare and Religion in a European Perspective.* (Uppsala: Institute for Diaconal and Social Studies).

Edgardh Beckman, N., T. Ekstrand and P. Pettersson (2006). 'The Church of Sweden as an agent of welfare: The case of Gävle'. In A. B. Yeung, N. Edgardh Beckman and P. Pettersson (eds) *Churches in Europe as Agents of Welfare – Sweden, Norway and Finland.* (Uppsala: Institute for Diaconal and Social Studies). 20–85.

Edvardsson, B. (2000). *New Service Development and Innovation in the New Economy.* (Lund: Studentlitteratur).

L'Eglise catholique en France (2002). *Annuaire statistique de l'Eglise.*

Ehrenreich, B. and A. R. Hochschild (2004). *Donne globali. Tate, colf e badanti.* (Milan: Feltrinelli).

Eisenstadt, S. (2000). 'Multiple modernities'. *Daedalus. Journal of the American Academy of Arts and Sciences*: 1–29.

Eisenstadt, S. N. (2002). *Multiple Modernities.* (New Brunswick, NJ: Transaction Publishers).

— (2003). *Comparative Civilizations and Multiple Modernities.* (Boston: Brill)

Ekstrand, T. (2002). *Folkkyrkans gränser: en teologisk analys av övergången från statskyrka till fri folkkyrka.* (Stockholm: Verbum).

Engvall, U. (ed.) (2002). *Gemensamt hushåll. Svenska kyrkans roll i den sociala ekonomin.* (Uppsala: Svenska kyrkans församlingsnämnd).

Enochsson, E. (1949). *Den kyrkliga seden, med särskild hänsyn till Västerås stift.* (Stockholm: Svenska kyrkans diakonistyrelse).

Equality Programme of the Finnish Government (1997). http://www.un.org/womenwatch/confer/beijing/national/finisnap.htm

Eriksen, G. F. (2004). Likestilling på autopilot. http://kilden.forskningsradet.no/nyhet/

Esmer, Y. R. and T. Pettersson (eds) (2007). *Measuring and Mapping cultures: 25 Years of Comparative Value Surveys.* (Leiden: Brill).

Esping-Andersen, G. (1990). *The Three Worlds of Welfare Capitalism.* (Cambridge: Polity Press).

— (ed.) (1996). *Welfare States in Transition: National Adaptations in Global Economies.* (London: Sage).

— (1999). *Social Foundations of Postindustrial Economies.* (Oxford: Oxford University Press).

— (ed.) (2002). *Why We Need a New Welfare State.* (Oxford: Oxford University Press).

European Union Committee of the Regions (2005). *European Union Committee of the Regions.* http://www.cor.eu.int/document/presentation/Delegationsnat.pdf

Evangelische Landeskirche in Württemberg (2005). http://www.elk-wue.de

Evangelischer Kirchenbezirk Reutlingen (2005). http://reutlingen.elk-wue.de

Faith in the City: A Call for Action by Church and Nation. (1985). Archbishop of Canterbury's Commission on Urban Priority Areas (London: Church House Publishing).

Falterbaum, J. (2000). *Caritas und Diakonie. Struktur- und Rechtsfragen.* (Neuwied/ Kriftel/ Berlin: Luchterhand).

Febvre, M. and L. Muller (2003). *Un français sur deux est membre d'une association en 2002.* (Paris: Insee Première).

Febvre, M. and L. Muller (2004). *12 millions de bénévoles.* (Paris: Insee Première).

Ferlie, E., K. McLaughlin and S. P. Osborne (eds) (2002). *New Public Management: Current Trends and Future Prospects.* (London: Routledge).

Ferrera, M. (1996). 'Il modello sud-europeo di welfare state'. *Rivista Italiana di Scienza Politica* no. 1: 67–101.

— (1997). 'General introduction'. In U. Ascoli et al. (eds) *Comparing Social Welfare Systems in Southern Europe.* (Paris: MIRE).

— (1998). 'The four 'social Europes': Between universalism and selectivity'. In M. Rhodes and Y. Meny (eds) *The Future of European Welfare. A New Social Contract?* (London: Macmillan). 79–96.

— (1998). *Le trappole del welfare.* (Bologna: Il Mulino).

Fix, B. and E. Fix (2002). 'From charity to client-oriented social service production: A social profile of religious welfare associations in Western European comparison'. *European Journal of Social Work* 5 (1): 55–62.

Forsberg, G., D. Perrons and L. Gonås (2000). 'Paid work: Participation, inclusion and liberation'. In S. Duncan and B. Pfau-Effinger (eds) *Gender, Economy and Culture in the European Union.* (London: Routledge): 27–48.

Frisina, Analisa (2006). 'The Catholic Church in Italy as an Agent of Welfare: The case of Vicenza'. In A. B. Yeung, N. Edgardh Beckman and P. Pettersson (eds) *Churches in Europe as Agents of Welfare – England, Germany, France, Italy and Greece.* (Uppsala: Institute for Diaconal and Social Studies). 182–217.

Fritzell, J. and O. Lundberg (2000). *Välfärd, ofärd och ojämlikhet.* Reports of the Government Commissions (Stockholm: Fritzes).

Furniss, N. (1990). *Idéer om välfärd.* Tidens idéserie (Stockholm: Tiden).

Gallup Ecclesiastica (2003). Data on Finns. (Tampere: KTK).

Garelli, F. (1991). *Religione e Chiesa in Italia.* (Bologna: Il Mulino).

Garelli, F., G. G. Guizzardi and E. Pace (2003). *Un singolare pluralismo. Indagine sul pluralismo morale e religioso degli italiani.* (Bologna: Il Mulino).

Gaskin, K. and J. Davis Smith (1995). *A New Civic Europe? A Study of the Extent and Role of Volunteering.* (London: Volunteer Centre).

Gävle Helga Trefaldighets församling (2001). *Församlingsinstruktion för Gävle Heliga Trefaldighets församling.*

Gävle kyrkliga samfällighet (2003). *Svenska kyrkan i Gävle. Årsredovisning 2003.* Annual Report (Gävle).

Gävle Maria församling (2001). *Församlingsinstruktion för Gävle Maria församling.*

Geertz, C. (1973). *The Interpretation of Cultures: Selected Essays.* (New York: Basic Books).

Gellerstam, G. (1971). *Från fattigvård till församlingsvård: utvecklingslinjer inom fattigvård och diakoni i Sverige 1871 – omkring 1895.* (Lund: Lunds universitet).

Giddens, A. (1991). *Modernity and Self-identity. Self and Society in the Late Modern Age.* (Stanford, CA: Stanford University Press).

Gilbert, N. (2002). *Transformation of the Welfare State: The Silent Surrender of Public Responsibility.* (Oxford: Oxford University Press).

Gonäs, L. and J. Karlsson (2006). *Gender Segregation: Divisions of Work in Post-industrial Welfare States.* (Aldershot: Ashgate).

Grözinger, H. and H.-D. Haas (eds) (2004). *Sozialraumorientierung in der Arbeit der Diakonischen Bezirksstellen. Grundlagen und Ergebnisse einer wissenschaftlichen Forschungsstudie.* (Stuttgart: Diakonisches Werk Württemberg).

Gulbrandsen, T. (2002). *Norske makteliter.* (Oslo: Gyldendal).

Gustafsson, G. (1995). 'Svenska folket, Estonia och religionen'. In L. Ahlin and G. Gustafsson (eds) *Två undersökningar om Estonia och religionen.* (Lund: Lund University). 7–46.

Gustafsson, G. and T. Pettersson (eds) (2000). *Folkkyrkor och religiös pluralism – den nordiska religiösa modellen.* (Stockholm: Verbum).

Habermas, J. (1997). *Solidarietà tra estranei.* (Milan: Guerini e Associati).

— (2005). *Religion in the Public Sphere.* Lecture presented at the Holberg Prize Seminar 28 November 2005.

Hansson, P. (2001). *Svenska kyrkans organisationskultur.* (Stockholm: Verbum).

Harling, P., G. Davie, H. Hartman and B. Murray (1995). *Tro i förorten: delrapport 1 från en seminarieserie om kyrkans uppgift och förutsättningar i förorten idag.* (Uppsala: Stiftssamfälligheten i Uppsala stift).

Harris, M. (1998). *Organizing God's Work. Challenges for Churches and Synagogues.* (London: Macmillan).

Harris, M., C. Rochester and P. Halfpenny (2001). 'Voluntary organizations and social policy: Twenty years of change'. In M. Harris and C. Rochester (eds) *Voluntary Organizations and Social Policy in Britain.* (Basingstoke: Palgrave). 1–20.

Heelas, P. (2006). 'Challenging secularization theory: The growth of "New Age" spiritualities of life'. *The Hedgehog Review. Critical Reflections on Contemporary Culture* 8: 46–58.

Heelas, P. and L. Woodhead (2005). *The Spiritual Revolution: Why Religion is Giving Way to Spirituality.* (Oxford: Blackwell).

Heino, H., K. Salonen and J. Rusama (1997). *Response to Recession. The Evangelical Lutheran Church of Finland in the Years 1992–1996.* (Tampere: Kirkon Tutkimuskeskus).

Heitink, G. (1999). *Practical Theology: History, Theory, Action Domains: Manual for Practical Theology.* (Grand Rapids: Eerdmans).

Helander, E. (2005). 'Churches and Nordic identity: Churches as welfare providers'. In A. Bäckström (ed.) *Welfare and Religion. A Publication to Mark the Fifth Anniversary of the Uppsala Institute for Diaconal and Social Studies.* (Uppsala: Uppsala Institute for Diaconal and Social Studies). 65–71.

Held, D. and A. G. McGrew (2002). *Globalization/Anti-globalization.* (Cambridge: Polity Press).

Herbert, D. (2003). *Religion and Civil Society: Rethinking Public Religion in the Contemporary World.* (Aldershot: Ashgate).

Hermans, T. (2003). 'Cross-cultural translation studies as thick translation'. *Bulletin of SOAS* 66 (3): 380–389.

Hernes, H. M. (1987). *Welfare State and Woman Power: Essays in State Feminism.* (Oslo: Norwegian University Press).

Hervieu-Léger, D. (2000). *Religion as a Chain of Memory.* (Cambridge: Polity Press).

— (2003). *Catholicisme, la fin d'un monde.* (Paris: Bayard).

Hervieu-Léger, D. and G. Davie (1996). *Identités religieuses en Europe.* (Paris: La Découverte).

Hettne, B. (1997). *Den europeiska paradoxen: om integration och desintegration i Europa.* (Stockholm: Nerenius & Santérus).

Hirdman, Y. (1998). 'State policy and gender contracts: The Swedish experience'. In E. P. Drew, R. Emerek and E. Mahon (eds) *Women, Work and the Family in Europe.* (London: Routledge). 36–46.

Hochschild, A. R. (1995). 'The culture of politics: Traditional, postmodern, cold-modern, and warm-modern ideals of care'. *Social Politics* 3: 331–346.

Home Office Faith Communities Unit (2004). *Working Together: Co-operation between Government and Faith Communities.*

Hoogvelt, A. M. M. (2001). *Globalization and the Postcolonial world: The New Political Economy of Development.* (Basingstoke: Palgrave).

Hooper, S. (1995). 'Reflexivity in academic culture'. In B. Adam and S. Allan (eds) *Theorizing Culture: An Interdisciplinary Critique after Postmodernism.* (London: UCL Press). 58–69.

Hort, S. E. O. (1990). *Social Policy and Welfare State in Sweden.* (Lund: Arkiv).

Hytönen, M. (2003). *Contemporary Ethical Questions and the Evangelical Lutheran Church of Finland.* (Tampere: Kirkon Tutkimuskeskus).

Il femminismo cristiano di Elisa Salerno e le sue prospettive (1989). (Vicenza: Centro Documentazione e studi Presenza Donna, Gestioni grafiche Tassotti).

Industrie- und Handelskammer Reutlingen (2008). *Industrie- und Handelskammer Reutlingen.* http://www.reutlingen.ihk.de

Ingelstam, L. (1995). *Ekonomi för en ny tid: lärobok om industrisamhället och framtiden.* (Stockholm: Carlsson).

Inglehart, R. (1977). *The Silent Revolution: Changing Values and Political Styles Among Western Publics.* (Princeton, NJ: Princeton University Press).

— (1990). *Culture Shift in Advanced Industrial Society.* (Princeton, NJ: Princeton University Press).

— (1997). *Modernization and Postmodernization. Cultural, Economic and Political Change in 43 Societies.* (Princeton NJ: Princeton University Press).

— (2007). 'Mapping global values'. In Y. Esmer and T. Pettersson (eds) *Measuring and Mapping Cultures: 25 Years of Comparative Value Surveys.* (Leiden: Brill). 11–32.

Ion, J. (1997). *La fin des militants?* (Paris: Les Editions de l'Atelier).

Ipsos Mori (2006). *MORI Polls.* http://www.mori.com/polls/trends/religion.shtml

Jegermalm, M. (2005). *Carers in the Welfare State: On Informal Care and Support for Carers in Sweden.* (Stockholm: Stockholm University, Department of Social Work).

Jenkins, P. (2002). *The Next Christendom: The Coming of Global Christianity.* (New York: Oxford University Press).

Jenson, J. (1997). 'Who cares? Gender and welfare regimes'. *Social Politics* 4 (2): 182–187.

Jeppsson Grassman, E. (1999). 'The voluntary sector in a welfare perspective: Sweden – with a comparison to France'. In D. Bouget and B. Palier (eds) *Comparing Social Welfare Systems in Nordic Europe and France.* (Paris: MIRE-DRESS). 193–213.

— (2001). *Socialt arbete i församlingens hägn.* (Stockholm: Verbum).

— (2003). *Anhörigskapets uttrycksformer.* (Lund: Studentlitteratur).

Jeppsson Grassman, E. and L. Svedberg (1996). 'Voluntary action in a Scandinavian welfare context: The case of Sweden'. *Nonprofit and Voluntary Sector Quarterly* 25 (4): 415–427.

— (1999). 'Medborgarskapets gestaltningar. Insatser i och utanför föreningslivet'. In E. Amnå (ed.) *Demokratiutredningen.* (Stockholm: Fritzes). 121–180.

— (2007). 'Civic participation in a Scandinavian welfare state: Patterns in contemporary Sweden'. In L.Trägårdh (ed.) *The State and Civil Society in Northern Europe: The Swedish Model Reconsidered.* (Copenhagen: Nordic Council of Ministers).

Jeppsson Grassman, E. and A. Whitaker (2006). 'With or without faith. Spiritual care in the Church of Sweden at a time of transition'. *Omega: Journal of Death and Dying* 53 (1–2): 153–172.

Johansson, L. (1991). *Caring for the Next of Kin: On Informal Care of the Elderly in Sweden.* (Stockholm: Almqvist & Wiksell International).

Julkunen, R. (2003). Womens' Rights in Finland. http://virtual.finland.fi/finfo/english/uskoeng.html

Kääriäinen, K. (2002). Religion and Churches in Finland. http://virtual.finland.fi/finfo/english/uskoeng.html

Kahl, S. (2005). 'The religious roots of modern poverty policy: Catholic, Lutheran, and Reformed Protestant traditions compared'. *European Journal of Sociology* 46: 91–126.

Kainulainen, S., T. Rintala and M. Heikkilä (2001). *Hyvinvoinnin alueellinen erilaistuminen 1990–luvun Suomessa.* (Helsinki: Stakes).

Kaiser, J.-C. (1998). 'Innere Mission und Diakonie'. In U. Röper and C. Jüllig (eds) *Die Macht der Nächstenliebe. Einhundertfünfzig Jahre Innere Mission und Diakonie 1848–1998.* (Berlin: DHM). 14–43.

Kaldor, M. (2004). *L'altra potenza. La società civile globale: la risposta al terrore.* (Milan: Università Bocconi Editore).

Kautto, M. (1999). *Nordic Social Policy: Changing Welfare States.* (London: Routledge).

— (2002). 'Investing in services in West European welfare states'. *Journal of European Social Policy* 12 (1): 53–65.

Kautto, M., J. Fritzell, B. Hvinden, J. Kvist and H. Uusitalo (eds) (2001). *Nordic Welfare States in the European Context.* (London: Routledge).

Keupp, H. (2000). *Eine Gesellschaft von Ichlingen? Zum bürgerschaftlichen Engagement von Jugendlichen.* (München: SOS).

Kirkon tilastollinen vuosikirja 2004. (2005). (Helsinki: Kirkkohallitus).

Kirkon tutkimuskeskus (2004). '*Kirkko muutosten keskellä*'. (Tampere: KTK).

Kjelstad, R. (2001). 'Gender policies and gender equality'. In M. Kautto, J. Fritzell, B. Hvinden, J. Kvist and H. Uusitalo (eds) *Nordic Welfare States in the European Context.* (London: Routledge). 55–78.

Kommittén Välfärdsbokslut (2000a). '*Välfärd vid vägskäl: utvecklingen under 1990-talet: delbetänkande*'. Statens offentliga utredningar 2000:3. (Stockholm: Fritzes).

Kommittén Välfärdsbokslut (2000b). *Välfärd, ofärd och ojämlikhet: levnadsförhållanden under 1990-talet: rapport från Kommittén Välfärdsbokslut.* (Stockholm: Fritzes).

Korvajärvi, P. (2003). Gendering Practices in Working Life. http://virtual.finland.fi/finfo/english/uskoeng.html

Kramer, R. M. (1981). *Voluntary Agencies in the Welfare State.* (Berkeley: University of California Press).

Kuhnle, S. and P. Selle. (1992). *Government and Voluntary Organizations: a Relational Perspective.* (Aldershot: Avebury).

Kulturdepartementet (1999). *Social ekonomi: en tredje sektor för välfärd, demokrati och tillväxt? Rapport från en arbetsgrupp.* (Stockholm: Regeringskansliet).

Kunta- ja palvelurakenneuudistus. (2006). http://www.intermin.fi/intermin/hankkeet/paras/home.nsf/pages/indexfin

Kyrkoordning (1999). *Kyrkoordning med angränsande lagstiftning för Svenska kyrkan* (Stockholm: Verbum).

Lahden kaupungin tulevaisuuspaketti, 2004 (2004). (Lahti: Lahden kaupunki).

*Lahden kaupunki, talouden seurantaraportti (*2004). Tammi-helmikuu 2004. (Lahti: Kaupungin Rahatoimisto).

*Lahden kaupunki, talousarvio 2004 ja taloussuunnitelma 2004–2006 (*2003). (Lahti: Kaupunginvaltuusto).

Lahden seurakuntayhtymä (2004). *Missio, visio, arvot ja strategiat vuoteen 2010.*

Lahden seurakuntayhtymä (2005). *Diakonia- ja yhteiskuntatyön toimintakertomus 2004.*

Lahden työttömyysaste 1990–2004 (2005). *Lahti, tilastoja ja kalvoja.* http://www.lahti.fi/kannat/tevi/tilastotjakalvot.nsf/Uusimmat%20tilastot?OpenView

Lamura, G. (2003). *Supporting Carers of Older People in Europe. A Comparative Report on six European Countries.* Paper presented to the eleventh European Social Services Conference, Venice

Landsberg, G. (2003). 'Alter. Der Generationenvertrag ist aufgekündigt'. In K. Deufel and M. Wolf (eds) *Ende der Solidarität? Die Zukunft des Sozialstaats.* (Freiburg im Breisgau/Basel/Vienna: Herder). 39–45.

Laville, J.-L. and R. Sainsaulieu (1997). *Sociologie de l'association.* (Paris: Desclée de Brouwer).

Lebrun, F. (1980). *Histoire des catholiques en France.* (Paris: Privat, Pluriel).

Leibfried, S. (1992). 'Towards a European Welfare State: On Integrating Poverty Regimes in the European Community'. In Z. Ferge and J. E. Kolberg (eds) *Social Policy in a Changing Europe.* (Frankfurt: Campus Verlag). 133–156.

Leira, A. (2002). *Working Parents and the Welfare State: Family Change and Policy Reform in Scandinavia.* (Cambridge: Cambridge University Press).

Leis, A. (2004a). *Den kyrkliga diakonins roll inom ramen för två välfärdssystem: en jämförande fallstudie av två diakoniinstitutioner i Sverige och Tyskland.* (Uppsala: Uppsala Institute for Diaconal and Social Studies).

— (2004b). 'Welfare, church and gender in Germany'. In N. Edgardh Beckman (ed.) *Welfare, Church and Gender in Eight European Countries.* (Uppsala: Uppsala Institute for Diaconal and Social Studies). 203–236.

Leis-Peters, A. (2006). 'Protestant agents of welfare in Germany: The case of Reutlingen'. In A. Yeung, N. Edgardh Beckman and P. Pettersson (eds) *Churches in Europa as Agents of Welfare – England, Germany, France, Italy and Greece.* (Uppsala: Uppsala Institute for Diaconal and Social Studies). 56–122.

Lervik, O. (2004). 'Får gave på 1,7 millioner'. *Drammens Tidende.* 24 March.

Levenskog, Y. (1997). *Institutionssjälavård i Sverige 1932–1989: med särskild hänsyn tagen till fängelsesjälavården.* (Stockholm: Almqvist & Wiksell International).

Lewis, J. (1992). 'Gender and the development of welfare regimes'. *Journal of European Social Policy* 2 (3): 159–173.

— (1997). 'Gender and welfare regimes: Further thoughts'. *Social Politics* 4 (2): 160–177.

Lipset, S. M. and S. Rokkan (eds) (1964). *Party Systems and Voter Alignments.* (New York: Free Press).

Lister, R. (1995). 'Dilemmas in engendering citizenship'. *Economy and Society* 24 (1): 1–40.

Liukko, M. (2004). *Lahden kaupungin sosiaali ja terveystoimialan tulevaisuuspaketti.* (Lahti: Lahden kaupunki).

Luckmann, T. (1967). *The Invisible Religion.* (New York: Macmillan).

Luhmann, N. (1982). *The Differentiation of Society.* (New York: Columbia University Press).

Lundström, T. (1995). *Staten och det frivilliga sociala arbetet i Sverige.* (Sköndal: Sköndalsinstitutet).

Lundström, T. and F. Wijkström (1995). *Från röst till service? Den svenska ideella sektorn i förändring.* (Sköndal: Sköndalsinstitutet).

— (1997). *The Nonprofit Sector in Sweden.* (Manchester: Manchester University Press).

Lusch, R. F. and S. L. Vargo (2006). *The Service-dominant Logic of Marketing: Dialog, Debate, and Directions.* (Armonk, NY: M.E. Sharpe).

Lyon, D., and M. Glucksmann (2008). 'Comparative configurations of care work across Europe'. *Sociology* 42 (1): 101–118.

Mabille, F., and C. Valasik (2004). 'Welfare, church and gender in France'. In N. Edgardh Beckman (ed.) *Welfare, Church and Gender in Eight European Countries.* (Uppsala: Uppsala Institute for Diaconal and Social Studies). 237–287.

Magnusson, L. (2000). *Den tredje industriella revolutionen – och den svenska arbetsmarknaden.* (Stockholm: Prisma/Arbetslivsinstitutet).

Mahler, J. and H. Green (2002). *Carers 2000.* (London: Office for National Statistics).

Manninen, M. (1999). The Status of Women in Finland. http://virtual.finland.fi/finfo/english/women/naiseng.html

Manow, P. (2004). 'The "Good, the Bad and the Ugly". Esping-Andersen's Welfare State Typology and the Religious Roots of the Western Welfare State'. Working paper 04/03, Max-Planck-Institut für Gesellschaftsforschung, Cologne.

Manow, P. and B. Palier (2009). 'A conservative welfare state regime without Christian Democracy? The French Etat-providence, 1880–1960'. In K. van Kersbergen and P. Manow (eds) *Religion, Class Coalitions and Welfare State Regimes.* (Cambridge: Cambridge University Press). 147–175.

Mårtenson, B. (2004). *Ekonomijournalistik som forskningsområde.* (Stockholm: SNS Medieforum).

Martin, C. (1997). 'Social welfare and the family in southern Europe: Are there any specificities?' In U. Ascoli et al. (eds) *Comparing Social Welfare systems in Southern Europe.* (Paris: MIRE). 315–337.

Martin, D. (1978). *A General Theory of Secularization.* (Oxford: Blackwell).

— (1990). *Tongues of Fire: The Explosion of Protestantism in Latin America.* (Oxford: Blackwell).

— (2002). *Pentecostalism: The World their Parish.* (Oxford: Blackwell).

— (2005). *On Secularization: Towards a Revised General Theory.* (Aldershot: Ashgate).

Maurin, E. (2004). *Le ghetto français. Enquête sur le séparatisme social.* (Paris: Seuil).

Messina, P. (2001). *Regolazione politica dello sviluppo locale. Veneto e Emilia Romagna a confronto.* (Turin: UTET).

— (2004). 'I contesti locali'. In A. Del Re (ed.) *Quando le donne governano le citta. Genere e gestione locale del cambiamento in tre regioni italiane.* (Milan: Franco Angeli).

Metzler, G. (2003). *Der deutsche Sozialstaat. Vom bismarckschen Erfolgsmodell zum Pflegefall.* (Stuttgart/München: Deutsche Verlagsanstalt).

Mingione, E. (2000). 'Modello sud europeo di welfare, forme di poverta e politiche contro l'esclusione sociale'. *Sociologia e politiche sociali* 3 (1): 87–112.

Mingione, E. and A. Andreotti (2001). 'Esclusione urbana e sistemi locali di welfare in Europa'. www.facolta.sociologia.unimib.it/wcms/file/materiali/200.pdf

Ministry of Social Affairs and Health (2002a). *Report on Social Affairs and Health 2002.* (Helsinki).

— (2002b). *Trends in Social Protection in Finland.* (Helsinki).

— (2003). *Sosiaali- ja terveysministeriön opas sukupuolivaikutusten arvioimiseksi lainsäädäntöhankkeissa.* (Helsinki: STM).

— (2004). *Promoting Social Welfare.* http://www.stm.fi/Resource.phx/eng/subjt/socwe/index.htx

Mintzberg, H. (1983). *Power in and around Organizations.* (Englewood Cliffs, NJ: Prentice-Hall).

Molokotos-Liederman, L. (2007). 'The Greek ID card controversy: A case study of religion and national identity in a changing European Union'. *Journal for Contemporary Religion* 22: 187–203.

Moor, R. de (1995). *Values in Western Societies.* (Tilburg: Tilburg University Press).

Morgan, K. L. (2009). 'The religious foundations of work-family policies in Western Europe'. In K. van Kersbergen and P. Manow (eds) *Religion, Class Coalitions and Welfare State Regimes.* (Cambridge: Cambridge University Press). 56–89.

Morrison, K. (1995). *Marx, Durkheim, Weber: Formations of Modern Social Thought.* (London: Sage).

Muller, S. (1997). 'Time to kill: Europe and the politics of leisure'. *The National Interest* 48: 26–36.

National Institute for Health and Welfare (STAKES) (2006). *Toimeentulotukea saaneet kotitaloudet kotitaloustyypin mukaan. 1990–2000.* http://www.stakes.info/files/pdf/Raportit/TT%20nettiin%204.xls

National Statistics Online (2004). *Focus on Gender: Work and Family.* http://www.statistics.gov.uk/cci/nugget.asp?id=436

— (2008). *Workforce Jobs by Industry.* http://www.statistics.gov.uk/statbase/tsdataset.asp?vlnk=495

Niemelä, K. (2002). 'Suomalaisten uskonnollisuus uuden vuosituhannen alussa'. In E. Helander (ed.) *Muutoksen tulkkina.* (Helsinki: Kirjapaja). 140–157.

Normann, R. and R. Ramírez (1994). *Designing Interactive Strategy: From Value Chain to Value Constellation.* (Chichester: Wiley).

Nussbaum, M. (2003). *Capacità personale e democrazia sociale.* (Reggio Emilia: Diabasis).

Observatoire national de la pauvreté et de l'exclusion sociale. (2002). *Les travaux de l'Observatoire national de la pauvreté et de l'exclusion sociale, 2001–2002.* (Paris: La Documentation Française).

OECD (2004). *Programme for International Student Assessment, Learning for Tomorrow's World. First Results from PISA 2003.* (Paris: Organization for Economic Co-operation and Development).

Offe, C. and J. Keane (1984). *Contradictions of the Welfare State.* (London: Hutchinson).

Office for National Statistics (2001). *Living in Britain: Results from the 2001 General Household Survey.* (London: ONS).

Olk, T. (2001). 'Träger der Sozialen Arbeit'. In H.-U. Otto and H. Thiersch (eds) *Handbuch Sozialarbeit/Sozialpädagogik.* (Neuwied/Kriftel: Luchterhand). 1910–1926.

Ormières, J.-L. (2002). *Politique et religion en France.* (Brussels: Editions Complexe).

Pace, E. (1998). *La nation italienne en crise. Perspectives européennes.* (Paris: Bayard).

Palme, J. (2000). *Welfare at Crossroads: Summary of Interim Balance Sheet for Welfare in the 1990s.* (Stockholm: Ministry of Health and Social Affairs).

Palme, J., A. Bergmark, O. Bäckman, F. Estrada, J. Fritzell, O. Lundberg, O. Sjöberg, L. Sommerstad and M. Szebehely (2002). *Welfare in Sweden: The Balance Sheet for the 1990s.* (Stockholm: Fritzes offentliga publikationer, Ministry of Health and Social Affairs).

Parjanne, M. (2004). *Väestön ikärakenteen muutokset vaikutukset ja niihin varautuminen eri hallinnonaloilla.* (Helsinki: Sosiaali ja terveysministeriö).

Parker, G. and D. Lawton (1994). *Different Types of Care, Different Types of Carers: Evidence from the General Household Survey.* (London: HMSO).

Paugam, S. (2002). *La Disqualification sociale.* (Paris: PUF).

Pelletier, D. (2002). *La crise catholique. Religion, société, politique en France (1965–1978).* (Paris: Payot).

Perin, L. (1989). *L'Affaire Lefebvre.* (Paris: Cerf).

Persenius, R. (1987). *Kyrkans identitet: en studie i kyrkotänkandets profilering inom Svenska kyrkan i ekumeniskt perspektiv, 1937–1952.* (Stockholm: Verbum).

Pestoff, V. (1991). 'Social service i kooperativ regi'. In *Kooperativ årsbok 1991.* (Stockholm: Föreningen Kooperativa Studier). 93–108.

Pettersson, P. (2000). *Kvalitet i livslånga tjänsterelationer: Svenska kyrkan ur tjänsteteoretiskt och religionssociologiskt perspektiv.* (Stockholm: Verbum).

— (2003). 'The Estonia disaster (Sweden 1994). The Church of Sweden as public service provider of rituals'. In P. Post, A. Nugteren, R. L. Grimes, P. Pettersson and H. Zondag (eds) *Disaster Ritual, Explorations of an Emerging Ritual Repertoire.* (Leuven: Peeters). 187–199.

Pettersson, T. (1992). 'Välfärd, välfärdsförändringar och folkrörelseengagemang'. In S. Axelson and T. Pettersson (eds) *Mot denna framtid. Folkrörelser och folk i framtiden.* (Stockholm: Carlssons). 33–133.

Pettersson, T. and Y. R. Esmer (2008). *Changing Values, Persisting Cultures: Case Studies in Value Change.* (Leiden: Brill).

Petts, R. J. and C. Knoester (2007). 'Parents' religious heterogamy and children's well-being'. *Journal for the Scientific Study of Religion* 46 (3): 373–389.

Pfau-Effinger, B. and B. Geissler (2005). *Care and Social Integration in European Societies.* (Bristol: Policy Press).

Pizzuti, F. R. (2005). *Rapporto sullo stato sociale. Anno 2005.* (Turin: UTET).

— (2006). *Rapporto sullo stato sociale. Anno 2006.* (Turin: UTET).

— (2007). *Rapporto sullo stato sociale. Anno 2007.* (Turin: UTET).

Plantenga, J. (1997). 'European constants and national particularities. The position of women in the European Union labour market'. In G. Dijkstra and J. Plantenga (eds) *Gender and Economics: A European Perspective.* (London: Routledge). 86–103.

Pollitt, C. (1995). 'Improvement strategies'. In C. Pollitt and G. Bouckaert (eds) *Quality Improvement in European Public Services: Concepts, Cases and Commentary* (London: Sage). 131–161.

Prévotat, J. (1998). *Etre chrétien en France au XXème siècle: de 1914 à nos jours.* (Paris: Seuil).

Putnam, R. (2000). *Bowling Alone. The Collapse and Revival of American Community.* (New York: Simon & Schuster).

Putnam, R. D., R. Leonardi and R. Y. Nanetti (1992). *Making Democracy Work: Civic Traditions in Modern Italy.* (Princeton, NJ: Princeton University Press).

Radford Ruether, R. (1995). 'Catholic women'. In R. Keller Skinner and R. Radford Ruether (eds) *In Our Own Voices. Four Centuries of American Women's Religious Writing.* (Louisville, KY: Westminster John Knox Press). 17–60.

Rake, K. (2001). 'Gender and New Labour's social policies'. *Journal of Social Policy* 30 (2): 209–231.

Regionfakta (2005). http://www.regionfakta.com/gavleborg

Reimers, E. (1995). *Dopet som kult och kultur: bilder av dopet i dopsamtal och föräldraintervjuer.* (Stockholm: Verbum).

Religionswissenschaftlicher Medien- und Informationsdienst e.V. (2006). http:// www.remid.de

Repstad, P. (1995). *Religion and Modernity: Modes of Co-existence.* (Oslo: Scandinavian University Press).

— (2004). 'Radikal kirkeelite – tegn på makt eller avmakt?' In O. G. Winsnes (ed.) *Tallenes tale 2003: perspektiver på statistikk og kirke.* (Trondheim: Tapir). 73–82.

— (2005). 'Why the Norwegian church elite is politically radical: Some possible explanations' *Informationes theologiae Europae: internationales ökumenisches Jahrbuch für Theologie* 13 (2004): 75–79.

Ricard, J.-P. [Président de la Conférence des évêques de France]. (2005). *Déclaration à la conférence des évêques de France.* Lourdes.

Rosanvallon, P. (2004). *Le modèle politique français.* (Paris: Seuil).

Rostgaard, T. and J. Lehto (2001). 'Health and social care systems: How different is the Nordic model?' In M. Kautto, J. Fritzell, B. Hvinden, J. Kvist and H. Uusitalo (eds) *Nordic Welfare States in the European Context.* (London: Routledge). 111–136.

Rothstein, B. (1994). *Vad bör staten göra?: om välfärdsstatens moraliska och politiska logik.* (Stockholm: SNS).

— (2003). *Sociala fällor och tillitens problem.* (Stockholm: SNS).

Ruud, S. (2002). 'Jaging av uønskede elementer har liten virkning'. *Drammens Tidende.* 22 August.

— (2003). 'Tanker rundt en innsamling'. *Drammens Tidende.* 22 November.

Sainsbury, D. (1999). *Gender and Welfare State Regimes.* (Oxford: Oxford University Press).

Saint-Blancat, C. and O. Schmidt Di Friedberg (2002). 'Mobilisations laïques et religieuses des musulmans en Italie'. *Cahiers d'études sur la Méditerranée orientale et le monde turco-iranien* 33: 91–106.

Salonen, K., K. Kääriäinen and K. Niemelä (2001). *The Church at the Turn of the Millenium.* (Tampere: The Research Institute of the Evangelical Lutheran Church of Finland).

Santi, E. (2003). 'Contratti di genere. Un'applicazione e confronti europei'. In F. Bimbi (ed.) *Differenze e disuguaglianze. Prospettive per gli studi di genere in Italia.* (Bologna: Il Mulino). 161–187.

Saraceno, C. (2003). *Mutamenti della famiglia e politiche sociali.* (Bologna: Il Mulino).

Sarpellon, G. (2002). *Chiesa e solidarietà sociale.* (Turin: Leumann).

Scharpf, F. W. (2003). 'Den europeiska sociala modellen och de nationella välfärdsstaterna'. In P. Blomqvist (ed.) *Den gränslösa välfärdsstaten. Svensk socialpolitik i det nya Europa.* 60–81.

Scharpf, F. W. and V. A. Schmidt (2000). 'Welfare and work in the open economy'. In F. W. Scharpf and V. A. Schmidt (eds) *From Vulnerability to Competitiveness.* (Oxford: Oxford University Press). 310–336.

Schein, E. H. (1985). *Organizational Culture and Leadership: A Dynamic View.* (San Francisco: Jossey-Bass).

Schilling, H. (1998). *Aufbruch und Krise. Deutschland 1517–1648.* (Berlin: Siedler).

Schloz, R. (2003). *Kirche: Horizont und Lebensrahmen. Weltsichten, Lebensstile, Kirchenbindung. Vierte EKD-Erhebung über die Kirchenmitgliedschaft.* (Hannover: Kirchenamt der EKD)

Schmidt, H. (2005). 'Churches and diaconal organisations as welfare providers: The German case'. In A. Bäckström (ed.) *Welfare and Religion. A Publication to Mark the Fifth Anniversary of the Uppsala Institute for Diaconal and Social Studies.* (Uppsala: Uppsala Institute for Diaconal and Social Studies). 72–80.

Sciolla, L. (2004). *La sfida dei valori. Rispetto delle regole e rispetto dei diritti in Italia.* (Bologna: Il Mulino).

Selander, S.-Å. (1986). *Livslångt lärande i den svenska kyrkoförsamlingen: Fleninge 1820–1890.* (Uppsala: Erene/Jala bok & musik).

Sennett, R. (2004). *Rispetto. La dignità umana in un mondo di diseguali.* (Bologna: Il Mulino).

Sigurdson, O. (2008). 'Beyond Secularism'. Paper presented to a Conference on Secularization and Secularism, Gothenburg October 20–21.

Siim, B. and A. Borchorst (2005). 'The women-friendly welfare states revisited'. In N. Kildal and S. Kuhnle (eds) *Normative Foundations of the Welfare State: The Nordic Experience.* (London: Routledge). 97–111.

Sinn, H.-W. (2004). *Ist Deutschland noch zu retten?* (Munich/Berlin: Econ/Ullstein Buchverlage).

Sipilä, J. (1997). *Social Care Services: The Key to the Scandinavian Welfare Model.* (Aldershot: Ashgate).

Sjödin, U. (2001). *Mer mellan himmel och jord. En studie av den beprövade erfarenhetens ställning bland svenska ungdomar.* (Stockholm: Verbum).

Slater, D. (1997). *Consumer Culture and Modernity.* (Cambridge: Polity Press).

Smith, G. (2004). 'Implicit Religion and Faith Based Urban Regeneration'. *Implicit Religion* 7 (2): 152–182.

Sociobarometer (2006). *Sociobarometer 2006.* (Helsinki: Sosiaali ja terveysturvan keskusliitto).

Sommier, I. (2003). *Les nouveaux mouvements contestataires.* (Paris: Flammarion).

SSB (2008a). Higher share of women working full time. http://www.ssb.no/english/ subjects/06/10/aku_en/— (2008b). Increase in church weddings. http://www. ssb.no/english/subjects/07/02/10/kirke_kostra_en/

— (2008c). Membership figures reached 400 000. http://www.ssb.no/english/ subjects/07/02/10/trosamf_en/

Stålhammar, B. (2002). *Kyrkoherdens ledningsvillkor.* (Stockholm: Verbum).

Stadt Reutlingen (2005). *Reutlingen im Spiegel der Statistik.* (Reutlingen: Stadtverwaltung).

— (2005). *Stadt Reutlingen.* http://www.reutlingen.de

Stark, R. and W. S. Bainbridge (1987). *A Theory of Religion.* (New York: Lang).

Statistics Norway (2006). *Population and Housing. Census 2001: Documentation and Main Figures.* (Oslo).

Statistics Sweden (2005). http://www.scb.se

Statistisches Bundesamt Deutschland (2006). http://www.destatis.de

Stephens, J. D. (1996). 'The Scandinavian welfare states: Achievements, crisis and prospects'. In G. Esping-Andersen (ed.) *Welfare States in Transition. National Adaptations in Global Economies.* (London: Sage). 32–65.

Strohm, T. (2000). 'Diakonisch-soziale Arbeit im europäischen Einigungsprozeß – Schwerpunkte und vorrangige Aufgaben". In T. Strohm (ed.) *Diakonie an der Schwelle zum neuen Jahrtausend. Ökumenische Beiträge zur weltweiten und interdisziplinären Verständigung.* (Heidelberg: Universitätsverlag C. Winter). 517–538.

— (2002). 'Wohin steuert das Gesundheitssystem?' *Zeitschrift für Evangelische Ethik* 46: 162–168.

Sulkunen, I. (2004). Finland – A Pioneer in Women's Rights. http://finland.fi/

Sundström, E. (2003). *Gender Regimes, Family Policies and Attitudes to Female Employment: A Comparison of Germany, Italy and Sweden.* Doctoral Dissertation. (Umeå: Umeå University, Department of Sociology).

Sunesson, S., S. Blomberg, P. G. Edebalk, L. Harrysson, J. Magnusson, A. Meeuwisse, J. Petersson and T. Salonen (1998). 'The flight from universalism'. *European Journal of Social Work* 1 (1): 19–29.

Swatos, W. H., Jr (2003). 'Differentiating experiences: The virtue of substantive definitions'. In A. L. Greil and D. G. Bromley (eds) *Defining Religion: Investigating the Boundaries Between the Sacred and Secular.* (Amsterdam: JAI). 39–53.

Szebehely, M. (1999). 'Concepts and trends in home care for frail elderly people in France and in Sweden'. In D. Bouget and B. Palier (eds) *Comparing Social Welfare Systems in Nordic Europe and France.* (Paris: MIRE-DRESS). 385–400.

— (2005). 'Care as employment and welfare provision – child care and elder care in Sweden at the dawn of the 21st century'. In H. M. Dahl and T. Rask Eriksen (eds) *Dilemmas of Care in the Nordic Welfare State.* (Aldershot: Ashgate). 80–100.

Taylor, C. (1989). *Sources of the Self: The Making of the Modern Identity.* (Cambridge, MA: Harvard University Press).

— (1992). *The Ethics of Authenticity.* (Cambridge, MA: Harvard University Press).

Thidevall, S. (2000). *Kampen om folkkyrkan. Ett folkkyrkligt reformprograms öden 1928–1932.* (Stockholm: Verbum).

— (2003). *När kartan inte stämmer. Svenska kyrkans församlingar i ett samtidshistoriskt perspektiv.* (Uppsala: Institute for Diaconal and Social Studies).

Thörn, H. (2002). *Globaliseringens dimensioner. Nationalstat, välfärdssamhälle, demokrati och sociala rörelser.* (Stockholm: Atlas).

Toffler, A. (1980). *The Third Wave.* (London: Collins).

Toimintakertomus 2004. (2005). Lahti: Lahden kaupungin sosiaali ja terveystoimi.

Torres Queiruga, A. (2004). *La Chiesa oltre la democrazia.* (Molfetta: Edizioni La Meridiana).

Trägårdh, L. (ed.). (2007). *State and Civil Society in Northern Europe. The Swedish Model Reconsidered.* (Oxford: Berghahn Books).

Trifiletti, R. (1999). 'Southern European welfare regimes and the worsening position of women'. *Journal of European Social Policy* 9 (1): 49–64.

— (2003). 'Dare un genere all' "uomo flessibile". Le misurazioni del lavoro femminile nel post-fordismo'. In F. Bimbi (ed.) *Differenze e disuguaglianze. Prospettive per gli studi di genere in Italia.* (Bologna: Il Mulino). 101–159.

Trigilia, C. (1986). *Grandi partiti, piccole imprese.* (Bologna: Il Mulino).

Trydegård, G. (2003). 'Swedish care reforms in the 1990s. A first evaluation of their consequences for the elderly people'. *Revue française des affaires sociales* 57 (4): 443–459.

Turina, I. (2005). 'Towards a Micro-Theory of Secularisation'. Paper presented to the International Conference of the Sociology of Religion, Zagreb, July 2005.

Twigg, J. (1993). *Informal Care in Europe.* (York: University of York, Social Policy Research Unit).

Valasik, C. (2001). *Les Intellectuels catholiques laïcs en France des années soixante à nos jours.* Doctoral thesis. (Paris: Ecole des Hautes Etudes en Sciences Sociales).

Van Kersbergen, K. and P. Manow (2009). 'Religion and the Western welfare state – the theoretical context'. In K. van Kersbergen and P. Manow (eds) *Religion, Class Coalitions and Welfare State Regimes.* (Cambridge: Cambridge University Press). 4–37.

— (eds) (2009). *Religion, Class Coalitions and Welfare State Regimes.* (Cambridge: Cambridge University Press).

Venuti, L. (1998). *The Scandals of Translation: Towards an Ethics of Difference.* (London: Routledge).

Vogel, J. (2003). *European Welfare Production: Institutional Configuration and Distributional Outcome.* (Dordrecht: Kluwer Academic).

Waerness, K. (2005). 'Social research, political theory, and the ethics of care in a global perspective'. In H. M. Dahl and T. Rask Eriksen (eds) *Dilemmas of Care in the Nordic Welfare State.* (Aldershot: Ashgate). 15–32.

Walter, T. and G. Davie (1998). 'The religiosity of women in the modern West'. *British Journal of Sociology* 49 (4): 640–660.

Weber, M. (1958). 'Science as a vocation'. In H. H. Gerth and C. W. Mills (eds) *From Max Weber: Essays in Sociology.* (New York: Oxford University Press). 129–156.

— (1978). *Economy and Society: An Outline of Interpretive Sociology.* (Berkeley, CA: University of California Press).

— (1996). *Religionen, rationaliteten och världen.* (Lund: Argos).

Weisbrod, B. A. (1988). *The Nonprofit Economy.* (Cambridge, MA: Harvard University Press).

Wijkström, F. and T. Einarsson (2006). *Från nationalstat till näringsliv? Det civila samhällets organisationsliv i förändring.* (Stockholm: Handelshögskolan i Stockholm, Ekonomiska forskningsinstitutet (EFI)).

Wijkström, F. and T. Lundström (2002). *Den ideella sektorn: organisationerna i det civila samhället.* (Stockholm: Sober).

Winter, J. (2001). *Staatskirchenrecht der Bundesrepublik Deutschland. Eine Einführung mit kirchenrechtlichen Exkursen.* (Neuwied/Kriftel: Luchterhand).

Wollebæk, D., P. Selle and H. Lorentzen (2000). *Frivillig innsats.* (Bergen: Fagbokvorlaget).

Wollmann, H. (2004). 'Local government reforms in Great Britain, Sweden, Germany and France: Between multi-function and single-purpose organisations'. *Local Government Studies* 30 (4): 639–665.

Woodhead, L. (2005). 'Gendering secularisation theory'. *Kvinder, køn og forskning* 14 (1/2): 20–33.

— (2008a). 'Gender differences in religious practice and significance'. In J. A. Beckford and N. J. Demerath III (eds) *The Sage Handbook of the Sociology of Religion.* (London: Sage). 566–586.

— (2008b). 'Gendering secularization theory'. *Social Compass* 55 (2): 187–193.

Woodhead, L. and P. Heelas (2000). *Religion in Modern Times: An Interpretive Anthology.* (Oxford: Blackwell).

Wrede, G. (1966). *Kyrkosynen i Einar Billings teologi.* Doctoral thesis. (Stockholm: Studia doctrinae Christianae Upsaliensia).

— (1992). *Folkkyrkan i framtiden.* (Stockholm: Verbum).

Yeung, A. B. (2004). *Individually Together. Volunteering in Late Modernity: Social Work in the Finnish Church.* (Helsinki: The Finnish Federation for Social Welfare and Health).

— (2006). 'A trusted institution of altruism. The social engagement of the Nordic churches'. In R. Harito and K. Inaba (eds) *The Practice of Altruism: Caring and Religion in Global Perspective.* (Cambridge: Cambridge Scholars Press). 98–124.

Yeung, A. B., N. Edgardh Beckman and P. Pettersson (eds) (2006). *Churches in Europe as Agents of Welfare – Sweden, Norway and Finland: Working Paper 2 from the Project Welfare and Religion in a European Perspective.* (Uppsala: Institute for Diaconal and Social Studies).

— (eds) (2006). *Churches in Europe as Agents of Welfare – England, Germany, France, Italy and Greece: Working Paper 2 from the Project Welfare and Religion in a European Perspective.* (Uppsala: Institute for Diaconal and Social Studies).

Index